Raising
Laughter

Raising Laughter

How the Sitcom Kept Britain Smiling in the '70s

Robert Sellers

First published 2021
This paperback edition published 2023

The History Press
97 St George's Place, Cheltenham,
Gloucestershire, GL50 3QB
www.thehistorypress.co.uk

British Library Cataloguing in Publication Data.
A catalogue record for this book is available from the British Library.

ISBN 978 1 80399 368 3

Typesetting and origination by The History Press
Printed and bound in Great Britain by TJ Books Limited, Padstow, Cornwall.

MIX
Paper from
responsible sources
FSC® C013056

Trees for L♈fe

Contents

Acknowledgments

The author wishes to express his sincere thanks to the following people. All of whom gave their time and assistance with great generosity of spirit.

This project dates back a number of years and sadly some of those who contributed have since passed away. I would like to pay special tribute to them and their services to comedy. They made us laugh, the greatest gift, and always will.

Daniel Abineri, Raymond Allen, Trevor Bannister, Humphrey Barclay, David Barry, Patricia Brake, Richard Briers, Duggie Brown, Ian Carmichael, Tony Caunter, Eric Chappell, Roy Clarke, Brian Clemens, Dick Clement, Con Cluskey, Dec Cluskey, Brian Cooke, Ray Cooney, Jilly Cooper, Wendy Craig, John Howard Davies, Priscilla Dunn, Norman Eshley, Ian La Frenais, Ray Galton, Liza Goddard, Mike Grady, Robin Hawdon, Melvyn Hayes, Philippa Howell, Nerys Hughes, Susan Jameson, Martin Jarvis, John Kane, Diane Keen, David Kelly, Matthew Kelly, Carla Lane, Bob Larbey, Peter Lewis, David Mallet, Troy Kennedy Martin, Brian Murphy, David Nobbs,

Francoise Pascal, Su Pollard, Jeff Rawle, David Roper, Peter Sallis, Tony Selby, Mike Sharland, Alan Simpson, Harold Snoad, Peter Spence, William G. Stewart, Richard Stilgoe, Christopher Strauli, Eric Sykes, Peter Tilbury, David Warwick.

Introduction

For many of us who grew up in the 1970s, it was a great time to be a kid. We raced around on Chopper bikes, recreated the Second World War in the garden with our Action Man doll or Airfix toy soldiers, read comics like *2000 AD* and *Commando*, played Scalextric or Subbuteo with dad, sucked on Spangles and guzzled down gallons of strawberry Cresta – 'It's frothy, man,' went the ads. All of this to a great soundtrack of glam rock, prog, disco and punk.

TV wasn't bad either. It could get a bit soulless on Sunday afternoons when the only thing on the box was either a religious service or some old codger trout fishing, but every night at prime time there was always something guaranteed to make you laugh: Morecambe and Wise, Benny Hill, Dave Allen, Dick Emery, The Two Ronnies, Tommy Cooper, and a sitcom. In the 1970s the sitcom was seen as the main ingredient of the television week. Most nights there was one on either the BBC or ITV (just two channels back then), sometimes on both and you could finish watching one and be able to turn over just as another was about to start. They were prolific and hugely popular. It's no surprise to learn that out of the top twenty most watched television programmes in Britain in the 1970s nine of them are comedies, with six of them being sitcoms.

Why did the sitcom flourish during the 1970s? Well, the general population needed cheering up somehow. For all the nostalgia, the 1970s was a bleak time in the UK's social history. Endless industrial disputes and strike action, power cuts, a three-day week, and other governmental failings left the economy flailing; by the end of the decade rubbish was piling up in the streets and dead bodies went unburied. The sitcom, then, was a welcome relief for the whole family, something that everyone from grandparents to children could enjoy and watch together.

As well as giving us some much-needed laughs, the sitcom also said much about the socio-political changes occurring at the time. Shows like *Love Thy Neighbour* and *Till Death Us Do Part* dealt with the thorny issue of race relations, often with too crude a palette for many tastes. Ideas of class and snobbery were highlighted in comedies as wide ranging as *Whatever Happened to the Likely Lads* and *The Good Life*. While workplace politics was scrutinised in shows like *Are You Being Served?* and *The Fall and Rise of Reginald Perrin*. Sexism and chauvinism and the role of women in society played a major part, too. This was a decade that started with women as sex objects for lecherous middle-aged bus drivers but finished with *To the Manor Born*'s Penelope Keith as a prototype Margaret Thatcher.

It's no accident then that the 1970s constitute a 'Golden Age' in television comedy, with the highest proportion of classic and popular sitcoms than any other decade. Just think of all those catchphrases: 'You stupid boy', 'I'm free', 'Don't panic', 'Ooh, Betty', 'You dirty old man', 'I 'ate you, Butler', 'You silly moo', 'Don't mention the war', 'Ooh, Miss Jones', 'I didn't get where

I am today …', 'Power to the people'. The '70s was truly the decade of the comedy catchphrase. It also gave us some of the most beloved comedy characters, from Basil Fawlty to Captain Mainwaring, Rigsby to Frank Spencer.

Here's a question – what exactly is a sitcom? In essence, they present much-loved characters in cosily familiar settings week-in, week-out. Vince Powell, the man behind '70s sitcom hits like *Bless This House* and *Mind Your Language*, believed a successful sitcom had to contain two certain ingredients: firstly, the situation and the characters must be believable. Secondly, it must have areas of comedy, drama and even pathos.

So, what's the difference between a sitcom and say a comedy series? The defining feature is that back in the 1970s the majority of sitcoms were recorded in front of a live studio audience. Some of the actors never liked or came to terms with the process, but an audience was essential, and very few sitcoms ever worked without an audience.

The biggest question of all is, what made those sitcoms from the 1970s especially unique and special? Hopefully you'll have a good idea by the time you've finished this book. In it we take a look at every single sitcom from that decade, with contributions from actors, writers, producers and directors. Not all of those 1970s' sitcoms were great, far from it – some were bad, some were downright weird and others make you scratch your head and go, what the hell were they thinking? Today, many of them represent a different world. Back in the '70s, television comedy and light entertainment was still very much rooted in the British traditions of music hall and variety. And television was made differently back then, too. The BBC, for example, was a totally different organisation than the one we have today. Those at the top, whether as the head of comedy or light entertainment, all seemed to have the power to make decisions, and it was very much the same situation over at ITV. Now, that seems to have gone, replaced by committees, focus groups and endless processes to go through. The industry has become huge and unwieldy compared to what it used to be. Does that make it better or worse, or maybe just different?

Chapter One

1970

Britain can proudly lay claim to producing the first ever regular half-hour sitcom. *Pinwright's Progress* was broadcast live from the BBC studios at Alexandra Palace every fortnight, beginning on the evening of 29 November 1946. Like many of the sitcoms that were to follow, *Pinwright's Progress* saluted the hardworking British labour force, set as it was in a high street store. Ironically, it's doubtful that anyone actually working in a shop was in a position to see it, television sets being prohibitively expensive at the time.

Only ten episodes were ever made and while a sprinkling of sitcoms did come after, it was the arrival of *Hancock's Half Hour* in 1956 that is generally acknowledged as the birth of the British TV sitcom. The show's creators, Galton and Simpson, must then be considered as the genre's grand architects. Alan Simpson and Ray Galton first met at Milford Sanatorium in 1948, where they were both undergoing treatment for TB. Listening to comedy shows on the wireless, both concluded that they could do a better job and so began a remarkable writing partnership.

With *Hancock's Half Hour* the aim was to produce 'a comedy with no jokes,'[1] in the words of Galton. Instead, the humour derived from the interplay between the characters and their reactions to the environment and situations in which they find themselves. And in Tony Hancock the writers had the perfect vehicle. 'Tony didn't do verbal jokes, really,' explains Simpson. 'He did comments, he did irony and sarcasm.'[2]

For several years Galton and Simpson formed part of a script-writing agency that also included Spike Milligan, Johnny Speight and Eric Sykes, which was run from offices five floors above a greengrocers' shop on Shepherd's Bush Green, west London. The pair arrived one morning to find an associate reading one of their scripts. 'Honestly, I don't understand your stuff,' he said to them. 'There's not one joke in here I can pinch.'[3]

The impact of *Hancock's Half Hour* cannot be underestimated. Running on the BBC across seven series until 1960 and garnering huge audiences, the show became the yardstick by which other sitcoms were measured. Far from resting on their laurels, in 1962 Galton and Simpson created one of the most beloved of all TV comedies in *Steptoe and Son*, which explored the fraught and often tragic lives of father and son rag and bone men. It was a concept that played to the writers' strength of exploring relationships between people trapped or living in close confinement. 'It never appealed to us writing for a large ensemble of actors,' says Ray. 'Didn't want that at all, just two guys in a room and what they get up to was enough for us.'[4]

Steptoe and Son broke new ground by introducing a note of gritty realism and by having established actors in the leads rather than comedians. Wilfrid Brambell, who began his career at Dublin's famous Abbey theatre, played Albert Steptoe, a grimy and grasping layabout who ate pickled onions in the bath and thought nothing of putting dentures back into his mouth after they'd fallen in horse manure. Harry H. Corbett's Harold aspired for the finer things in life and an existence beyond the gates of the family business, but his every effort was rendered useless by the need to care for his father. A much-admired actor in the 1950s, Corbett played Shakespeare and Ibsen at Joan Littlewood's Theatre Workshop and was an exponent of the Method style of acting, whose techniques he brought to bear in his interpretation of Harold Steptoe. 'Harry was always examining the part to try and bring a new edge to it,' says Alan. 'In rehearsals he could give three or four different performances, while Wilfrid was from the old school of acting, where you learnt your lines and played them the same way each time.'[5]

The popularity of *Steptoe and Son* was such that half the UK population regularly tuned in. Harold Wilson even successfully pressured the BBC to move a transmission of one episode from the day of the 1964 General Election fearing that Labour voters might prefer to stay in and watch it rather than go out to the polling station. Then, after four series and at the peak of its popularity, Galton and Simpson pulled the plug in 1965. 'We simply got fed up with it,' confesses Ray.[6] It was becoming increasingly difficult to come up with fresh storylines and the writing duo had begun to diversify into movies, including a stint in Hollywood that didn't quite work out.

Fittingly, it was to be *Steptoe and Son* that kicked off what many people regard as the golden age of British sitcom when it returned to television screens early in March 1970.

Galton and Simpson are unclear as to exactly whose idea it was to bring them back, perhaps Tom Sloan, then the BBC's head of light entertainment. Whoever it was, the writers took kindly to the notion, as enough time had passed and there was a wealth of new possibilities with the dawning of a new decade. They were, however, at first daunted about the new series being broadcast in colour. 'We were very worried about it,' confesses Ray, 'because we thought it might take away the greyness and the bleakness of it all.'[7]

In the intervening five years little had changed at Oil Drum Lane; the family coffers were routinely empty and Harold remained a virtual prisoner in his own home, unable to leave the clutches of his father, who'd feign a heart attack every time he so much as sniffed the scent of freedom. Interestingly, Galton and Simpson were never tempted to kill off the old bugger and thus free Harold, or to change their financial situation. 'We never ever thought of doing what they did in *Only Fools and Horses*, turning them into millionaires,' says Alan. 'And I think John Sullivan realised he'd made a mistake there because he almost immediately had them lose it all again.'[8] It's true, the British public much prefer the underdog, they like to see their sitcom characters struggle. 'Success is not funny, is it?' says Ray.[9] And he's absolutely right.

Much has been documented about the 'supposed' fractious relationship between Corbett and Brambell, but the writers found them a delight to work with. 'We had no real problems,' says Alan. 'Although Wilfrid could be quite acerbic at times.'[10] He was also some distance from the 'dirty old man' he played on screen. Brambell was a bit of a dandy in real life, usually dressed in a waistcoat with beautifully creased trousers and shiny shoes, with an accent that could cut glass. His transformation into Steptoe was simple yet brilliant; he'd stop shaving for a couple of days before a recording and use another set of false teeth. Brambell was just 50 when the series first started but already wore false teeth. This new set was specially made and all blackened up, and Brambell simply popped them into his mouth for the performance. His tatty clothes came courtesy of BBC wardrobe. 'And when the show was finished,' recalls Alan, he'd go into his dressing room and after about twenty minutes emerge like a butterfly. He'd be shaved, have his proper teeth in, immaculately dressed with a cane and an overcoat dragged over his shoulders, hair in a slick parting, and he used to stride out and walk past the audience, if they were still mingling around, and they wouldn't recognise him. While Harry, who used to dress better on the show than he did in real life, used to come out and everybody recognised him immediately.[11]

On one occasion Brambell was refused permission to enter the BBC bar, dressed as he was in his posh togs. 'They telephoned me,' remembers Ray, 'and said, 'There's a gentleman here claims he's Wilfrid Brambell, doesn't look anything like him.' I had to go across and say, yeah that's him.'[12]

And then there was the famous catchphrase, 'You dirty old man', which the writers slipped into one of the scripts and it got such a laugh they decided to use it again. That, of course, can lead to problems, when a catchphrase becomes so famous audiences are expecting it and writers become either reluctant to use it or use it too much. 'It can become too much of a gimmick,' says Alan. 'But at times it was so right you couldn't think of anything else that would be better. I don't think we used it that often.'[13]

Neither Corbett nor Brambell contributed to the scripts in any way. It had been much the same with Hancock, who contributed no ideas of his own. 'Tony never used to ring up and say, here, what about if this week he does so and so. Never, not once,' says Alan.[14] In many ways the 1970s scripts of *Steptoe and Son* are superior to their 1960s counterparts, with a higher proportion of them standing out as classics, like 'The Desperate Hours', which saw a pair of prison escapees hide out at Oil Drum Lane, and 'Divided We Stand', where Harold builds a partition in the house, effectively quarantining him from his father. This was an idea based on a story that Ray's brother told him years before about relatives in a brewery who hated each other so much they built a wall inside their house. Then there was 'A Star is Born', in which Albert ends up an unexpected sensation at a local amateur dramatic production. 'That was the terrible thing about the old man,' says Alan:

> He'd always win. It wasn't very true to life, but if ever Harold took up a hobby, the old man could do it better, anything, didn't matter what it was. He beat Harold at things like monopoly and scrabble. In the snooker episode if you remember he turned out to be a crack billiards player.[15]

Having written the script, Galton and Simpson always made sure to be present for the first day of rehearsal and then for the actual day of recording, making the odd suggestion and maybe altering the odd line. 'We'd sit in the control room, watching all the camera angles,' recalls Ray. 'If you're on the studio floor you can't get the whole picture.'[16] Alan even took on the role of 'warm-up man' and kept the audience laughing and engaged in between set ups. Most shows generally had a 'warm-up man' to welcome the audience and to explain what was happening when the crew stopped for any retakes that were necessary, costume or scenery changes and the moving of cameras and sound booms to the next set that was going to be used. This was because a large number of the audience had probably never been to a studio recording before and it was rather different from going to the theatre, with which they may have been more accustomed.

The success of *Steptoe and Son* second time round came as something of a surprise to the writers. 'It was in the second batch that we got the highest viewing figure ever,' claims Alan.

'Twenty-eight and a half million.'[17] Such was its success that a spin-off film was made in 1972 and proved a massive hit. 'They used to send us the box office results every week, because we had a share of the profits,' says Alan. 'And it broke eighty-four box office records in the UK.'[18] A second movie was hurried into production but when that opened in 1973 it struggled to even get its cost back. Alan has a theory as to why the second film flopped so badly:

> I suspect, and I've got no reason for thinking this but it's the only satisfactory explanation, I think everybody flocked to see the first one because it was a big thing on television still, and they must have been disappointed with it so when the second picture came out, they didn't bother to go and watch it.[19]

It's ironic because the second film is much more in tune with the TV series. 'And from our point of view a far better film,' says Ray.[20] It's also a lot broader as Albert and Harold fight off local gangsters, invest in a decrepit greyhound and hatch a plot to pass Albert off as dead and claim on his life insurance. It's a beautifully judged film, although Alan reveals that Brambell hated the director. 'He thought he was a coarse brute.'[21]

It's also probably the best example of how to turn a sitcom into a movie, despite the writers' protestations that they always found the transition from TV to film a difficult one. 'First of all, you're going against all the things we wanted, like the claustrophobic atmosphere,' says Ray.[22] By their very nature films are expansive. 'We used to find the biggest problem with film was construction,' admits Alan, 'because you'd be used to doing thirty minutes and in a strange way you don't need any construction with thirty minutes. If a script lasted twenty pages, the first scene could last nineteen pages, especially with *Steptoe*, whereas a film needs construction, it needs peaks and lows, and I don't think we ever mastered that.'[23]

There were just as many complexities involved when it came to adapting *Steptoe and Son* for the American TV market. 'We first went over there in 1967,' recalls Alan. 'And the first thing they asked us to do was Americanise the script, which took us about half a day, replacing yes with yeah and elevator instead of lift, the usual stuff. They said, that's fine, thank you very much, it will take a week now for us to read it, so you just sit round the pool and enjoy yourself. And that's what we did.'[24]

When a production meeting was finally called the executives expressed a major problem as to where they were going to locate the show. 'If they put it in New York people might say, oh it's Jewish,' recalls Ray. 'In Boston they'd say they're Irish. If it was Chicago, they're Italian. In Los Angeles, they'd be Mexican.'[25] The executives were at pains not to upset any particular ethnic group. 'They were very sensitive,' says Alan. 'They didn't think the Mexicans and the Jews would be happy if it was suggested that they were poverty stricken.'[26]

After much debate Ray suggested, 'What about making them black?' One of the executives stood bolt upright in his chair. 'Oh wonderful, great idea, but impossible.' The political climate of the time just wasn't right, according to Alan. 'Any black characters on TV had to be doctors, politicians, they had to be upwardly mobile. Then about four years later we were called by Turner Productions, who'd picked up the option, and they said to us, would we mind if they cast it black, and we said, "Well, wonderful, we thought of that four years ago." They said, "You couldn't do it four years ago, but you can do it now."'[27]

Sanford and Son starred Red Foxx as the cantankerous Fred Sanford and Demond Wilson as his frustrated son Lamont. It ran from 1972 to 1977 on the NBC network and was a ratings smash, although Galton and Simpson hardly had anything to do with it. 'The first season they used some of our scripts,' says Alan. 'But in the end, they did what they always do, get a team of writers in and write their own.'[28]

Back in Britain Galton and Simpson decided to call time on their creation. The final episode was a Christmas special aired on Boxing Day 1974. One of the reasons for not wanting to do any more was the fact that a little bit of tension had started to creep into the relationship between the two actors. 'Nothing terribly serious,' admits Alan. 'But it was noticeable that they were getting a bit short with each other. The old man would say things like, "God, I was acting when he was a f★★★ing nipper."'[29]

Brambell's habit of taking a few drinks during rehearsals leading to the odd fluffed line also began to irk Corbett. Remember these were two very different people, with very different working methods. They also led totally separate lives, hardly seeing each other outside of the studio. 'We never socialised with them either,' says Alan. 'Harry used to socialise with us during the day, he'd come to our office and we'd have lunch quite often, but we never, ever went to his house.'[30] His wife didn't allow it, according to Ray. 'I think his wife discouraged show business people being there.'[31]

Another reason for stopping was that eight series in total was probably enough. 'It was becoming harder to come up with completely fresh subjects without plagiarising yourself,' admits Alan. 'So, we thought, well, perhaps now the time has come.'[32]

That wasn't quite the end, however. In 1977 Corbett and Brambell flew to Australia to appear in a sell-out touring theatrical production. After several months on the road, they landed in Christchurch, New Zealand, for the second leg and were invited on to a local breakfast TV show. Whether or not he was homesick, tipsy or plain mischievous, Brambell replied to an innocuous question about the merits of Christchurch with a four-letter outburst and the station hurriedly cut transmission and went to an ad break. Embarrassed, Corbett stormed out of the studio vowing never to work with his old partner again. Four years later Corbett was dead at just 57.

Galton and Simpson always resisted returning to their most famous TV creation but in 2006, after much pestering by Ray's new comedy writing partner John Antrobus, 'Murder at Oil Drum Lane', a new Steptoe and Son play, was produced in London. 'I said to Antrobus that the only way I would be interested in doing a play, was that Harry murders his old man,' reveals Ray. 'Accidentally, but nevertheless, skewered him.'[33] The play, which ran for a limited season at the Comedy Theatre, brought the Steptoe and Son saga to a fitting end.

Interestingly, that wasn't the first time Albert had been killed off. At the end of the third series back in 1964, Brambell suddenly announced out of the blue that he wouldn't be available for the next series because he was going to Broadway to appear in a musical called *Kelly*, which was expected to run for years. 'We had a choice to either cancel the show or recast,' recalls Alan:

And Ray and I, probably out of sheer pique, decided to open the next series with a funeral. At the graveside you see Harold looking miserable, and we find out the old man has finally dropped dead. We take Harold back to the house, and Harry would have played it beautifully, all the little bits in the house reminding him of the old man, and his own guilt, that he didn't do enough and all the rest of it. Then there's a knock at the front door and he opens it and there's a boy standing on the doorstep, about 21 years old, saying, 'Harold Steptoe, my mum told me that if ever I was in any trouble to come and look you up.' And it turns out that he's Harold's son. So, it was going to be Steptoe and Son, but down a generation. And we'd even cast it, we were going to ask David Hemmings.[34]

In the end, the musical *Kelly* was a disaster and closed after just one performance and Brambell came scurrying back saying, 'I'm ready to do another series now.'

★★★

The first 'new' sitcom of the decade appeared just two weeks after the return of *Steptoe and Son* over on BBC 2 and arrived very much from left field. File under fascinatingly forgotten, *Charley's Grants* was a satirical piss-take of the arts grants system from the pen of N.F. Simpson, a surrealist playwright closely associated with the Theatre of the Absurd. Writing support came from John Fortune and John Wells, a fine comedian best remembered for his impersonation of Denis Thatcher and as one of the original contributors to *Private Eye*.

The plot revolved around the machinations of an on-his-uppers aristocrat, played by rotund character actor Willoughby Goddard, who attempts to solve his financial difficulties by scrounging grants from Hattie Jacques as head of the Heritage Trust. Keeping this highly creative bunch of artists in order was producer Ian MacNaughton, who'd recently scored great success with *Monty Python's Flying Circus*. He didn't manage the same here, *Charley's Grants* lasted just six episodes.

Meanwhile, over at BBC 1 something very big indeed was happening. Michael Mills, the station's Head of Comedy, had recently enjoyed a short break in Italy. Wandering around the ancient ruins of Pompeii, Mills nudged his companion and joked that he half expected Frankie Howerd to come loping around the corner. It was back in 1963 that Howerd took the London stage by storm in the ancient Rome-set musical *A Funny Thing Happened on The Way to The Forum*. Obviously, Mills' memory of Howerd as a comedic slave had not dimmed, and seized by the possibilities of using such a character as the basis of a sitcom, he approached Carry On writer Talbot Rothwell to come up with a pilot script.

Mills' rather highbrow hopes was for something based loosely on the comedy works of the Roman-era playwright Plautus. Rothwell briefly looked through a Penguin translation of Plautus Mills had lent him, tossed it away and fell back on what he was best at, innuendo and coarse humour. Rothwell created a world that revolved around the daily life of Lurcio, a mischievous Roman slave in the somewhat chaotic household of senator Ludicrus Sextus and his wife Ammonia. Rothwell was to admit later that he wrote the script with Kenneth Williams in mind but Mills remained adamant that Howerd do it. The comic liked the material well enough but voiced reservations about whether it was too bawdy for the nation's living rooms. Howerd never saw himself as a blue comedian and couldn't abide filth; the last thing he wanted to do was offend the public. In the end he came to regard Rothwell's scripts as, 'vulgar without being dirty'.[35]

The pilot aired in September 1969, with the *Radio Times* describing the new show as, 'A sort of Carry On up the forum'. Predictably, Mary Whitehouse scolded it for being both sordid and cheap. The public thought so too and lapped it up. A series was quickly commissioned, going out after 9 p.m. at the close of March 1970.

Up Pompeii was a personal triumph for Howerd. Much of the programme's success was down to his ability to seamlessly break the fourth wall and talk directly to the audience, a typical example being when Ludicrus remarks that his daughter Erotica is, 'delightfully chaste', Howerd turns to camera muttering, 'Yes, and so easily caught.'

Howerd brought all his personal angst and insecurity to the role. Regular cast members and guest stars were to remark how nervous and tense he was before a recording. The show's producer David Croft claimed that he had to reluctantly get rid of quite a number of talented artists simply because they didn't get on with Howerd, or Howerd didn't get on with them. 'If Frankie wasn't happy you haven't got a show.'[36] One senses that Croft and Howerd did not get on. 'When the audience arrived, he was magic. He was absolutely wonderful. And then two minutes after the show was over, he was horrible again.'[37]

A ratings winner, a second series was hurried into production and arrived on screens that autumn. This time Rothwell was assisted by *The Army Game*'s creator Sid Colin, but the jokes remained pretty much the same. The script's reliance on broad humour, stale puns and double entendres drew criticism from some quarters. Mills defended the programme against such snobbish attacks, that something so common did not have a place on the BBC. '*Up Pompeii* is outrageous, of course,' he said. 'And the innuendo is awful. You wouldn't be able to do it except for three things – one, it's funny, which excuses almost anything, and two, it's Frankie Howerd. If it were Benny Hill or Terry Scott doing the same script it would be horrid, but because it's Frankie with that pursed-up, outraged schoolmistress look, it's marvellous. Thirdly, it's done very well, with great style, lovely sets, good costumes and good artists. So, it doesn't look like a tatty music-hall sketch that's been put on to get a dirty laugh.'[38]

After fourteen episodes Howerd declared himself fed up with the show. It had run its course, he felt, and concerns began to take root about being swamped by the character; that people think Lurcio instead of Frankie Howerd. He did though agree to resurrect the character a year later in a film spin-off, shot for just £200,000 at Elstree studios on sets left over from Charlton Heston's film of Julius Caesar. Ending up the eighth most popular film at the 1971 UK box office, it spawned two cinematic sequels that followed a variation of Lurcio through history, not dissimilar to what *Blackadder* later did: *Up the Chastity Belt* (1971) was set in medieval times, while *Up the Front* (1972) took place during the First World War.

All three films were directed by Bob Kellett with Ned Sherrin acting as producer. Sherrin's relationship with Howerd was uneven at best. When Howerd was given time off shooting to attend Elizabeth Taylor's legendary 40th birthday party in Budapest, he returned nursing a hangover and found little sympathy from Sherrin, who insisted he went straight back to work.

Lurcio was to return in a one-off BBC Easter special in 1975 called *Further Up Pompeii*, with much of the original cast and a script by Rothwell, who had not worked on any of the movie outings. It was directed by David Croft, who again did not enjoy the experience much. Besides taking an age to learn the script, Howerd had other odd habits. He wore not the most realistic wig, but insisted that the make-up department pretend this wig was in fact his natural hair and plonk his stage wig on top. Then after a young male assistant refused to go anywhere near Howerd's dressing room, Croft began only using female assistants, who didn't face the same problems. Despite all this, Croft saw a master comedian at work: 'He played the audience as a master fisherman plays a trout. He had complete control. They loved him. He was magic.'[39]

Then, in a bid to exploit the cult status Howerd was to enjoy shortly before his death, ITV revived the show in 1991 for another one-off special. But the old magic just wasn't there any more.

April

David Nobbs began his career in comedy as a writer for the iconic 1960s BBC satirical show *That Was the Week that Was*. On the strength of its success, Nobbs and his then writing partner Peter Tinniswood were asked by the BBC to come up with a sitcom for one of the show's regular cast members, Lance Percival:

> They wanted Lance to be as free as the wind, to go and do whatever he wanted to do, there were no other main characters. That was the brief, which of course was a complete and utter disaster. That is a brief that possibly only Jacques Tati and Chaplin, and people of that ilk, can survive; even Hancock had to have regular characters each week. It was impossible.[40]

Nobbs quickly recovered from that setback and by 1970 was established as a top comedy writer, working for the likes of Tommy Cooper, Frankie Howerd, Dick Emery and Ken Dodd. He returned to the world of sitcom with *Shine a Light*, written with Peter Vincent and David McKellar for Yorkshire Television. 'And it was awful. And it's a shame that it was awful because it really could have been very good.'[41]

The setting is a lighthouse, stationed miles out to sea, manned by elderly Timothy Bateson and his junior, played by Tony Selby. It's no surprise that in such a confined space the pair get up each other's noses, spending much of their time finding new ways to disagree with one another. 'In some senses,' says Nobbs, 'a lighthouse is a wonderful place for comedy because characters are trapped. But looking back on it, if you compare it to say *Steptoe and Son*, in that show they're trapped by something far more interesting than the fact they're entirely surrounded by water, they're trapped because they need each other and they can't get away from each other, which is brilliantly dramatic. I think it was too easy to have people trapped in a lighthouse.'[42]

It was certainly a brave idea, but with such a limited subject everything ended up taking place on virtually the same set. 'I do think we made a big mistake only having two main characters, it wasn't enough,' Nobbs admits. 'And neither of them on the surface were very likeable, neither of them had much warmth, so I think we'd shot ourselves in the foot before we started. As the most experienced writer I should have seen some of the mistakes but we were all in it together. We were sort of doomed.'[43]

Nobbs doesn't blame the two actors, they simply played what they were given. Bateson was a veteran performer, who'd appeared in the first British production of Beckett's *Waiting for Godot* in 1955, while Selby would make a name for himself later in the decade with the army sitcom *Get Some In*. The only respite in the action came from an occasional visiting captain of a supply ship and, in one episode, a relief lighthouse keeper, played by John Le Mesurier. 'We created a marvellous gag for John,' recalls Nobbs:

His character read Dickens all the time, but because you couldn't take much luggage to the lighthouse, he read it from memory. He'd say, 'Excuse me, I'm reading,' and he'd got no book. And then he'd laugh to himself, 'Oh he is a master isn't he,' and the whole thing sprang to life. We were capable of writing a good sitcom, we knew how to write funny lines and character situations, and we had quite good plots, but there just wasn't enough light and shade, and there wasn't enough charm to sustain it.[44]

It was doomed, as Nobbs puts it, and lasted all of six episodes.

★★★

Norman Wisdom had been unquestionably Britain's biggest comedy film star during the 1950s and early '60s, but as time wore on his seaside-type humour began to look stale and shopworn and he turned instead to television and his first sitcom, which was for ITV. The hope was to move away from his slapstick-clown persona towards a more sophisticated style of comedy, but *Norman* proved a fruitless exercise with a plot that could have derived from any number of his movies. Wisdom plays a man bored to death of his soul-destroying, nine-to-five job working for the Inland Revenue and leaves to pursue his love of music, which inevitably leads to a series of accident-prone situations.

The pedigree of the show looked solid enough. Wisdom's former marquee value alone should have been enough to grab a sizeable TV audience, and the writers were Ray Cooney and John Chapman, the brains behind a number of stage farces. I contacted Cooney, who predominately wrote for the theatre, with the intention of grilling him about his one and only TV sitcom. He very kindly got back only to apologise profusely that he couldn't remember a damn thing about *Norman*, it had been entirely erased from his memory banks. 'We only did a pilot anyway, didn't we?' he said. I had to inform Mr Cooney that in fact six episodes were made. 'Six!' he bellowed over the phone incredulously. 'We made six of them! Good God. Well, there you go.'[45]

***

ITV really hit paydirt with the gentle comedy *For the Love of Ada* that paired two old comic veterans together, Irene Handl and Wilfred Pickles, who had been a big radio star in the '40s and '50s. Handl ranks among that group of character actresses that Britain regularly used to churn out; instantly recognisable, comforting and quite potty. Appearing in numerous films and TV comedies from *Hancock's Half Hour* to *The Italian Job*, it was *For the Love of Ada* that gave Irene her biggest success, even though she was nudging 70 at the time.

The basic premise is boy meets girl, the twist being that the boy and girl in question are claiming their old age pensions! During a visit to her husband's grave, Irene's Ada meets the very gravedigger who put him six feet under, Pickles' Walter. The two begin an unlikely friendship, which over time blossoms into love and eventually marriage. Irene herself never married in real life. Those who worked on the show remember her constant companions being two chihuahuas that she brought to rehearsals inside a discreetly curtained cage.

This affair comes as something of a surprise to Ada's daughter, played by Barbara Mitchell, and son-in-law Jack Smethurst, later the uber bigot Eddie Booth in *Love Thy Neighbour*. And there are tangible glimpses of that infamous character to come in Smethurst's repeated outbursts of 'Bloody Nora' and other choice bits of dialogue. In bed with his wife, Jack complains he hasn't had it for a long time. 'Is that all you think about, sex and chips?' she complains. 'I don't get enough bloody chips either,' is the weary response.

For the Love of Ada came courtesy of one of the 1970s' most prolific writing partnerships, Vince Powell and Harry Driver. The two first met when Powell put an ad in a newsagent's window for a straight man for his comedy double act and Driver answered. Working the northern club circuit, it looked like their association was doomed when Driver contracted polio in 1955 and spent eighteen months in hospital. Paralysed from the waist down, Driver spent the rest of his life in a wheelchair. Unable to perform comedy, the duo decided to write it and got their break furnishing scripts for Harry Worth before working on shows such as *Coronation Street*.

The pair established themselves as a comedy writing force, devising a succession of hit sitcoms: *George and the Dragon* (ITV, 1966–68) starred Peggy Mount as an indomitable housekeeper to a rich, retired colonel; *Never Mind the Quality, Feel the Width* (ITV, 1967–71) was about a pair of tailors of contrasting religious and political views running a business in London's Whitechapel; and *Two in Clover* (ITV, 1969–70) paired Sid James with Victor Spinetti as two insurance company clerks who ditch the rat race to run their own farm.

Coming up with the idea of *For the Love of Ada*, Powell and Driver encountered misgivings from television executives that audiences might find a love affair between geriatrics unappealing or not very funny. The writers' first choice to play Ada, the 51-year-old Beryl Reid, refused the role on the grounds she didn't want to play a pensioner. But the British warmed to this senior romance and four series were made in rapid succession, ending with a Christmas special on Boxing Day 1971. Just a month later the cast reassembled for a disappointing feature film version, financed by Tigon, a company associated more with the horror genre and films such as *Witchfinder General*.

Although in its manner and execution *Ada* was excessively British, the theme of people finding love in later life was a universal one and the format was picked up in America by ABC and ran for twenty-two episodes under the title *A Touch of Grace* during 1973. It was never screened in Britain.

★★★

Meanwhile, the BBC tried to entice audiences with the medical-set *The Culture Vultures*, which had more than a whiff of the famous Doctor film series about it. Not least in the casting of super-smoothie Leslie Phillips as Dr Michael Cunningham, senior lecturer in anthropology at the University of Hampshire. Phillips, who appeared in four Carry On movies and took over from Dirk Bogarde as the Doctor series' regular medical nincompoop, brings all of his poised comedy elegance to the role of a laid-back rogue whose passion for gambling and physical pleasures invariably leads to clashes with his seniors, in particular stuffy Professor George Hobbs, played by Peter Sallis.

A medical drama of a different kind occurred halfway through production when Phillips was rushed to hospital with an internal haemorrhage. 'It shook me a little,' he told the *Radio Times*. 'It's the first time I've been seriously ill in my life.'

Although Phillips continued with rehearsals from his hospital bed and managed to return to the studio for filming, he was far from fit and the series had to be halted after just five episodes.

May

The month of May saw the welcome return to ITV of a couple of old favourites that had begun life in 1968 and were still huge ratings winners. First another Powell and Driver hit, *Nearest and Dearest*, which teamed the music-hall comedians Jimmy Jewel and Hylda Baker as warring siblings who inherit a Lancashire pickle factory.

Inspired casting this may have been but the two veterans did not get on. According to Powell, it began at the recording of the very first episode when Hylda objected to a scene in which Jewel was getting all the laughs. Later she, 'went berserk,' in Powell's words, that the episode finished on a close-up of Jewel. 'Stop the show,' she screeched, waving her hands in front of the cameras. 'I'm not having this. I'm the star of the show, not him.' To pacify matters it was decided to end with both of them in the final frame. But the die was cast. 'From that day on, it was open warfare,' remembered Powell. 'For the next five years during the run of the series, they barely exchanged a word, save for the ones which were written for them in the script.'[46]

When Baker was the subject of *This Is Your Life* in March 1972 and the cast of *Nearest and Dearest* was introduced, Jewel was conspicuous by his absence. Hylda got her revenge by not showing up for Jewel's *This Is Your Life* two years later.

Nearest and Dearest became one of Granada's most successful shows, running for forty-six episodes from 1968 to 1973; an estimated 20 million were watching in 1971. There was even a stage version put on at the Blackpool Grand during the summer season. Written by Powell and Driver, it played to capacity audiences and starred both Jewel and Hylda, who far from burying the hatchet brought their mutual animosity for each other on to the stage every night, trading insults that the audiences loved, believing them to be all part of the show.

There was also the by now obligatory cinema version, made by Hammer Films, and released in 1972. The following year the series was adapted for the American market as *Thicker than Water*, with Julie Harris and Richard Long as the squabbling siblings. Networked by ABC, it was cancelled after thirteen episodes.

***

Rivalling Powell and Driver as ITV's most prolific comedy writers were Brian Cooke and Johnnie Mortimer of *Man About the House* and *George and Mildred* fame. Their first big success came in 1968 with *Father, Dear Father*, a generation-gap comedy that was inspired by the state of television around the late '60s. 'You had *Steptoe and Son*, Alf Garnett and a number of other working-class shows,' says Cooke,

So, we said, what about doing one where we get a middle-class family. We made the lead character a writer of rubbishy novels, gave him two daughters, a dog and a nanny, very middle class. And we went to Thames [the franchise holder for ITV serving London and the surrounding area on weekdays] and said, 'We know the guy who would be perfect for this, Patrick Cargill.' And they said, 'Who's Patrick Cargill?' We said, 'You know, the doctor in Hancock's "The Blood Donor", that's Patrick Cargill.'[47]

Cargill fitted perfectly the role of supercilious author Patrick Glover, left to bring up his two nubile teenage daughters in trendy Hampstead when his wife runs off with another man. But there was an unforeseen situation, unforeseen, that is, by the writers. 'We didn't realise that Patrick was gay,' admits Brian. 'Looking back on it now, it was obvious.'[48] The penny finally dropped after they wrote an episode featuring a gay window cleaner and their script was sent back. The producer William G. Stewart told them, 'Patrick won't do it.'

'Why not,' asked Brian. 'It's perfectly good.'

'He won't do it because there's a gay in it.'

'So.'

'Well, you know,' said Stewart. 'He's a bit …'

'We should have realised,' admits Brian, 'because he was always with four or five different fellas, all younger than him. That shows you almost how naïve we were.'[49]

Cooke and Mortimer began their careers as cartoonists. Brian worked for years writing the storylines for the *Daily Mirror* strip The Larks, 'whose only claim to fame was that it was underneath Andy Capp'.[50] Besides paying the mortgage, writing those strip cartoons was a great training ground for life as a sitcom writer. 'We were used to selling humour,' says Brian. 'And that was a good start, we knew the value of a gag.'[51]

Moving from strip cartoons to radio in 1965, Cooke and Mortimer wrote several episodes of *The Men from the Ministry*, a parody of the British civil service, and *Round the Horne*. Their TV break arrived in 1966 when Frank Muir, then a producer at the BBC, told them one day, 'You are the dirtiest writers in radio and I've got a dirty TV show that you're perfect for.' The show in question was a Whitehall-set sitcom called *Foreign Affairs* starring Leslie Phillips, Ronnie Barker and Richard O'Sullivan. 'It's being written by somebody but they're not very good,' said Muir. 'Can you have a look at it?' Cooke and Mortimer took the script away with them, did a total rewrite and sent it back. 'That's great, we'll do that,' said Muir. 'And here's the next one.' In the end the pair were asked to write the entire series and were quickly poached by Thames Television, where they ended up working for most of their careers. 'Philip Jones was the head of light entertainment at Thames and he was a genius,' affirms Brian. 'He didn't discover us, he let us discover ourselves.'[52] Their first offering was *Father, Dear Father*.

Not only did Cooke and Mortimer create the show, but they insisted on writing every single episode. Brian explains the secret to making sure a long-running sitcom never goes stale:

What you do is you people your sitcom, you begin to add various new characters. We introduced, for instance, Richard O'Sullivan as one of the girl's boyfriends. We introduced a brother, played by Donald Sinden. You have Glover's agent who's naturally a gorgeous female and he fancies her like mad. All that's essential to keep the whole thing fresh. But you've got to be careful because otherwise you'll spread things too much. You've got to keep a sense of gravity around the people you start with, while introducing other elements.[53]

And there was the dog, of course, a large and lumbering St Bernard named after Glover's favourite author, H.G. Wells. 'He was easy to work with,' says Brian. 'Apart from the time he did try to mount one of the girls during the course of a show; he had a real go – and it's there on screen.'[54]

But it was Cargill's show and he excelled. 'I think of all the people I worked with,' states William G. Stewart. 'I learnt more in the area of comedy from Patrick than anybody. He was the most accomplished actor in comedy that I ever came across. And because of Patrick's stature in the business, we were able to attract big name guest stars, people like Rodney Bewes, Ian Carmichael, Beryl Reid and June Whitfield.'[55]

Each episode was recorded in front of a live studio audience, and not everything always ran smoothly. In one scene, Patrick had to light a cigarette from a lighter that looked like an antique gun. On the first try the damn thing didn't work, so it had to be explained to the audience what was happening and Patrick tried again. 'Fifteen times it didn't work,' recalls Brian. 'We were up in the control room and said to the producer, "Let's just forget it." Anyway, the sixteenth time it worked and the audience burst into spontaneous applause, and we had to do it again otherwise the viewers at home wouldn't know what the hell was going on.'[56]

In spite of such hiccups, Brian believes having that live audience was essential, not least because of the special atmosphere it brought to all of the recordings:

I prefer a live audience, a lot of the actors don't, but it is the immediacy that you get. I worked a lot in America and over there they had a machine where you had someone twiddling knobs to produce laughs to sweeten a show. They do that in Britain now, but back then they didn't. And I talked to this

guy who had this machine and said, 'Where do you get the
laughs from?' And he said, 'From shows my father used to
work on like Milton Berle and Jack Benny.' And I said, 'That
means that all the people laughing on this show are probably
all dead.' And he said, 'Oh yes.' That's creepy.[57]

While not a classic by any means, *Father, Dear Father* was hugely
popular. 'It got great reviews,' recalls William G. Stewart. 'And
several times got to number two in the national ratings. It was
always number one in the London region. And it was great fun
to make. We were like a real family.'[58]

After seven series and forty-nine episodes the show finally
came to an end in 1973. 'Patrick and I went to Philip Jones one
day,' says Stewart, 'and said, "We both feel we can't do any
more." Philip was a little disappointed, but Patrick wanted to
stop at the top.'[59]

That didn't prevent a feature film spin-off being made, of
course, which Cooke and Mortimer wrote in three weeks by
reworking the first two episodes. Featuring the original cast and
costing, according to Stewart, the princely sum of £116,000, it
opened in May 1973. However, this wasn't to be entirely the end
of the *Father, Dear Father* story. One afternoon, Brian received a
phone call from a producer in South Africa. At the time Britain
weren't selling television shows to that country due to apartheid,
but this producer had taken all the *Father, Dear Father* episodes
and dramatised them on radio with a cast of local white actors:

And this producer said to us, 'You haven't got any more have
you?' We didn't because we'd moved on to other shows by then,
and he said, 'Well would you mind if I write them?' We told
him to go ahead and he wrote something like 170 new episodes,
they went out every week. And when the movie came out over

there it out grossed *Jaws*, they were queuing round the block
to see the heroes that they'd heard on radio, which were completely different from the ones that were in the film.[60]

Still, this wasn't quite the end. In 1978 Cooke and Mortimer
were asked by the 7 Network in Australia, where numerous
British sitcoms and comedy shows had played successfully, to
make a down under version. The scenario they came up with
was that Glover and nanny jet off to Sydney to stay with a
previously unmentioned brother. This brother suddenly ups
and leaves, and Glover is left to look after the house and – wait
for it – two attractively nubile teenage daughters! Cooke and
Mortimer happily wrote the first two episodes and then left the
remaining twelve to be authored by other writers.

They'd been less happy with a one-off television special called
Patrick Dear Patrick that was broadcast back in 1972. 'That was a
right f*cking rip-off if I ever saw one,' blasts Brian:

And not only that, he [Patrick] produced a record called
Father Dear Father Christmas. It was a full LP with the children, the dog, and we looked at it in astonishment because
we didn't know anything about it. It had all our characters on
it and we said, 'What is this?' 'Oh, we're terribly sorry,' they
said. We let it go, we weren't that arrogant. Patrick gave us a
copy each and for years and years I played this record every
Christmas for my family, who hated it.[61]

★★★

There were a few other hold-over shows from the late '60s that
carried into the 1970s, still pulling in audiences. *Dear Mother …
Love Albert* was very much a personal project for its star Rodney

Bewes, who not only created this show about working-class aspiration, but also co-wrote it with Derrick Goodwin. Bewes plays a young innocent northern lad who comes down to London and scrapes a living as a confectionery salesman, only in his letters back to his mother he romanticises and exaggerates the painful truth of his humdrum existence. The scenario derived from Bewes' own real-life letters to his mum when he arrived in London from Yorkshire and worked odd jobs to pay for his studies at drama school. The series began in 1969 and ran on ITV over the course of four series, ending in 1972.

There was *Mr Digby, Darling* from Yorkshire Television, which reunited Peter Jones and Sheila Hancock from the hit sitcom *The Rag Trade* (BBC, 1961–63). This time Jones works at a pest extermination company called Rid-O-Rat and Sheila is his devoted secretary. The show ran from 1969 to 1971 and the idea behind it was based on an observation the writers Ken Hoare and Mike Sharland made while working at the BBC. 'There were a fair number of middle-aged secretaries working for bosses in their fifties,' says Mike. 'They often had an office marriage, non-sexual, but with many of the problems of a real marriage. He was inefficient, she was over-protective, he was lazy, she would cover for him.'[62] It was an idea both writers intended to develop at some point in the future. Their chance came when an old friend, the writer Sid Colin, was setting up the Light Entertainment department at Yorkshire Television, and asked them to join.

Ken and Mike had worked with Peter Jones in the late '60s on the successful BBC show *Beggar My Neighbour* (announcers had to be very careful how they pronounced that one!) and liked him enormously. 'Peter was sometimes far funnier than he ever knew,' confirms Mike, 'and he was ideal for the Mr Digby character. Rehearsals were a muddled joy and I think Peter left more laughs in the rehearsal room than on the screen.'[63]

Both Sheila and Peter had a great audience following and *Mr Digby, Darling* took off straight away and ran for three series.

Lastly, *Me Mammy* chronicled the adventures of Irishman Bunjy Kennefick, a successful London executive desperate to take advantage of a bachelor's existence but hampered by his ever-present, domineering mother. Written by Irish playwright Hugh Leonard and starring celebrated Irish actor Milo O'Shea, this gentle comedy mocked institutions like the Roman Catholic Church and English misconceptions of the Irish. Among the fine supporting cast was Ray McAnally, Yootha Joyce and David Kelly.

Me Mammy was one of the first shows to take advantage of the BBC's brand spanking new rehearsal rooms in North Acton, later dubbed 'the Acton Hilton', which opened in May 1970. Here the rehearsal spaces were exactly the same size as the BBC studios, each included its own green room, and there was a wonderful restaurant on the top floor. 'It was very glamorous,' remembers David Kelly:

> These were rehearsal spaces made for the purpose, no scout halls or Territorial Army rooms, and we shared it with *Dad's Army*. I think we were the first two in there. There was no bar, but being Irish a bottle of wine was sneaked in and during lunch we used to drink it using cups and saucers, which went down very well. I remember John Le Mesurier passing by with a certain envy saying, this must be the Irish table. Eventually we brought in bottles of wine quite openly and finally the BBC saw sense and opened a bar in the restaurant.[64]

This saved the actors the needless journey of going to the rather ropey pub next door, although they were not averse to downing a few pints in there. Kelly recalls a condom machine that stood outside the saloon bar. 'And some wag, no doubt Irish, had written on it – "This is the worst chewing gum in London!"'[65]

Running on the BBC from 1969 to 1971, O'Shea and Leonard decided to call it quits after three series of *Me Mammy*, agreeing that the format had run its course, despite the fact it was still attracting a large audience.

June

Yorkshire Television's *Albert and Victoria* was set in the late nineteenth century, when men ruled the roost and women knew their place. As for the kids, they were probably locked up in the nursery with a nanny that looked like Billie Whitelaw out of *The Omen*.

Alfred Marks stars as the ultra-conservative Albert Hackett, with his brood of nine children and a frankly exhausted wife, played by renowned stage actress Zena Walker. By the second series Barbara Murray stepped into Zena's role of Victoria, only to be replaced herself after just two episodes following a miscarriage. Frances Bennett was drafted in to finish the series.

Some of the twelve episodes were directed by David Mallet, later a pioneering director of pop videos. Then in his early twenties, Mallet was a staff director at the BBC before defecting to Yorkshire Television in 1969, where he helped create the sketch show *Sez Lez*, the first TV starring vehicle for stand-up comic Les Dawson.

Mallet remembers that for some strange reason never explained to him the rehearsals for *Albert and Victoria* took place in London at the Duke of York's barracks off the King's Road during the week, and then the whole cast and crew caught the train up to Leeds to record the show in front of a live audience at Yorkshire Television's studios. 'Compared to nowadays when studio audiences have seen everything,' says David. 'Back then we were fortunate, particularly in the provinces like Leeds. It was a major day out for people to come and see a TV show recorded, so one tended to be lucky with their responses. But there were occasions when they were just puddings and wouldn't laugh and that just destroyed everybody.'[66] In the days before the advent of the laughter track on British television, Mallet always managed to get around these deathly silences. 'I think I was one of the first people ever to add a laugh where I thought there should have been one. I had my own little laughs which I nicked from the pre-show warm-ups and I used to add it in the editing.'[67]

★★★

Yorkshire Television and David Mallet joined forces again for *His and Hers*, a (for its time) progressive sitcom starring Ronald Lewis as a hopeless freelance journalist happy to play the role of house husband while his wife, played by Sue Lloyd, commutes to the City as an executive accountant more than capable of holding her own in the boardroom. It was probably a little too progressive for Donald Baverstock, who ran Yorkshire Television, when the writers Ken Hoare and Mike Sharland made their pitch. He had strange ideas about men who worked at home, one of them that a man would push a wheelbarrow full of cleaning materials around the house. 'At that point, Ken and I were careful not to catch each other's eyes,' recalls Mike, 'otherwise we knew we'd end up rolling around the floor with laughter.'[68]

David Mallet saw his role as director primarily as getting the show up and running in the rehearsal stage, because come the day of recording he was out of reach of the actors up in the control box organising the technical bits:

> You've got to remember that back then video was a bit of tape two inches wide and you were lucky to have one machine. I think they cost something like £50,000 in the late '60s, which was a hell of a lot of money, so you weren't going to have the luxury of recording a show on ten VTR machines. In fact, the whole of Yorkshire Television didn't have ten VTR machines.[69]

Oddly, it would be two years before *His and Hers* returned for a second and final series, by which time the role-reversal premise had been largely dropped in favour of a gamut of silly sitcom situations, like defecting Russian ballet dancers hiding out in suburban bathrooms.

Sue Lloyd was also missing. A familiar face on British TV and film since the early '60s, thanks to roles in *The Ipcress File* and *The Saint*, Sue would achieve soap immortality later in the decade when she joined the cast of *Crossroads*. Her replacement was Barbara Murray.

Sadly, series two did not find favour with audiences and suffered the ignominy of its last three episodes being replaced by repeats of *On the Buses* in the London region.

August

Another product of Yorkshire Television was *Never Say Die* and concerned life in a male-only hospital ward, with much of the humour deriving from the patients' various skirmishes with the staff. It was written by Liverpudlian Peter Tinniswood, who later found great success as a novelist and playwright, and drew upon his student days as a hospital porter when his nemesis was an ancient washing machine. 'It was old and it wheezed and spat steam, and gave me permanent catarrh,' he told the TV Times. 'But out of those steamy days came this series.'

The two leads were well known TV faces. Reginald Marsh was almost a permanent fixture in '70s sitcom land; there was his role as Paul Eddington's boss in *The Good Life*, Yootha Joyce's brother-in-law in *George and Mildred* – who visited only when his wife had a new material possession to show off – and Terry Scott's boss in *Terry and June*. But his most enduring role was probably flash bookmaker Dave Smith in *Coronation Street*.

Patrick Newell was another instantly identifiable small screen personality, or should that be shape, since his Billy Bunter-like proportions were his stock in trade. In his entry in *Who's Who on Television* in the late '70s, Newell defined himself as, 'Actor with a weight problem – the more he diets, the less work he seems to get.' It certainly contributed to his signature role of Mother, John Steed's boss in *The Avengers*.

Never Say Die unfortunately did not live up to its name, meeting a premature end after just one series.

***

If it Moves, File it, a short-lived sitcom from London Weekend Television, may well be the precursor to *Yes Minister*. It saw satirist John Bird and Dudley Foster play ineffectual civil servants obsessed with secrecy and constantly trying to avoid the attention of their boss, played by John Nettleton, who curiously would later appear as a Whitehall mandarin in *Yes Minister*.

But by far the most interesting thing about this comedy was the man who wrote it – Troy Kennedy Martin, the creator of

Z Cars. A sitcom seemed an odd choice for Martin, even though he'd handled comedy before with his screenplay for the classic Michael Caine crime caper *The Italian Job*. 'It was really just an attempt to see how far I could push my own comic potential,' Martin recalls. 'And the sitcom seemed an ideal vehicle.'[70] It was to prove a dispiriting experience. For starters, he'd written one of the characters with Brian Murphy in mind, but John Bird was cast instead. 'The two characters were quite different. The Dudley Foster character was stern and very much played by the book and quite lofty, and the other one, played by Bird, tended to panic and was semi-working class, but it was always the John Bird character who came out on top.[71]

In one episode both men are transferred to the intelligence services and sent out to keep watch on a house. Sitting on a bench, they get to thinking, supposing there are actually some very dangerous criminals inside, and Bird comes out with this flight of fantasy of people bursting out of the building guns blazing. 'In fact, that's exactly what happens,' says Martin. 'The door opens and these men come out shooting, but Bird and Foster just turn on their heels and run away. It's as if the fantasy had created reality, and if he hadn't have actually said it, then it wouldn't have happened.'[72]

In another episode both of them get walled in when workers arrive to refurbish the building; their office door gets nailed up and plastered over. 'They suddenly realise they can't get out,' recalls Martin. 'And it becomes a test of nerves. The Dudley Foster character says to the other guy, "Don't lose your nerve, we're going to get out." It becomes almost like a submarine picture where someone panics because the air's running out. And, of course, it's the Dudley Foster character who breaks down first.'[73]

Sadly, after submitting the scripts, Martin felt totally left out of the creative process, the total opposite of his experience on *Z Cars* where the writer worked closely with the director and the actors. At the time *If it Moves, File it* went into production Martin was living in France doing rewrites on the Clint Eastwood war picture *Kelly's Heroes*. 'I didn't feel I was part of a team. Being stuck in a room hundreds of miles away just sending the scripts in and being unable to be there and help steer it along was a soul-destroying experience. And I was really disappointed with the outcome.'[74] What began life as a quite anarchic satire, cocking a snoot at authority, became more and more outlandish and after just six episodes LWT pulled the plug on it.

That was it as far as sitcoms were concerned, Martin had no desire to write another one. 'They're much harder to write than you think.'[75] By the middle of the decade Martin had slipped back into familiar territory writing episodes of *The Sweeney* and in the '80s enjoyed further hits with *Reilly, Ace of Spies* and the conspiracy thriller *Edge of Darkness*.

September

Bachelor Father was a welcome return to situation comedy for Ian Carmichael, who'd previously scored with television audiences as perennial upper-class ass Bertie Wooster, opposite Dennis Price as Jeeves, in *The World of Wooster* (BBC, 1965–67). *Bachelor Father* was based on the extraordinary true-life story of a man called Peter Lloyd Jeffcock, a foster-father to twelve children. 'He was an ex-RAF gentleman,' Carmichael recalled. 'And quite rich, who developed a burning desire to give to children who had been less fortunate than himself the same happy and contented upbringing. Now, as you will imagine, there was a bit of a problem with a bachelor gentleman adopting, but somehow he won the authorities over and got permission.'[76]

All of Jeffcock's charges came from broken homes and by the end his 'family' consisted of six boys and six girls. 'This brood he reared entirely on his own,' said Carmichael. 'Unaided, he shopped for them, cooked, ironed, nursed, ensured that they all had a sound education and provided them with succour and affection.'[77]

Michael Mills, the BBC's Head of Comedy, thought this perfect source material for a sitcom and bought the rights to Jeffcock's autobiography and gave it to Richard Waring, who'd written many of the *Wooster* shows. It was also Mills' decision to cast Carmichael. It was an interesting role for the vastly experienced actor, who hitherto had specialised in playing bumbling innocents and dithering dolts in a succession of droll 1950s British film comedies including *I'm All Right Jack*, *Lucky Jim* and *School for Scoundrels*.

By its very nature the show necessitated a herd of little sprogs scurrying around Carmichael's feet, though it never bothered him and he ignored the old cliché about acting with children. 'I can only say that anyone who doesn't realise the reflected glory in which one can bask when they are good – and all mine were – must be extraordinarily unperceptive. I just encouraged them, tried to help them and let them get on with it. They really did all the work for me.'[78] One of the little girls, then aged just 12, was Geraldine Cowper, who went on to play the missing child Edward Woodward searches for in *The Wicker Man*.

Bachelor Father was relatively well received by critics, but perhaps better appreciated by the public and lasted two series. 'It was clean, wholesome, family viewing,' said Carmichael, who was especially proud of his involvement. 'Frequently funny, occasionally moving, and at its worst, inoffensive.'[79]

★★★

Another offering from Yorkshire Television and written by Sid Colin, *On the House* stars John Junkin as a harassed foreman continually at odds with Carry On stalwart Kenneth Connor's militant shop steward. Trading on that classic 'them-against-us' situation rife in blue-collar trades in post-war Britain – one thinks also of *The Rag Trade* and *Are You Being Served?* – *On the House* takes place on a building site, with a proposed estate of desirable bijoux residences looking unlikely to ever become reality if it's left to this bunch of workers.

A second series followed where *Play School* presenter Derek Griffiths was added to the regular cast, along with Robin Askwith as a long-haired layabout not dissimilar to the character he'd soon be essaying in the Confession films. There was also an impressive array of guest stars including Brian Glover, Imogen Hassall, Madeline Smith, Patrick Troughton and Paula Wilcox.

David Mallet was once again in the director's chair and probably had his best time working on any sitcom. 'The cast were great. Kenneth Connor was a very outgoing, broad comic player and John Junkin was the same, but he was a very withdrawn sort of person, extremely nice, but very withdrawn. Robin Askwith was a hoot all day and all night.'[80]

On the House proved to be Mallet's final sitcom gig before he changed tact completely and became one of the most innovative and significant pop video directors in the world, working for the likes of David Bowie, U2, the Rolling Stones, Elton John, Queen and Madonna. Today Mallet looks back on his days working at Yorkshire Television as largely a grind:

Normally you never had a chance to go back and change anything. On *Friends* they had twenty-five sets of writers and they did each gag ten ways in front of an audience and then chose the one that went best; that's the way modern

Hollywood sitcoms work. We did it once live and that was it, and if something went wrong during the filming you didn't stop the tape, you just carried on. Later on, we could regroup and fix it, but if there were more than three edits in a sitcom it was considered a bit of a disaster.[81]

***

That September audiences also welcomed back two old favourites: *Dad's Army* and *Please, Sir!*

By 1970 *Dad's Army* was already in its fourth series, having begun in 1968, and would run for several more years yet. On many people's list as their favourite sitcom of all time (this author included) *Dad's Army* was 'born out of desperation', in the words of its creator Jimmy Perry. After seventeen years of slogging his guts out in weekly rep and small roles on television, Perry had achieved absolutely nothing as a performer. There was, he decided, only one course of action left, to sit down and write a comedy himself, making sure it had a good part in it for him. The idea he came up with drew upon his own experiences serving with the Home Guard during the war as a 16-year-old before being called up to the regular Army.

After writing a pilot episode, and not really knowing what to do with it, Perry was cast in an episode of the BBC sitcom *Beggar My Neighbour*, playing the uncouth brother of Reg Varney. The producer was a certain David Croft. During rehearsals Perry approached Croft to ask if he'd take a look at his Home Guard script. Croft, who had served in the Royal Artillery during the war, immediately recognised the idea's potential and passed it on to Michael Mills. Against the advice of some senior BBC executives, notably Paul Fox, Controller of Programmes, who was worried about the potential negative effects of a series mocking the British war effort, Mills commissioned a series. Perry was forever beholden to Mills and liked him very much:

> He had been a lieutenant commander in the navy during the war and was inclined to shout at you as though he was on the ship's bridge in a force ten gale. But he was in my opinion the best Head of Comedy the BBC ever had – a bit of a fanatic and slightly potty, he had the knack of making things work and was a tremendous enthusiast, always looking for new ideas.[82]

Croft was asked to help the inexperienced Perry write the scripts, and so began a partnership that was to last more than twenty-six years. Their work pattern was never to change, meeting up for two or three days, drinking endless cups of coffee, discussing plots for a couple of episodes, taking notes and then off they'd go to write an episode each.

For the all-important role of Captain Mainwaring, bank manager for the fictional Walmington-on-Sea, who takes it upon himself to lead the platoon, Croft favoured Jon Pertwee. The BBC had offered the role to Thorley Walters, who rejected it out of hand. At the time John Howard Davies was one of Croft's personal assistants:

> David did have this fixation about Jon Pertwee playing Captain Mainwaring, even though he kind of knew it wasn't right. And I remember being in his office when his other PA, who was a lady, said, 'What about that chap who used to be in *Coronation Street*, Arthur Lowe.' So, it was this lady that suggested Arthur and that's how it came about.[83]

It turned out to be an inspired piece of casting and at the age of 52 Lowe became one of the most instantly recognisable faces on television. 'Arthur was rather like his character,' recalls Harold Snoad, who worked as production manager then later directed several episodes:

> in as much as he was very pedantic about how he was regarded by other people. The first example I witnessed of his slightly pompous attitude (which made him ideal for Mainwaring) was on the first day of location filming. Myself and all the other members of the cast were sitting on the coach outside the hotel waiting to be taken to the location. Arthur was late – presumably because he'd complained about something wrong with his breakfast. When he finally emerged and got on the coach, a member of the platoon extras called out, 'Morning, Arthur.' He sat down in horror alongside me and said, 'Arthur! – that'll have to change.'[84]

John Le Mesurier, at 56, was a veteran television and film actor and perfect casting as Mainwaring's right-hand man, Sergeant Wilson. Prior to agreeing to take on the role, the BBC wrote to Le Mesurier with a strange request – could he run. Le Mesurier replied in the positive but admitted years later, 'The answer was actually no, but so what. I could remember the real Home Guard and I never saw any of them run, save possibly to the pub.'[85] This laissez-faire attitude typified the actor and the way he played the role. 'John was totally impractical,' says Harold Snoad. 'On the first day's filming I pointed out to him that his watch had stopped and he thanked me and asked me if I could wind it up!'[86]

The relationship between Wilson and Mainwaring is at the heart of the comedy and although Lowe and Le Mesurier appreciated each other's talents they never clicked personally, so different were they as people. Their on-screen chemistry, however, is one of the treasures of British comedy. Perry considered Lowe to be one of the greatest comedy actors of the period.

The rest of the key platoon members were cast with a brilliant eye; indeed, *Dad's Army* may be the most perfectly cast comedy show of all. To play the spirited if inept Corporal Jones, Croft knew he couldn't cast a veteran performer due to the number of stunts and physical comedy he would be asked to do. Jack Haig was first choice but when he proved unavailable Croft remembered a much younger actor he'd worked with and been impressed by. The actor was asked to come in and read and was quite brilliant, but the decision was taken that it would be too time consuming to drastically age him up all the time. The actor in question was David Jason. Clive Dunn, then in his mid-40s, was cast instead.

It was Michael Mills' suggestion that one of the platoon members should be Scottish and that John Laurie was ideal for the doom-laden undertaker Frazer. Arnold Ridley was cast as the gentle Godfrey, with his iffy water works. By far the oldest members of the cast, Snoad remembers that Laurie and Ridley did exhibit a touch of jealousy, 'because each of them somehow thought that the other one was being looked after better than himself during long spells of filming'.[87]

The youngest member of the platoon was the soppy Private Pike, a character based very much on Perry's own personal experiences. It was Croft's wife Ann, who happened to be an agent, that discovered the perfect candidate for the role, a 22-year-old actor she'd just taken on as a client, Ian Lavender. As for Walker, the town's black marketeer and general wide boy, Perry was keen to play that part himself but was cautioned by Mills that he had to decide which end of the camera he wanted to be on. James Beck was cast instead.

One of Harold Snoad's first responsibilities as production manager was to find suitable locations for many of the exterior scenes. After a lot of research, he came up with the ideal place, the Stanford Practical Training Area in Norfolk. It was ideal because it was a large area of countryside containing a village including houses, stables, a church and a pub. The army had bought up the area, everyone had moved out and it was now used purely for military training purposes. It was not unknown for the cast during a tea break to see real soldiers emerge suddenly from the undergrowth to share a cup of char with them. Once the crew were hurriedly moved off because jets were coming in to launch a practice air strike. As for Walmington-on-Sea itself, that was in reality the small town of Thetford, Norfolk, chosen by Snoad because the high street and many of the houses retained much of the same look they would have had during the war.

Launched in July 1968, the first series faltered slightly with the public. 'The viewing figures and reaction hadn't been that strong,' recalls Harold, 'and the bosses decided that it probably wasn't worth doing any more. David Croft and myself went to the Head of Comedy and the Controller of BBC 1 and encouraged them to change their minds and we all know how successful the series became.'[88]

Indeed, by the time of the fourth and fifth series it was regularly clocking viewing figures in excess of 16 million. By 1971 there had been a movie version made, though Croft and Perry were shocked when they met the director Norman Cohen on set and heard he had not seen a single episode. The *Dad's Army* movie is entertaining enough if a little unoriginal, reprising the first ever episode in which the platoon is formed. Most who worked on it considered the picture to have been a disappointment.

In 1975 Croft and Perry were approached to adapt *Dad's Army* for the stage. Determined this time not to rehash old material, the writers presented a mixture of sketches and popular war-time songs. Highlights included the platoon attired as Morris dancers and Arthur Lowe and John Le Mesurier doing their best Flanagan and Allen. Opening at the Shaftesbury Theatre in the West End, it ran for five months before embarking on a success-ful nationwide tour in the spring and summer of 1976.

Bizarrely, in the same year, the show's huge success tweaked the interest of the American networks and Croft and Perry were invited to Los Angeles to watch the recording of a pilot episode for ABC. The writers were left scratching their heads to see Mainwaring turned into a Jewish tailor and Wilson hail-ing from Italian stock. The American producers had chosen the classic German U-boat episode as a try-out, but according to Croft the whole proposition of transferring the show to the USA was something of a lost cause and in the end died a natu-ral death. Not surprising really given that America was never threatened with invasion in the way Britain had been, so it seemed odd why executives over there believed the show would resonate with audiences.

Back in Blighty, *Dad's Army* continued to be hugely popu-lar with the public, although by that time it had lost one of its pivotal cast members. In 1973 James Beck died suddenly at the age of 44. The series was never really the same again without his cheeky and edgy persona and it wasn't long before Croft and Perry voiced dissatisfaction about carrying on. It was only due to the enthusiasm and persuasive skills of BBC 1's Controller that they agreed to write further series.

By the ninth and final series in 1977, many of the cast were showing their age and shooting was, in the words of Croft, 'an ordeal'. Le Mesurier looked ill and desperately thin having recently collapsed with liver failure due to his drinking habit. Lowe was having trouble remembering his lines and would keep bits of script in Mainwaring's office drawer and refer to them during scenes. And poor Arnold Ridley had ripped a cartilage in his leg and needed to be ferried by limo to and from the studio. Croft himself directed the final episode, and it was a very emotional evening. By the end of recording everyone had a lump in their throats and a tear in their eye.

Fondly remembered today, the appeal of *Dad's Army* appears to be in no danger of waning. There are endless TV repeats, a 2016 film remake was viewed as moderately successful, and there is a *Dad's Army* museum and walking tours in Thetford itself. 'I loved working on *Dad's Army*,' Harold Snoad sums up. 'All the cast were very friendly and we all got on very well together. In fact, going away on location was almost like going on holiday with a lot of friends – except that it was very hard work.'[89]

***

Back in 1968 LWT, the ITV network franchise holder for Greater London at weekends, began broadcasting. Frank Muir, he of the pink bow tie, tweeds, plummy voice and endearing lisp, was its first Head of Comedy. His track record was exemplary; with Denis Norden he'd written some of Britain's most beloved post-war radio comedies including *Take it from Here* (1948–60) and in the 1960s he was the BBC's Assistant Head of Light Entertainment.

One of Muir's first actions at LWT was to collect up as many comedy writers as he could to see if they had any ideas that might work on the fledging station. Bob Larbey and John Esmonde had been childhood friends and written comedy for the radio but only had one TV sitcom to their name, the short-lived *Room at the Bottom* (BBC, 1966), about a team of maintenance men working in an office block. 'We had a couple of ideas for Frank,' recalls Bob:

> One was about a failed actor and his faithful valet, which he hated! The other one was only half-formed, about a young teacher at a tough school who was less worldly-wise than the kids he was teaching. Luckily, Frank liked that one and commissioned a pilot script, bless his heart, and the rest is history.[90]

Unbeknown to Muir, Larbey and Esmonde first offered the school idea to the BBC but the corporation turned it down on the grounds that one of the pupils was 'educationally subnormal', and that it was dubious at best to make humour out of a person's afflictions. In the end the character of Dennis, played by Peter Denyer, was handled with sensitivity, although Denyer did later admit that he got the part because he looked stupider than anyone else at the auditions. So, the BBC's loss was LWT's gain and *Please, Sir!* lasted fifty-seven episodes in total, running from 1968 to 1972.

The series was also to make a star of John Alderton. Muir cast him as young teacher Bernard Hedges after an amusing guest appearance as an asthmatic teacher-cum-lodger in the opening episode of the spicy marital sitcom *Never a Cross Word* that aired soon after LWT launched. The newly qualified Hedges arrives at Fenn Street Secondary Modern, a school in a particularly rough area of south London, full of ideals and modern teaching methods. In an effort to curb this naïve enthusiasm, his fellow teachers put him in charge of 5C, a class full of delinquents and no-hopers.

With little chance of finding good enough actors of school age, director Mark Stuart decided to cast young adults to play the kids. David Barry was coming up to 23 years old when he was cast as the loutish Frankie Abbott but had been a child actor since the age of 12, touring with the likes of Laurence Olivier. 'That's why the casting worked,' he states, 'because we were all quite experienced already. Malcolm McFee, who played Peter Craven, had been in the film of *Oh! What a Lovely War* and stuff like that, and Peter Cleall, who was Duffy, had also done a lot of work. I think you do need experience to play comedy. I don't think it matters quite so much with straight drama, but comedy, and especially working in front of a studio audience, you need that experience.'[91]

From its earliest episodes *Please, Sir!*, while hugely popular with audiences, was not favoured by the critics. 'They lambasted it,' says David. 'They really did. And we got a few complaints from schoolteachers. It's tame stuff now but at the time they thought, this appeals to children and should Duffy be advising Hedges, when he's going to do some boxing, to guard his cobblers, stuff like that. And Mary Whitehouse would complain, but I think she was pretty much ignored.'[92]

In the ratings, however, the show never failed to make the top ten and was LWT's first big comedy success. 'I remember that John and myself were surprised by how quickly it took off,' admits Bob Larbey. 'It's hard to say why it became popular. I suppose it was the first "grown up" series about school life and we were blessed with an excellent cast and director.'[93]

From complete unknowns the cast were suddenly recognised everywhere they went. David Barry remembers regularly being mobbed by schoolchildren. 'Unfortunately, we always used to finish rehearsals at half three or four in the afternoon when the senior schools were coming out, so we'd don the dark glasses and the newspaper broadsheets to hide behind on the train home.'[94]

Most episodes switched between the classroom and the staff room, which featured Hedges' much-put-upon colleagues, including Noel Howlett's incompetent headmaster and his besotted deputy head, played by Joan Sanderson, famous for her immortal portrayal of Mrs Richards, the hotel guest with hearing problems in *Fawlty Towers*. There was also Deryck Guyler's caretaker, a former Desert Rat with delusions of grandeur.

In the classroom scenes John Alderton almost comes across as the straight man, he's the feed and it's the kids who get most of the laughs. 'It was great teamwork,' says David Barry. 'And John was wonderful to work with in the beginning. Towards the end it got a little bit tiring. John very much saw himself as a classical actor.'[95] During one of the breaks between series, Alderton went across to the BBC to appear in a production of *Macbeth* and one of the newspaper critics likened the performance to his Hedges character and half expected to see Duffy and Frankie Abbott bounding across Dunsinane Hill. When work started again on a new *Please, Sir!* David Barry went up to Alderton and said, 'Great, John, we got a review in Macbeth and we weren't even in it.'[96]

Despite Alderton's growing antagonism towards the series, filming was largely a happy affair. 'It was lots of fun,' recalls Bob Larbey. 'Memories of improvised cricket matches in the rehearsal room and ideas from various cast members if the script was short – featuring, funnily enough, the character the cast member played!'[97] David Barry recalls that Larbey and Esmonde encouraged the cast to ad lib on set and to introduce nuances to their characterisations, which the writers in turn would pick up on. 'Rehearsals were great. Frank Muir used to come in and sit next to us and chuckle at the read throughs.'[98]

After four days of rehearsal everyone moved into the studio, where the episode was recorded as live, with barely any retakes since editing in those days was expensive and cumbersome. 'Our producer/director Mark Stuart used to go ape if you fluffed a line or needed a retake,' recalls David:

> We were gibbering wrecks by the end, we had fear instilled into us – no retakes. So, every episode was recorded rather like a play with multi-cameras. We used to start the warm-up around eight in the evening and Mark used to boast about how we were in the bar before nine o'clock.[99]

Studio audiences were a further hindrance, especially in the things they found funny. There was one episode featuring actor Geoffrey Hughes playing a painter and decorator in the classroom. Duffy remarks, 'Look, it's Rembrandt,' and Hedges has to apologise. 'That's OK chief,' says the decorator. 'The name's Turner actually.' It didn't get a single titter. 'The studio audience just didn't get it,' recalls David. 'Whereas if Duffy said knickers or something, they'd hoot with laughter.'[100]

The obligatory film spin-off arrived in 1971 and was an exciting time for the young cast. 'Strangely enough,' says David, 'there was less pressure in making the movie than there was doing the TV series because it was more of a leisurely pace. It took hours to light each scene so you could get to play silly games and chat.'[101] Filmed over at Pinewood Studios, David recalls everyone got excited when they found out the latest James Bond movie, *Diamonds Are Forever*, was being shot at the same time. One lunchtime David and the others visited the big sound stages to look around the gigantic sets being used for the 007 film.

By the fourth series, the original kids had left to star in their own spin-off show, *The Fenn Street Gang*. Alas, the new intake of pupils failed to make any sort of impression on audiences.

Combined with Alderton finally leaving, the magic that had made the earlier episodes so special was lost and the series finished in February 1972.

October

The Lovers ranks as one of the finest sitcoms ITV ever made, a warm and witty spin on the traditional 'boy meets girl' storyline given an added spice by its gentle knocking of the perceived 'permissive' society.

It's a story about a normal young Manchester couple. Football-mad Geoffrey wants what all young men want and is forever trying to get his end away with girlfriend Beryl, who is determined to stay chaste until her wedding night and not give in to 'Percy Filth', as she calls it. The pair are forever playing an exhaustive game of verbal foreplay, with Beryl usually landing the best lines. When Geoffrey bemoans, 'Beryl, we live in a permissive society.' She replies, 'Not on this street, we don't.'

The Lovers was the creation of Jack Rosenthal, one of the most prolific and celebrated of British television dramatists. Born in Manchester in 1931, Rosenthal started his career at fledgling Granada Television, where his first job entailed ordering toilet-roll holders. He went on to write 129 early episodes of *Coronation Street* and the popular sitcom *The Dustbinmen* (ITV, 1969–70). *The Lovers* was Rosenthal's attempt to document the enormous strain heaped upon teenagers tentatively entering their first serious sexual relationship and it won him the Writers Guild Award for best TV comedy script.

Besides perfectly capturing its era, *The Lovers* made small screen stars of its young leading players. Paula Wilcox, later to achieve even greater success in *Man about the House*, was just 17 years old when she was first spotted in a play with the National Youth Theatre of Manchester and later cast as Beryl. Paula brought delightful charm and innocence to the role, and Rosenthal cast her because she was able to convey the sweet side and wily side of her sex.

When it came to casting Geoffrey, every actor who read for it said the same thing, that there was only one person who could play the part – Richard Beckinsale. 'One actor talking himself out of a job is unusual enough,' said Rosenthal. 'But six?'[102] Rosenthal had never heard of this Richard Beckinsale, so tried to find out firstly who he was and then where he was. It turned out he was doing a play in Hull and an informal meeting was arranged at the only time he could manage, which was in between shows. Rosenthal waited for him to arrive. 'The doorbell rang and in walked the perfect Geoffrey.'[103] Beckinsale, then 23, was an instant hit in the role, largely due to his relaxed attitude in front of the camera, which very much mirrored his real-life personality and allowed him to portray the innocence that was so integral to Geoffrey.

In spite of its large ratings and critical acclaim, only two series were ever made. Perhaps it was thought that viewers would eventually grow tired of plots never advancing further than Beryl and Geoffrey constantly falling out of love and then making up again. A feature film version was made in 1972, directed by Herbert Wise, and looked back at how the young couple first met and the early rocky months of their relationship. Besides being a historical document of the sexual mores of the early '70s, the film also offers a fascinating glimpse of the city of Manchester itself, with scenes taking place at such well-known spots as Old Trafford and the long-gone George Best boutique.

November

Diana Dors was Britain's answer to Marilyn Monroe in the 1950s, a blonde bombshell with a mischievous sense of humour and more curves on her than Silverstone race track. But as her film career declined, Diana increasingly turned to television to make ends meet, and Yorkshire Television's *Queenie's Castle* gave her one of her most memorable roles.

Devised and written by Keith Waterhouse and Willis Hall, the men behind the stage play and film of *Billy Liar*, it cast Diana as the indomitable Queenie Shepherd, matriarch to three good-for-nothing grown-up sons. With no father around the flat, one is left to presume he's serving time somewhere. Queenie's offspring spend their days either in the pub or terrorising the neighbours, especially hapless Residents' Association secretary Mrs Petty, played by Lynne Perrie, who is forever trying to get Queenie's unruly family evicted.

Another member of the household is Queenie's wheeler-dealer brother-in-law Jack. Originally producers went for the novelty casting of Alan Lake, Diana's real-life husband, until he got involved in a fracas in a pub that resulted in someone being stabbed. Luckily jobbing actor Tony Caunter had already been up to see the director about the show, only nothing came of it:

And then out of the blue my agent telephoned to say, 'Will you stand by until the end of the week because there's a possibility you might be taking over as the brother-in-law.' I said, 'What do you mean might be?' He said, 'Well, Alan Lake's trial is on and it's a question of whether he goes down or not.' And he did. I remember the phone call, it was, 'Hello Tony, pack your bags, you're off to Leeds, Alan's been given 12 months.'[104]

Delighted with the news, Tony felt more than a little anxious about playing opposite the legend that was Diana Dors, especially under such circumstances:

> You can imagine my feelings, there I was, wow, I've got a leading role in a sitcom, but oh dear, what a way to get it. I went up to Leeds and was introduced to Diana, who was sitting in make-up, poor love, still in tears, floods of tears, mascara running all over the place. And I thought, how is this lady going to respond to me arriving in place of her husband, and she could not have been kinder, she was adorable.[105]

Queenie's Castle is a real time capsule of a show, about as 1970 as British television got with its earthy, broad humour and sprinkling of bad language. Even today some of the material seems quite strong for early teatime viewing. Some people working on the show felt a similar unease at the time, that the balance being struck wasn't quite right. 'The content was very funny,' recalls Tony. 'But I think it was the producer or director's choice that we went for a certain reality that I thought was totally out of keeping with comedy. There was this one scene, where we had this poor guy on the floor and we were going to put the boot in, and I remember protesting strongly at the time saying, this ain't funny. I did feel it was a little bit too close to the reality of the situation.'[106]

When the cast returned for the second and third series the approach was much broader and more comical, and as such everyone felt happier, especially Diana, 'Because we were terribly working class,' says Tony. 'In fact, lower than working class, we were layabouts and poverty stricken, and Diana had just got fed up with it, she wanted to glam up a bit.'[107]

Although the location was unspecified on screen, parts of the series were filmed in Quarry Hill flats in Leeds. Built in the late

1930s, Quarry Hill was at the time the largest social housing complex in the country, and because of its modernist design was something of a showcase. 'People came from all over the world to look at this marvellous new concept,' says Tony. 'But by the time we were doing our series it had become very much a working-class tenement area. We did do bits of location filming there and I seem to remember some of the local heavy lads showed up. But if you had a clever first assistant, he would bring them into the fold as it were and they would become our security.'[108] Due to social problems and poor maintenance, Quarry Hill was demolished in 1978. The West Yorkshire Playhouse now stands on the site.

Chapter Two

1971

January

The year kicked off with a show that was only really beginning to establish itself with audiences but would soon become a fixture for the remainder of the decade, *The Liver Birds*. It also saw the early flowering of one of Britain's most popular sitcom writers, Carla Lane.

A Liverpudlian housewife, Carla didn't know she could write comedy. 'I didn't know I could write much at all. I just wrote a lot of poetry.'[1] It was at a local writers' club that she met Myra Taylor and together they began coming up with funny little sketches. Never imagining it was possible to become a professional writer, some of these sketches were sent to the BBC and one idea in particular, about two Liverpool girls sharing a bedsit, a sort of female version of *The Likely Lads*, landed on the desk of Michael Mills.

Produced as a pilot in April 1969, Carla remembers watching it at home. 'I was embarrassed because I didn't know whether it was good, bad or indifferent. I was so scared. I liked it because I'd written it and thought a lot about it, but I was really nervous and troubled when the first one came out, but people were so kind about it.'[2]

Happy with the result, Mills commissioned a series but suggested that Carla and Myra be given a mentor and so an experienced writer was brought in called Lew Schwarz, who'd written for Dick Emery and *The Army Game*. 'They gave me someone who taught me the rules of television,' says Carla. 'And by the end of that first series I knew exactly what I was doing. It was amazing the things I didn't know. It was all very exciting, but it was also very frightening. But after a while it just slowly settled upon me that I could do it, you're a writer, don't argue against it, just pick up your pen and do another episode.'[3]

Television at that time was such a male-dominated environment that at meetings and script conferences Carla was usually the only woman in the room. Certainly, she wasn't involved in things such as casting. 'I wasn't important enough. I was very much the shy, quiet writer in the corner, frightened of everybody.'[4] Intimidated by everything that was going on, Carla kept a low profile during those early days until one of the actors at rehearsals gave a bad line reading and she found herself putting her hand up. 'I half expected to get my head bitten off, instead she was so charming and so thoughtful about it and from that time on I knew where I was. I just needed someone to give me the belief that I was reasonably important.'[5]

With women beginning to enjoy new freedoms at the start of the 1970s, both financially and sexually, *The Liver Birds* followed the exploits of Dawn and Beryl, played by Pauline Collins and Polly James, their trials and tribulations with boyfriends, work, parents and each other. For Carla the most important thing was for the characters to speak with an authentic voice. 'I wanted to get it right. I didn't want to write anything that women wouldn't say or that men would find trivial.'[6]

When the show returned in January 1971 for a second series, Collins had joined the cast of ITV's *Upstairs, Downstairs*. Fortunately, producer Sydney Lotterby remembered working with Nerys Hughes on an episode of *The Likely Lads* and offered her the part of Beryl's new flatmate Sandra. So began the show's golden era, with Nerys' more refined character contrasting nicely with the streetwise Beryl. Indeed, much of the reason behind the success of *The Liver Birds* was due to the chemistry between the two actresses, who became firm friends in real life. 'We sparked off each other so much,' recalls Nerys. 'And we used to improvise a lot, too. Later on, Carla didn't like that, she wanted the scripts how she had written them. And we thrived on a live audience because what you get from an audience is waves of love. But you don't play to them as if to a theatre audience because then it comes across as overacting on the telly. You play as if the audience is eavesdropping on your conversation.'[7]

It was a very friendly company, everyone got on and had fun. Nerys and Polly always threw a party for the cast and the technicians after recording was finished on the Saturday night. 'Half the time when we were doing the rehearsals, we'd be working out what to give them all to eat,' recalls Nerys.[8]

The city of Liverpool itself played an important role in the series. The opening titles, accompanied by a theme song by The Scaffold, a group that included Paul McCartney's brother, Mike, features the famous waterfront, notably the two sculpted birds perched atop each tower of the Royal Liver Building at Pier Head, from which the series takes its name.

All location shooting was always done first in Liverpool before recording went ahead in the studio. At one point, Nerys gave birth to a son and knew that in the opening episode of the forthcoming series she was going to have to be seen in a bikini. She had something like six weeks to get her weight down and flatten her stomach:

> Then I had to leave Ben to go up to Liverpool for filming and I came out in a rash from head to toe. They called a doctor and he said, 'She's missing her baby.' It was psychological. So, we couldn't film on me that day because I was just covered in this rash. And the next evening, when we returned to our hotel after filming other scenes, there was a pram in the hall, and I said to Polly, 'That's ever so like Ben's pram.' And it was Ben, my husband had brought him up, and my rash just disappeared.[9]

By the third series Myra Taylor left the show and Carla took over main script duties of what was now one of the BBC's biggest comedy hits. 'They couldn't get enough of them. I was amazed at the reception it got. I never got over it.'[10] Nerys recalls being recognised everywhere she went, but the reaction was never a negative, it was always genuine and warm. 'There was no starriness about us, we were ordinary, and so the reaction people had was that they thought they knew us.'[11]

With a hit show behind her, Carla was now living in a world that she never anticipated and being treated with an importance that was often baffling. 'People used to say, "Is it alright if I speak to Carla?" Is it alright, I used to think, what are they on about?'[12] Something else that turned out to be a surprise was how much value was placed on the writer, and how involved they were throughout the entire process. It got to a point where Carla used to deliberately stay away from the studios sometimes, only to get a phone call, 'Are you coming in today?' and she'd say, 'Well, I decided to give you a break,' and they'd answer, 'We don't need a break, we'd like you to be here, we want to get it right.'[13]

In 1976, when Polly James left the show, Sydney Lotterby was faced yet again with the challenge of finding another new leading actress to keep the series going. As luck would have it, Nerys Hughes had just seen a new Willy Russell play:

> And there was this goofy girl in it, and it was Elizabeth Estensen, and I went back and said to Sid, she's brilliant. He'd seen hundreds of girls already but he agreed to see her. Liz was the most shy and unassuming girl, she sat on this chair in front of Sid Lotterby and he had to lean over the desk to see her because she was sort of disappearing down into it. Anyway, she got the job so almost immediately I had another partner who was quite different from Polly but still incredibly fun.[14]

Elizabeth's feisty, flame-haired Carol also brought along with her an extended and dysfunctional family – the Boswells, clearly the inspiration for Carla Lane's 1980s series *Bread*.

While Carla never thought *The Liver Birds* ever lost its energy or became stale, by series nine in 1978 the time had come to call it a day. 'I just felt there was somewhere else I had to go. I wanted to be a bit more serious. To be honest, I didn't want to be a comedy writer to begin with. I like the drama of life. I never can write without putting drama in.'[15] By 1978 Carla had already begun work on perhaps her most accomplished sitcom, *Butterflies*, which beautifully balanced both comedy and drama.

Carla did try to introduce more dramatic elements into *The Liver Birds* but always found resistance, with the emphasis on it remaining lighthearted. Although she did succeed in bringing in a few realistic scenarios, such as getting the girls to think about longer-term relationships with men and giving Sandra a boyfriend, which provided an early role for future *Bergerac* star John Nettles.

Nerys, too, felt that the series had come to a natural end:

> I loved doing it, it was joyous for me, but we all thought, yes, it's time to finish. I was definitely ready to go. I kind of a bit had to be persuaded at the end to do them because after a while you do feel that you've had enough. Ultimately, the way I felt was that I didn't want it to end, but I didn't mind at all that it did.[16]

In 1996, seventeen years after the final episode was broadcast, the BBC revived the series, reuniting Polly's Beryl and Nerys' Sandra as they contemplated life after divorce. It was something that Nerys didn't want to do, feeling it was being done for the wrong reasons and that going back rarely works. But everyone was involved so it felt a bit churlish not to accept. As it happened the new series failed to connect with audiences and only seven episodes were made. It was a personal disappointment for Carla, who always retained a huge fondness for the show. 'I loved doing *The Liver Birds*. I learnt everything writing that.'[17]

***

Things took a decidedly macabre turn with *That's Your Funeral*, a darkly Gothic sitcom written by *Daily Mail* theatre critic Peter Lewis. The idea derived from his early days as a jobbing reporter covering funerals and hearing about some of the undertakers' stories and experiences. 'What occurred to me was that there was room for comedy if you saw the two sides of the undertaking business, the very business-like public front and what they're really like off duty, when they're not on public show.'[18]

Peter began writing for television on *That Was the Week that Was* back in 1963, but what he really wanted to do was a half-hour comedy play rather than sketches. Sending off his funeral idea to the BBC, he was summoned to see Michael Mills. Peter remembers Mills as, 'A small man of very unsmiling aspect and very Napoleonic manner.'[19] The meeting took place in Mills' office at Television Centre. 'We love your script,' he announced. 'But you'll have to write six more.'

'Well,' replied Peter. 'It's just one funny idea meant to last half an hour.'

'That's all very well,' Mills continued. 'But we are not really interested in it except as a series. Everything has to be a series these days and a series must be at least six.'[20]

Peter didn't think the idea could stretch that far but was confident enough in the characters to give it a bash.

With his frosty countenance and gravelly voice, Bill Fraser was perfect casting as Basil Bulstrode, a bombastic and abusive funeral director with a knack for rubbing people up the wrong way. Fraser had been a regular face in sitcoms since the late '50s with *The Army Game* and *Bootsie and Snudge*. His equally cynical partner was played by Raymond Huntley, usually cast on film and television as supercilious bureaucrats or Whitehall figures.

It's too long ago for Peter to bring to mind any of the storylines he dreamt up, save for one in which a customer asked the firm to bury their beloved alligator, which had gotten too large and died. The problem was to find a coffin to fit the creature. 'In the end we had an alligator-shaped coffin to put it in, which did look extremely amusing.'[21] Peter also recalls guest star Fenella Fielding:

She played a customer who wanted somebody buried and ended up fancying Basil. She would advance on him and he would back away. Well, in real life Bill Fraser did in fact back away and was very nervous of Fenella and tried to get as far from her as possible. She said to me, 'Of course, I'd forgotten that Bill was gay.'[22]

Fraser was well suited to his role but a little over the top for Peter's taste. 'One of his tricks was to put in a set of false teeth and at some point, during the episode, you could absolutely count on him bending over the coffin lid and his teeth would fall out with a great clatter. I remember begging him towards the end saying, "Bill, this week don't do the teeth," but he'd do them just the same.'[23]

Rehearsals took place at the 'Acton Hilton', a bleak multi-storey building directly opposite North Acton tube station that was the BBC's main rehearsal facility. 'Every floor housed a comedy in rehearsal,' says Peter. 'But we had no scenery and hardly any props, and you had to somehow work the thing out and rehearse it with minimal support. We did have a couple of real coffins. I remember Bill sniffing at one and saying, "That's been used."'[24]

On Friday, after a week's rehearsal, they moved into the studio for an afternoon run-through and then the audience would start arriving for the live recording that evening. 'The nature of the audience is a limiting factor,' states Peter. 'It certainly was in those days because they were nearly all works outings, people who had come out for a jolly good time and you've got to play up to that. Subtlety is not what's required. That's what Bill Fraser needed his tricks for.'[25]

Prior to the series going out, Peter stressed in interviews that it was not his intention to mock death or people's bereavement, but the inevitable complaint arrived from a woman who had buried her uncle that afternoon only to return home to see *That's Your Funeral* on the telly and was personally affronted by it. 'Michael Mills took this very badly and actually went on BBC

1 to apologise,' recalls Peter. 'I thought, oh well that's put the kibosh on that. A few days later he sent for me and said, "Well, of course, there won't be a second series." And I said, "Thank goodness for that, I don't think I could write another one," because I was at my wit's end producing this one.'[26]

That didn't stop Hammer studios reuniting the cast for a 1972 film version. Directed by John Robins and written by Peter, the plot centred around a rival undertaker's firm being used as a front for drug smuggling and featured a high-speed car chase with hearses (a cinema first?), along with a finale in which several hundred quid's worth of hash hidden in a coffin goes up in smoke. Shot cheaply and with undue haste at Pinewood studios, it performed poorly at the box office to nobody's great surprise.

February

One of ITV's most successful and best-loved sitcoms surely has to be *Bless this House*. It was created by Vince Powell and Harry Driver and quickly became a permanent fixture in the viewing habits of the nation, featuring in the top ten ratings throughout most of its six-year run. Principally though *Bless this House* was a great starring vehicle for Sid James, presenting him in a new and unfamiliar light, as suburban family man Sidney Abbott, although his cheeky Carry On persona was never far from the surface.

Bless this House rose out of the ashes of failure. While Sid's 1969 sitcom *Two in Clover*, also written by Powell and Driver, lasted two series, it never really caught on with the public, but Thames were keen to retain the services of James. Powell and Driver went through a succession of potential ideas: one had Sid as the landlord of an East End pub, another as a boxing promoter, then as the owner of a betting shop. All quite viable, but nothing that really caught anyone's imagination. 'Then Sid went off and did a seaside summer season,' recalls producer William G. Stewart. 'It was a comedy play in which he portrayed a family man. Philip Jones at Thames sent Vince and Harry off to see this play and they came back with an idea of putting Sid in a sitcom with a wife and a couple of teenage kids. Then Philip said to me, "Would you take it on," and I said, "Absolutely."'[27]

Stewart was a former holiday camp redcoat who worked his way up the ladder at the BBC from shifting scenery to directing comedy shows. He moved to ITV in the late '60s and was responsible for a string of sitcoms starting with *Father, Dear Father*. Stewart later achieved television fame himself as the host of Channel 4's long-running quiz show *Fifteen to One*.

Bless this House was the first time Stewart had worked with Sid James, and during early rehearsals found the veteran comic's performance curiously lacklustre:

> I quietly said to Sid, 'It's a bit flat, you know. I think it needs a bit more energy.' He said, 'I know kid.' I said, 'Let's try it again.' And he said, 'It'll be there.' Sid had done some boxing as a young man and he lent over towards me and whispered, 'Trust me. I never leave the fight in the gym.' He always had these little witticisms and several times over the years he used that expression, just trust me. And I did. Come on, if Sid James says trust me, you've got it made.[28]

Stewart went on to both produce and direct all sixty-five episodes, and from the very beginning he and Sid bonded and over time became extremely close friends. On set Sid was incredibly creative, but not in a demonstrative way. Instead, he might quietly suggest something to Stewart and nearly always it added to the humour in the scene or to a colleague's performance. On one occasion there was a complicated scene in the studio with something like five actors involved. Sid sensed that something was wrong.

'Is everything OK kid?' he said to Stewart.

'I just haven't got enough cameras to follow all the actors Sid, that's all.'

Sid looked around. 'I'll tell you what you do. Where's my camera?' Stewart pointed to one. 'Put that on me,' said Sid. 'I won't let you down.'[29]

The cameras rolled. 'And we played the scene with me just leaving that camera on Sid,' recalls Stewart, 'leaving me with enough cameras to do the rest of it. And every time somebody said something, he'd pull a face or give a reaction so that every line got a laugh. He was a hugely professional actor. And it's not talking out of turn to say that he did not think highly of some of his fellow Carry On stars, people like Kenneth Williams and Charles Hawtrey. Sid took his work very seriously. He never mucked about.'[30]

Sid's long-suffering but devoted wife was played by Leeds-born Diana Coupland, who was chosen by Stewart after seeing her in an episode of *Please, Sir!* However, much of the show's humour derives from watching Sid trying to understand and relate to his children. 'You know that generation gap they keep going on about,' he says, alluding to his son, Mike. 'It's between his ears!' Certainly, Powell and Driver set out from the start to exploit the friction that exists in most families made up of middle-aged parents and teenage children. 'The Abbott family live in a state of perpetual turmoil, varying between hysterical neutrality, punctuated with occasional moments of veiled hostility, and open warfare,' they told the *TV Times*.

Sid's teenage children were played by Sally Geeson and Robin Stewart. During the auditions, it was actually Robin Askwith who made the biggest impression on William G. Stewart:

As he walked out of the door I said to Sid, 'He's perfect,' but Sid said, 'Yeah, OK, but let's just see the others.' Then after Robin Stewart walked out Sid and I looked at each other and said, 'It's got to be him.'[31]

Robin was cast and his success in the role earned him fleeting heart-throb status.

Such was the runaway success of the show that within a year a spin-off movie was made by the Carry On team of producer Peter Rogers and director Gerald Thomas.

Most of the regular TV cast appear with the exception of Robin Stewart, who had prior work commitments. In an ironic twist, his replacement was Robin Askwith. It's no surprise to learn that the film isn't particularly good, though much enjoyment is derived from the supporting cast of familiar faces like Terry Scott and June Whitfield as next-door neighbours, a sort of trial run for their sitcom *Terry and June*.

It was an odd trend in the early to mid-'70s to regularly churn out film versions of sitcoms. Many of them were timed for the summer holidays and for good reason. With the likelihood of several downpours, almost everybody who went to a seaside resort, be it Great Yarmouth, Blackpool or Brighton, visited the cinema at least twice. Savvy managers used to change the programme, so you'd have an *On the Buses* movie say Sunday to Wednesday and then another sitcom movie would go on Thursday, Friday, Saturday. 'It made sense because they cost nothing to make,' says William G. Stewart. 'They also sold well in the Commonwealth, places like Australia, New Zealand, Canada, South Africa where all these British sitcoms were shown on TV. They nearly always made a healthy profit, not like *Star Wars* or Bond, but they did make money.'[32]

On television the show continued to go from strength to strength, largely due to Stewart's adoption of the American sitcom policy of commissioning episodes from a variety of writers, including Carla Lane. Stewart sometimes asked her for little bits of help and script doctoring and then offered her the chance to write some full episodes.

Carla didn't want to do it at first, then after agreeing went down to the studio to meet the cast, including Sid James. 'We acted as though we'd known each other for years,' Carla remembers. 'We had a laugh together and he liked what I did for the show. He was not really a funny guy. He was a very serious man to work with.'[33]

Brian Cooke also wrote several episodes and remembers all too well working with Sid. 'He was a gambler, Sid, and borrowed money from everybody; everyone told me about it. And one day Sid came up to me and said, "Do you have a tenner on you?" I said, "Of course Sid," and gave it to him thinking, that's the end of that. About three weeks later he came up to me and handed me forty quid, so you never know.'[34]

Sid was loved by all the *Bless this House* team. 'Sid was a much better actor than people gave him credit for,' says William G. Stewart. 'He wasn't always blowing raspberries. In real life he was a quiet, serious, very intelligent person who happened to discover this persona that was worth gold.'[35] His appeal was universal. 'It's a ghastly cliché,' says Stewart, 'but Sid was really loved. I mean, he couldn't go anywhere in the street. When we went out filming on location, we'd have bigger crowds there than we would in the studios. For example, he never went into a pub alone, he couldn't. Someone, myself or an assistant, would have to go in with him.'[36]

In 1974, with the show still among the highest rated on television, *Bless this House* came to an end. After a gap of two years

Sid was talked into reviving the series, but these episodes were of an inferior quality and Sid himself looked old and tired on screen. Then in April 1976, just a few days after the last episode was broadcast, Sid James collapsed on stage at the Sunderland Empire on the opening night of a play called *The Mating Season*. He'd suffered a massive heart attack and died on the way to hospital. He was 62.

***

At LWT Frank Muir surrounded himself with able young producers, some with little experience, but full of enthusiasm. One such individual was Humphrey Barclay. A member of the Cambridge Footlights revue, Barclay began his career on BBC radio producing the long-running *I'm Sorry, I'll Read that Again* before moving in 1967 to Rediffusion (soon to become Thames Television) to work on the comedy sketch show *Do Not Adjust Your Set*, featuring three soon-to-be members of Monty Python: Michael Palin, Terry Jones and Eric Idle. It was the success of this show that brought Barclay to Muir's attention and into a job at LWT. 'Frank was a joy to work with,' says Barclay. 'He was an avuncular figure. I don't think you'd necessarily call him a leader of men, but you wanted to do your best for him. He gave you a feeling of total confidence in your ability and in the task ahead of you all as a team.'[37]

Muir must have had enormous faith in Barclay since he gave him LWT's opening programme, the comedy sketch show *We Have Ways of Making You Laugh*, which wasn't strictly true unfortunately. After that Barclay worked on several light entertainment shows when Muir asked him to take charge of a new sitcom planned for the summer of 1969, *Doctor in the House*, based on the highly successful comedy novels of Richard Gordon about a bunch of ne'er-do-well medical students. The immediate problem facing Barclay was the concern that the show would be seen as a pale imitation of the famous Doctor film series starring Dirk Bogarde, again based on Gordon's books and still very current in the public's mind; would they miss Sir Lancelot Spratt, for example, so wonderfully played by James Robertson Justice? Wisely the decision was made to create a totally different set of characters doing much the same kind of knockabout stuff.

The new central character was to be Michael Upton, a young innocent medical student recently arrived at St Swithin's teaching hospital. Barclay's strong candidate for the role was David Jason. 'I thought he was a very talented comedy actor and would be ideal as the young doctor. But it was our director David Askey who steered us towards Barry Evans for his lovability over David's knockabout comedic qualities, and I think we made the right choice.'[38] Evans had made a recent splash in the 'Swinging Sixties' movie *Here We Go Round the Mulberry Bush* and was ably supported by a group of young actors including Robin Nedwell, Geoffrey Davies and George Layton.

As Barclay remembers it, the very first episode, written by John Cleese and Graham Chapman, while very good was a bit untidy and needed some fixing. Step forward Frank Muir, who came to a rehearsal one morning to watch a run-through. In the scene that was to play just before the commercial break, Michael Upton has just been interviewed about getting a place at St Swithin's. Outside he's asked by one of his mates how it went. In the script Evans was supposed to reply, 'I really don't know.' End of part one. Muir watched this and said, 'Do you know, I don't think that's going to keep people through the commercial break. Why don't you make it more positive?' And so, it was changed to Evans, his face opening up into a broad smile, saying, 'I think I'm in.' End of part one. 'And that was a wonderful lesson,' says Barclay, 'because it taught me so much about the architecture of the commercial half hour, that you've got to have the audience go and make the coffee saying, "It's good, isn't it," and ready to come back for part two.'[39]

Barclay saw what a good combination Cleese and Chapman were, two friends who liked writing together, one of them a medical professional; Chapman was a qualified doctor. He didn't have to look very far to find a similar team from among his acquaintances: Graeme Garden (another qualified doctor) who was happy to write with Bill Oddie. 'The combination of Bill, slightly more knockabout, and Graeme, slightly more cerebral, made for some jolly good scripts,' says Barclay.[40] Garden and Oddie, of course, would soon become *The Goodies*.

Doctor in the House was another big hit for LWT. 'We had a wonderful time on it,' says Barclay. 'The joy of it was that most of the team were in their 20s and it was just fun for all of us.'[41]

By the time the second series finished in mid-1970 Muir had left LWT and been replaced by Barry Took. One of the first decisions Took made was to cancel *Doctor in the House*. 'He said he didn't believe in it at all,' recalls Barclay. 'He only allowed us to continue, after we'd picked our jaws off the floor, by saying, well get it out of the hospital, then.'[42]

Doctor at Large saw the gang qualifying as doctors, including new recruit Richard O'Sullivan, and embarking upon their professional careers away from St Swithin's. Arriving in February 1971, it ran for an incredible twenty-nine consecutive weeks. Little wonder that Barclay at one point became short of writers. 'I rang up Cleese, who'd just had the gas bill in, and so he said yes he would write six episodes.'[43]

Just before the next series, *Doctor in Charge*, which began in 1972, Barry Evans suddenly announced that he was refusing to sign a new contract and leaving the show. 'He became discontented with being in the series,' reveals Barclay. 'He found it very difficult to cope with the stardom.'[44] Instead, Barclay elevated Robin Nedwell to the central role and as a result the series changed direction. 'We'd really run out of things that the young innocent doctor could do, so instead of just trying to replicate Barry's performance I brought in a kind of bull in the china shop character instead. And that was a different approach which carried us through another three series.'[45]

Replacing the larger-than-life presence of James Robertson Justice's Sir Lancelot was the equally imposing Sir Geoffrey Loftus, who ruled St Swithin's with an iron rod. The part was played by Ernest Clark, an actor who took himself terribly seriously and there wasn't much difference between how he was in the show and how he was off the show. He brought a copy of *The Times* to the set every day and it was always folded immaculately, and as far as he was concerned it was sacrosanct. One day at rehearsal John Kane, appearing as one of the medical students, decided to play a prank and asked Clark if he could borrow his *Times*. He agreed reluctantly, 'Be careful with it.' John took it, carefully substituting it with a copy he had brought in himself, and then pretended to get very angry at something, 'This is absolute garbage,' and tore it to pieces. Clark went apoplectic. Everyone was in on the joke except Clark. Then, of course, John produced his immaculate *Times* from behind his back.

Following *Doctor in Charge* came 1974's *Doctor at Sea*, 'which we did because there was a mistaken belief that the show needed more crumpet,' reveals Barclay. 'And after that sank, we came back to the hospital, which is, of course, where people wanted us to be.'[46]

Barclay was always throwing his net far and wide collecting all manner of new writers to work on the show, including Douglas Adams, a year before *Hitchhiker's Guide to the Galaxy* exploded on to the radio. Another time Barclay was having a drink at the studio bar after recording the last episode of a series, looking forward to taking a break, when a message came through from on high. They'd had a disaster and had to cancel an upcoming show, could Barclay carry straight on and do another thirteen *Doctors*. 'F*ck me,' says Barclay. 'Of course, I said yes, and I got to the stage of being so desperate for ideas that I would pick up on the slightest scrap. A 17-year-old schoolboy wrote in and said, I think this is a good idea for a *Doctor*'s episode. I got back to him and said, well, flesh that out into a full story and write one scene.'[47] It turned out to be Phil Redmond, later creator of *Grange Hill* and *Brookside*.

There was also a young writer who came from Canada called Gail Renard; 'and she couldn't quite get the writing style right,' admits Barclay.[48] The series' regular writer Bernard McKenna did such an extensive patch-up job on one of her episodes that Barclay insisted he take a co-writing credit. When McKenna refused, Barclay suggested he take a pseudonym, which ended up being an anagram of his name. So that episode went out as being written by Gail Renard and Brenda Crankmen. Amusingly, one newspaper commented how refreshing it was to see two young female scriptwriters.

Doctor on the Go arrived in 1975 and then again in 1977, by which time the series finally had a cardiac arrest and could stagger on no more. To be fair, the *Doctor* series was great fun and enormously enjoyable to watch, boasting some terrific supporting players, really the cream of the crop of '70s TV comedy performers from Arthur Lowe to Roy Kinnear, Hattie Jacques to James Beck. There were also early appearances for David Jason and Tony Robinson.

Like many other British sitcoms of the period, the *Doctor* series was enormously popular in Australia. Robin Nedwell and Geoffrey Davies took a stage version out there in 1974, playing to packed houses. In 1979 both actors were invited back to star in the not very imaginatively titled *Doctor Down Under*. Lasting just thirteen episodes, the UK didn't get to see them until 1981. There was also an early '90s revival with much of the old cast returning, but *Doctor at the Top* was really scraping the bottom of the barrel sadly and didn't progress further than seven episodes.

***

Ted Willis had a variety of jobs connected with amateur theatre and journalism before moving into television, where he made his name writing the first British television police series – BBC's *Dixon of Dock Green*, which first screened in 1953. His subsequent work mostly revolved around police stories and drama. Even his solitary dip into the world of sitcom had a police storyline, one that could have come straight out of an old Will Hay or Ealing comedy.

Coppers End was set in an isolated country police station where the local bobbies, including Bill Owen and Richard Wattis, do their best to avoid having any involvement with crime. Instead, they spend their days pursuing various money-making schemes, such as hiring out the patrol car for weddings and funerals. Their serenity is broken by the arrival of WPS Penny Pringle (Josephine Tewson), who is determined to shake things up. Alas, even the cast didn't give the series much hope and only one series was made for ATV. Bill Owen told the *Yorkshire Post* in 1990: 'All you could do was keep your fingers crossed someone would laugh.'

April

Playing a middle-class housewife in an almost constant state of domestic discord was nothing new to Wendy Craig, she'd already been through the rigors of raising kids in the popular sitcom *Not in Front of the Children* (BBC, 1967–70). That had been the creation of Richard Waring, a close friend of the actress. In the 1960s Wendy was seen very much as a dramatic actress, having appeared in Joseph Losey's *The Servant* and in *The Nanny* opposite Bette Davis. But Waring was determined to change all that. 'He was such a laugh was Richard,' Wendy recalls. 'We had a lot of fun together. And one night we were having dinner and he said to me, "You know there's a comedienne lurking inside of you and I'm determined to bring her out."'[49]

The success of *Not in Front of the Children* received a strange reaction from Wendy's acting colleagues:

> A lot of quite important people were rather disappointed in me and felt that I'd taken the wrong route, that I ought to have aimed for being a more classical type of actor. But I was so happy making people laugh and I had such a happy time doing it that I just thought, why not. There's nothing demeaning in making people laugh.[50]

When the series ended, Wendy and Richard Waring were approached by Thames to see if they would like to do a comedy series for them:

> They asked if we had any ideas so Richard, along with my husband Jack Bentley and I, got together this idea of a widower, Sally Harrison, trying to hold down a job while at the same time trying to bring up two boys on her own. We thought there was a lot of value to be got out of a situation like that.[51]

... *And Mother Makes Three* was among the first television series to tackle the subject of single parents and was a huge departure for a sitcom, so many of which revolve around the family unit. When it became a runaway success, it brought an altogether different kind of fame to Wendy:

> We had huge viewing ratings. I really couldn't go anywhere in England without being recognised. The thing was, because I was playing this quite sympathetic woman, people in the street were really friendly towards me. You didn't have people being vicious or spiteful, they usually came up and said, 'Hello, how are you, lovely to see you, you do make us laugh.' You had this feeling that you were surrounded by friends, really.[52]

Much of the reason for the show's success was down to Wendy's endearingly scatter-brained performance. In this and the later *Butterflies* she seemed to single-handedly express the frustrations and melancholy of mothers up and down the country. 'Sally was quite sweet really. I did like playing her. She was trying awfully hard to hold it all together.'[53]

The series was enormous fun to make for Wendy, especially working with her two young co-stars. Robin Davies was already familiar to home audiences as Carrot in the children's programme *Catweazle* (ITV, 1970–71), and David Parfitt, then just 13, would go on to become an independent film and theatre producer with credits such as *The Madness of King George* (1994) and *Shakespeare in Love* (1998), for which he won an Oscar:

> The boys were absolutely lovely and great to work with. Sometimes child actors are better than grown-ups. They're

always polite, they know their lines and they're always on time. And children have no fear, they don't think about it, they just go and do it, whereas it's grown-ups who think, 'Oh, supposing I dry, supposing it goes wrong, supposing I faint.' They have all these fears and trepidations, but children are not like that.[54]

Each episode was filmed in front of a live audience and for someone like Wendy, who was theatrically trained and began her career in the theatre, this was nothing new. However, there was a subtle difference. The trick was not to get too excited about the reactions of the audience, instead try and pitch one's performance for the camera. 'You can't milk the reaction; you've got to play it quite straight as if you were in an empty studio or making a film. But you have to at the same time leave room for the laughs. You mustn't talk over the laughs. It is quite a delicate operation.'[55] One made almost impossible by the responses you can sometimes get:

There were a couple of times when the audience were so sympathetic about my character they went, ahh, or they gave you a huge round of applause because you'd just done a scene rather well. And, of course, we had to do it again and say, 'Much as we love the applause ladies and gentlemen, can you not do that because otherwise we won't be able to cut.'[56]

Four series were made of ... *And Mother Makes Three*. In the final episode Sally marries antiquarian bookseller David Redway, a widower with one daughter, leading directly to the equally popular ... *And Mother Makes Five*.

May

Johnnie Mortimer and Brian Cooke had long expressed a desire to write something about the chancier side of the entertainment business, those plying their trade as buskers and street performers. They got their wish in 1968 when Ronnie Barker was asked by ITV to do a comedy series encompassing six different stories. 'We wrote two,' recalls Brian. 'One was called *The Fastest Gun in Finchley* and the other one was called *The Incredible Mister Tanner*, which turned out to be the best one. It was Ronnie as the world's worst escapologist, and Richard O'Sullivan as his young partner.'[57]

Three years later the writers developed this promising idea into a full series, *Kindly Leave the Kerb*, but this time equalising the ages of the two main characters and casting Peter Butterworth as the second-rate Houdini and Peter Jones as the man with the gift of the gab who passes his hat around the punters. The pair live in a basement flat, earning just enough to keep themselves going.

Sadly, *Kindly Leave the Kerb* ran for only one series on ITV. 'It just didn't work,' confesses Brian.[58] But the writers were still not finished with the idea and returned to it ten years later in the wake of the sad passing of Yootha Joyce. 'We had lined up to do more *George and Mildred*s,' says Brian, 'and Thames Television were going to lose a lot of money if we didn't do something. "Well, the only thing we've got is *Kindly Leave the Kerb*," we told them, "which we think is great."'[59] And so, a third version was made, back to the old title of *The Incredible Mr Tanner* and starring Brian Murphy and Roy Kinnear. That didn't work either and only six episodes were produced. 'So, we finally gave up on that idea,' admits Brian. 'We really thought it would work every time. Maybe something was missing each time. It's a three-legged stool, as Frank Muir used to say, it's the performer, the producer and the writer and if any one of those legs fail the stool goes down.'[60]

★★★

Granada's *The Last of the Baskets* was a well written and highly amusing vehicle for Arthur Lowe, going some way to prove to audiences that he was much more than just Captain Mainwaring. Here he plays Bodkin, a somewhat pompous butler to the slightly dying 12th Earl of Clogborough. When the Earl finally pops his clogs, it turns out that his only heir is a rather common factory worker from up north, played by Ken Jones, who moves into Clogborough Hall with his mother, played by Patricia Hayes.

Not surprisingly, Bodkin doesn't approve of his new uncouth masters, serving them their bottles of brown ale on a silver platter, but agrees to remain in his post for the sake of the family name. Besides, the new heir is in for a rude awakening as his inheritance turns out to be a poisoned chalice of unpaid bills and debts.

Lasting two series, *The Last of the Baskets* was written and created by John Stevenson, former northern theatre critic/showbiz reporter for the *Daily Mail*. It appears that Stevenson had a crusty relationship with Lowe. He told of one incident that occurred during rehearsals after Lowe had invented a neat bit of comedy business:

> Pleased with himself, and wishing to needle me, he said loudly, 'We don't need writers, do we Bill?' [Bill was series producer/director Bill Podmore, a friend of Stevenson and a director who liked and valued writers.] Bill turned to the actor and replied, 'Of course we don't, Arthur. Not once we've got the script.'[61]

June

Strange as it may seem, there does exist a sitcom featuring Richard Briers that wasn't a success. *Birds on the Wing* was a tale of a one man/two women team of confidence tricksters who spend more time swindling each other than the public. 'It never really worked,' Briers admitted:

It was a bit of a flop and lasted just six episodes. Trouble is, in my day if you had a flop, and we all have flops, you took it off your CV, like a play that ran ten days, you didn't put it in *Spotlight*. Naturally you put up your good notices and the losers went out the window. Now with these bloody computers and the internet you can't get rid of it. *Birds on the Wing*, why would I want that on my credits, it was terrible; sorry love, it's there. All your sins are remembered.[62]

Briers began his sitcom career way back in 1961 with *The Seven Faces of Jim* featuring Jimmy Edwards and followed that up with *Brothers in Law* in 1962, his first starring role on television at the age of 27:

Then I met Richard Waring, who played with me as an actor, and he said, 'I've written this thing called *Marriage Lines*.' We found Prunella Scales, almost discovered her as far as television is concerned, she was a terrific stage actress but the public didn't know who she was, and that show really took off.[63]

Marriage Lines, about the domestic ups and downs of a suburban couple, ran on the BBC for five series from 1963 to 1966. There followed a long gap afterwards where Briers worked predominantly in West End theatre until the ill-fated *Birds on the Wing* came along. He wouldn't have to wait too long, though, for another shot at sitcom stardom.

July

The Trouble with Lilian was originally a hit on BBC Radio 4 in the late '60s and written by Jennifer Phillips, a prolific writer for radio and one of the very few females writing any kind of comedy at the time. It starred Beryl Reid and Patricia Hayes as ladies of a certain vintage living together whose friendship is often strained due to the fact that one of them is the tenant while the other is her lodger.

It was Patricia's idea to transfer the show to television, but the BBC weren't interested; step forward LWT. With Beryl Reid unavailable, Dandy Nichols was a more than adequate replacement. Only six episodes were made.

★★★

You're Only Young Twice was a warm-hearted comedy set inside an old people's home, Twilight Lodge, where the residents are determined to grow old disgracefully. The message was clear, that even at pensionable age you can still enjoy life, even if Adrienne Corri's matron was usually around to spoil the fun.

It was written by prolific novelist and screenwriter Jack Trevor Story, whose television output was largely drama-led: *No Hiding Place*, *Public Eye* and *Budgie*. His very first novel, *The Trouble with Harry*, had been turned into a film by Alfred Hitchcock back in 1955. He did occasionally dabble in comedy and came up with the idea for *You're Only Young Twice* when a letter from a matron of an old people's home arrived on his desk one day at ATV suggesting there might be the basis of a series in her job. Story agreed. 'I like downbeat situations and I thought that as a humourist I could make something of it.'[64]

Alas, audiences stayed away and only one series was made. Curiously, six years later Yorkshire Television launched their own sitcom based in a retirement home. They even had the audacity to use the exact same title, *You're Only Young Twice*. Despite the obvious similarities, no one sued.

★★★

Not quite *Rebel Without a Cause*, but *Alexander the Greatest* was the nearest a sitcom set in the middle-class environs of the Jewish community in Golders Green ever got to it. Sixteen-year-old Alexander Green is intent on rebelling against his schooling and his comfortable home life, seemingly determined to give his poor parents a hard time. This intriguing premise was based on the writer Bernard Kops's own experiences of his wayward Jewish teenage son.

Starring Gary Warren, the young boy in the 1970 family classic *The Railway Children*, this ATV series also featured Adrienne Posta as Alexander's big sister, and a theme song sung by Barry Green, who later changed his name to Barry Blue and had a string of hits in the mid-'70s. It ran for two series.

September

Returning to screens, and showing no signs of losing its vast popularity, was *On the Buses*, already in its fifth series after first going on the air in 1969. It was created by established sitcom writers Ronald Chesney and Ronald Wolfe, most famous for

The Rag Trade, one of the BBC's top comedy hits of the early '60s. And it was to the BBC that they took their new idea, only for it to be derisorily rejected. The executives at the BBC didn't see what was funny about buses. A week later Chesney and Wolfe sat in Frank Muir's office over at London Weekend Television. The reception there was resolutely more positive and within twenty minutes a deal was agreed. Having already scored a sitcom hit with *Please, Sir!*, *On the Buses* would cement LWT's reputation for populist fare.

Unashamedly working class, and peppered with bawdy, seaside postcard humour, sometimes bordering on the vulgar, *On the Buses* took a battering from the critics but the public made it a smash hit, sometimes knocking the mighty *Coronation Street* from the top of the ratings. Taking place at a fictional east London bus depot, the show revolves around the antics of bus driver Stan Butler and his lecherous conductor Jack. Reg Varney, who came from a music hall and variety background and scored in the role of foreman in Wolfe and Chesney's *The Rag Trade*, played Stan, while Jack was essayed by the classically trained Bob Grant.

Laughs at work are counterbalanced by Stan's miserable domestic arrangements; he still lives at home with his over-bearing mother, frumpy sister Olive and her layabout husband. Veteran performer Cicely Courtneidge played mum in that opening series, sharing star billing with Varney, before the arrival of Doris Hare, who immediately made the part her own.

Stan and Jack's eternal nemesis is Inspector Blake, played by Stephen Lewis, whose authoritarian manner and Hitler-esque moustache gave rise to Nazi comparisons. His eternal cry of 'I 'ate you, Butler!', Lewis' own invention, it wasn't in the script, became a national catchphrase. Lewis enjoyed playing up to his 'Blakey' image. It was not unknown for him to visit bus depots, if he was appearing locally in a play or panto, and have fun shouting at the inspectors and drivers in character as 'Blakey'.

The early shows were recorded at the old LWT studios in Wembley, big enough to allow not one but two double-decker buses on to the studio floor. Later, when LWT moved to the purpose-built TV centre on the South Bank, the studio's restrictive space meant that the buses were fibreglass mock-ups. Varney, who hung around a real bus depot for two weeks prior to starting the series in order to pick up a few tips, also had to undertake a PCV driving test. Funnily enough, Bob Grant had actually once been a bus driver, not for very long because he was sacked after crashing one of the buses.

On the Buses is often held up as an example of the sort of sexism that was rife in society at the time and mirrored in popular culture, not least in TV sitcom land. Olive, played by Anna Karen, was made up to look like some kind of Gorgon in pebble glasses and was the butt of numerous jokes about her looks. Husband Arthur, played by character actor Michael Robbins, often snarls at her for being, 'a stupid great lump', and when she gets into a swimming costume she is told, 'You look positively obscene, woman!' A former model, Anna turned up at her audition glammed up, only to be taken to one side and told to scrub off her make-up in order to look dowdy. She got the role.

We also have the unpalatable sight of Stan and Jack, two middle-aged men ogling every minidressed dolly bird in sight like Sid James on valium. Some episodes also featured the black actor Glen Whitter, saddled by the scriptwriters with the character name of Chalkie.

A total of seventy-four episodes of *On the Buses* were broadcast over seven series. To give some idea of its impact on the nation, a board game was produced and a comic strip appeared in the children's magazine *Look-in*. There was also a marked increase in applications to become bus drivers up and down the country.

Not only was there the obligatory spin-off movie, but a record three of them, all produced by Hammer Films. The first arrived in 1971 and according to the *Daily Express* broke eighty-eight box office records in its opening week, and within five days had already covered its production cost of £98,000. The plot sees Stan and Jack scheming to put a stop to a liberal company policy that allows the employment of, perish the thought, female bus drivers. The prevailing snobbish attitude towards the show was clearly evidenced when an examiner at the British Board of Film Classification referred to the picture as, 'simple, good-hearted dirt for the working chap'.[65]

Mutiny on the Buses and *Holiday on the Buses*, set in a holiday camp, followed in quick succession. Wolfe and Chesney even managed to sell the *On the Buses* concept to the American network NBC, where the scripts were reworked by the team behind *The Dick Van Dyke Show*. Renamed *Lotsa Luck*, the Reg Varney role went to Dom DeLuise, not a bus driver here but a lost property clerk for the New York bus department. *Lotsa Luck* didn't come close to matching the success of its British cousin, running for just the one series of twenty-four episodes during 1973–74.

The wheels had started to come off back home, too. Wolfe and Chesney had taken a step back from scripting duties, allowing a number of other writers on to the team, with varying results. Michael Robbins was the first to call it quits, leaving before the seventh series went out early in 1973. He was soon followed by Varney himself, who walked out halfway through. The makers were faced with the challenge of keeping a sitcom on air without its main character. The decision to move Inspector Blake into the Butler household as a lodger probably made sense but the series was clearly coming to its end.

In 1990 plans were unveiled to revive the show and the original cast were reunited on the BBC's *Wogan* show. A pilot episode was devised that saw Stan and Jack running their own bus company in the newly deregulated market in direct competition with another company in the same town owned by 'Blakey'. The pilot was never made and the series didn't leave the depot.

Although he did find other work, Varney never escaped the spectre of his 'Cor Blimey' persona from *On the Buses*. Things were much worse for his cohort Bob Grant. Struggling for years with a lack of acting jobs and suffering from depression, he committed suicide in 2003, gassing himself in his car.

***

Now Take My Wife developed from a single episode on Comedy Playhouse, the BBC's breeding ground for sitcoms at the time. Entitled, *Just Harry and Me*, it focused on the generation-gap problems between a suburban middle-class couple and their teenage daughter. When the series began in earnest the focus shifted more on to the zany situations caused by the mother, played by Sheila Hancock, thus becoming a comedy vehicle for the actress. Years later, Hancock indicated that she had issues with the show, seeing it as an example of the sort of stereotyped ditzy blonde roles actresses were usually lumbered with in television comedy. Each episode began with her husband Harry turning exasperatingly to the camera saying, 'Now … take my wife.'

Harry was played by Welsh star Donald Houston, who came to prominence as the juvenile lead in *The Blue Lagoon* (1949) and continued working regularly in British films such as *Doctor in the*

House (1954) and *Where Eagles Dare* (1968). The show was not a success and ran for one series.

★★★

After the failure of *Shine a Light*, David Nobbs returned to Yorkshire Television with *Keep it in the Family*, an amusingly warped view of suburban bliss co-written with Peter Vincent. James and Yvonne Bannister are a married couple each burdened with an elderly widowed parent. One weekend James invites his mother Norah to stay, while Yvonne invites her war veteran father Des. Unfortunately, both decide to move in on a more permanent basis, in spite of the fact they loathe each other on sight.

Des was played by Jack Haig, later of *'Allo 'Allo!* fame, and very much a performer of the old school, as David remembers:

> He came from a music hall tradition and was a bit difficult to deal with because he could see that the scripts were not as good as they could have been. I don't think they were awful, but I don't think they were stunning. So, he would keep making suggestions. The most irritating of which was, he said, 'I've got a wonderful comedy sneeze,' and I kept having to resist him putting in his comedy sneeze.[66]

By the time of *Keep it in the Family*, Nobbs and Vincent had become a fairly well-established team, contributing sketches for the Two Ronnies and Frankie Howerd. Unlike a lot of writing partnerships, they sat working behind desks in the same room.

'When I talk to most writers who collaborate,' says David, 'one of them fleshes out the story, while the other expands the dialogue, it's that sort of thing, they don't sit in a room discussing every line. But most of the time Peter and I did sit in a room discussing every line. Looking back on it I think we probably approached that in the wrong way because it doesn't take half the time, it actually takes longer because you're discussing everything. Plus, you're getting half the money.'[67]

Keep it in the Family didn't exactly catch on, lasting just six episodes. David doesn't blame the actors or the scripts so much, instead highlights a lack of a leading character that stood out from the rest of the cast. 'I don't think I understood the extent to which a comedy is driven by a leading role. I think it was a bit too evenly spread. I don't think you knew who the star was, because there wasn't one.'[68] It was a lesson David would rectify brilliantly on his first solo sitcom featuring a certain Reginald Perrin.

***

Now, here's an odd one, *Under and Over* starred the three members of the popular Irish vocal trio the Bachelors: Dec Cluskey, Con Cluskey and John Stokes. Although highly experienced performers with a string of hits to their name and numerous TV variety appearances, it was something of a gamble to cast them as Irish navvies working on the London underground. 'It came as a real surprise to us when we were asked to do it,' recalls Con. 'And we took it as a bit of an honour.'[69]

Hedging their bets, the BBC made a pilot first for their Comedy Playhouse strand. It was directed by David Askey, who worked well with the trio and gained their trust and confidence. What happened next Dec always classed as, 'a tragedy'. For whatever reason, Askey was not asked back for the series, instead another director took over. 'And he was an alcoholic,' claims Dec. 'He did over-imbibe on a regular basis – and that was every day. Whereas we'd had the very strict regime of rehearsal with David Askey, now everything was extremely loose with no direction whatsoever and we were left to our own devices.'[70]

In the early 1970s there seemed to be a more laissez-faire attitude to boozing in the television industry. Even members of the cast got stuck in, including Jack Smethurst. Much of the show's action took place in awkward and claustrophobic sets. 'Jack was absolutely pissed out of his brain for one of the very complex special effects that we did where the actual tunnel had to fall in on top of us,' according to Dec. 'So, they weren't very amused when Jack forgot his lines and they had to recreate this complex effect all over again. Not very amusing.'[71]

Part of the plot revolved around Dec's character running this big scam, where there are supposed to be twenty fellas down in the hole digging away while in actual fact there was only two of them, but he was collecting money for the twenty. 'Dec was the clever one,' says Con. 'He was the Dublin entrepreneur type. And then there was myself who was supposed to be as thick as two short planks, and John who was the northern Irish protestant.'[72]

For one episode the cast and crew popped over to Ireland for some location filming. 'And it was absolutely sensational,' Dec recalls. 'The location people found a square in a village that had all these pubs. We arrived on the Sunday morning, the day after they'd had the all-Ireland hurling final so every pub was absolutely wrecked. There was about half an inch of broken glass on the floor of every pub we went into.'[73]

Back in the studio, Dec's patience with the director was near breaking point:

> I actually got quite upset with the whole thing. It had started off good but just gradually got looser and looser and by the time we came to the sixth episode it was just a shambles. You can't work with a drunken director, it's as simple as that. The

shows were recorded on the Sunday and his proud boast was that he didn't drink on the day of production, so all he did all day was shake, and that is not an amusing experience from an artist's point of view.[74]

Further bad luck arrived when the show was put up against the Tony Curtis/Roger Moore action series *The Persuaders*. 'And that was probably the most hyped series ever in the history of television,' says Dec. 'It was just advertised to death. It was on every hoarding, and it was directly up against us each week, and of course we lost out completely.'[75]

As a result, only one series was ever made, but the brothers enjoyed the experience immensely. 'People who saw it loved it,' recalls Con. 'We got a terrific reaction and we were hoping it would be continued, but unfortunately the powers that be didn't see it that way.'[76]

★★★

By the end of the third series of *Please, Sir!* LWT's decision to cast actors in their early 20s to play unruly teenagers was starting to look faintly ridiculous as some of them had begun to look even older than the teachers. The obvious solution was to recast the entirety of form 5C, this time more realistically with 18–19-year-olds. As for the old brigade, they were rewarded with a series of their own, *The Fenn Street Gang*, which saw them as school leavers cast out into the harsh real world. 'But I think when we did *Fenn Street*, LWT still thought of us as kids,' recalls David Barry, back as Frankie Abbott. 'They thought, would we be able to carry a series on our own?'[77]

To be on the safe side, John Alderton was pressed into agreeing to do the first three episodes to see it launched safely. 'And it's my recollection that he would only do it if he got a grand an episode,' recalls David, 'which was an incredible amount in those days, plus a role in a straight drama series, which turned out to be *Upstairs, Downstairs*. That was all written into his contract. So, he managed to kill off his Bernard Hedges character playing the welsh chauffeur in *Upstairs, Downstairs*.'[78]

Confident of success, LWT ordered a first run of twenty-one episodes for the opening series. 'It was hard work,' recalls David. 'Everybody was under a lot of pressure because you'd go into the studio to record an episode sometimes two days before it was broadcast, so they were cutting it really fine.'[79]

With the original series carrying on that autumn, along with the arrival of *Fenn Street*, writers Bob Larbey and John Esmonde were so busy they could only act as script editors on the new show, so a whole batch of fresh writers were brought in. 'I thought a lot of these new writers missed the point of the show,' says David. 'I don't think they really got the characters. Some of them were coming up with the most ridiculous ideas. Frankie Abbott, who fantasised about being a private detective, actually became a private detective and I felt like saying, "Heh, come on, you've missed the point." It was like making Billy Liar successful. It didn't work.'[80]

To keep things familiar for audiences, the former classmates kept in close contact with one another throughout the new series. But as time went on some of the characters were written out or cast members got pregnant and had to leave. 'In the end there was just four of us,' recalls David. 'We used to make jokes that it was like Agatha Christie's *And Then There Were None* because we were dropping like flies.'[81]

To compensate, new characters were introduced, notably a local racketeer called Mr Bowler, played by George Baker, who ended up getting his own spin-off series, essentially a spin-off from a spin-off. For a while there were plans for another spin-off show, this time featuring Duffy and Sharon, now played by Carol Hawkins, who had also taken the role in the *Please, Sir!* movie. They'd begun dating at school and by season three of *Fenn Street* got married. The premise was that Duffy's painting and decorating business was doing so well the couple could afford to go up in the world by moving to a posh housing estate. The idea was later dropped.

Although there was a general paucity of good comedy situations, the public's affection towards these characters was enough for three series to be made. It's David's belief that when Larbey and Esmonde returned to writing them the standard of the show went up, but LWT just didn't want to do any more. 'I always got the impression that LWT were rather resentful of their own success with *Please, Sir!* and *Fenn Street*. You would wander into LWT's office reception and they'd have photos of all their hit shows, but never *Please, Sir!* And it wasn't just me being paranoid, people used to remark on it saying, "Why are there no photos of *Please, Sir!*?"'[82]

October

After appearing successfully together in a West End revival of J.B. Priestley's *When We Are Married*, Peggy Mount and Hugh Lloyd asked *Dad's Army* creator Jimmy Perry to come up with a sitcom for them to star in. The result was Perry's only comedy with a domestic setting, the warm but unmemorable *Lollipop Loves Mr Mole*, in which the comedy veterans play husband and wife Maggie and Reg, whose affectionate nicknames for each other provided the title.

Perry had written for Lloyd before, the obscure 1969 BBC 2 sitcom *The Gnomes of Dulwich* co-starring Terry Scott, and tailored the part of Reg to suit his personality, that of the well-meaning underdog. Lloyd, who'd been straight man to the likes of Benny Hill and Tony Hancock, described the show as a combination of drama and comedy, where the best comedy comes out of character and not out of funny lines.

For Perry, on the other hand, there were problems from the start. Peggy Mount had made a virtual career out of playing, to use an outmoded term, battleaxes, and Perry had written Maggie as a domineering woman but with a heart of gold, in order to contrast with Lloyd's quiet and timid Reg. In the first week of rehearsal Perry grew concerned that Mount was playing her role in a restrained and understated manner and enquired why. 'Oh, I don't want to play aggressive, shouting women anymore,' she replied, which sort of torpedoed Perry's entire scenario.[83]

Perry feared the worst for *Lollipop Loves Mr Mole* but Bill Ward, head of ITV's Midlands franchise ATV, asked for another series. Perry was incredulous. 'But it's rubbish. It doesn't work.'[84] Ward told Perry not to argue with the viewing figures, which were good, so one more series was made.

November

In the same year that he found TV immortality through his partnership with Ronnie Barker in *The Two Ronnies* (BBC, 1971–87), diminutive comic actor Ronnie Corbett was cast as an insurance salesman who still lives at home with his domineering mother in *Now Look Here*; an early prototype of his portrayal of mummy's boy Timothy Lumsden in the '80s sitcom *Sorry!*

Desperate to spread his wings, Ronnie gets his chance when he meets soulmate Laura, played by Rosemary Leach, and begins a courtship, which by the start of the second season has resulted in the pair getting married and setting up home together.

For so conventional a sitcom it's rather a surprise to learn that its writers were Monty Python's Graham Chapman and gag meister Barry Cryer, who had also scripted Corbett's successful late '60s sitcom *No – That's Me Over Here!*

★★★

It was a chance meeting at a dinner party that led the editor of *The Sunday Times Magazine* to ask Jilly Cooper to write a piece for him on the difficulties of being a young working wife. As well as being typically outrageous, it was very funny and, as a result, *The Sunday Times* took her on as a regular columnist. Remarkably these columns, in which Jilly, among other things, wrote about marriage, sex and housework, ran from 1969 to 1982.

It was after one of these columns came out that the BBC rang up and asked Jilly if she'd like to have a go at doing a sitcom. 'I was thrilled and very excited.'[85] The result was *It's Awfully Bad for Your Eyes, Darling* and it was about four girls sharing a London flat and their hysterical lifestyle. 'Mothers were always turning up at the wrong time,' says Jilly. 'And people were always getting off with people they shouldn't and there was general bad behaviour and fun.'[86] It was loosely based on Jilly's own experiences. 'One of the funniest times in my life was living in a flat with two girls, one was a very beautiful air hostess and she used to smuggle back brandy in her bra.'[87]

Jilly sat down and wrote a pilot, 'and I had a lovely director called John Howard Davies'.[88] It was after the BBC commissioned a series that the problems started. First of all, they sent in a script doctor called Christopher Bond. 'He was a darling man,' Jilly recalls, 'and came and sat on my sofa for ages and ages where

I lived in Fulham and we drank a lot of gin. But I'd never had to write with another person and it was terribly difficult and I don't think it worked at all.'[89]

Much worse was the departure of John Howard Davies. 'Instead, they moved in this Australian director who was terribly anti the whole thing. He was a perfectly nice man but he just thought the whole thing was deeply silly and set about changing everything.'[90]

Coming as Jilly did from Fleet Street and journalism, where there was a fair sprinkling of women writers and editors, though not many, television was almost completely male dominated and she found herself almost without any kind of creative influence:

> I had a reputation for being a very sexy writer in those days and maybe that's why they had a script doctor and a rather tough director to take all the naughty bits out. But I just hated coming in and finding out a whole scene had been completely changed. I found that very difficult to deal with. It was one of the more unhappy experiences of my life.[91]

Some compensation arrived with the good relations she built up with the cast. 'That part of it was fun.'[92] The cast were certainly well chosen: Jane Carr, for instance, had recently appeared in the film *The Prime of Miss Jean Brodie*, and there was model-turned-actress Joanna Lumley as the personification of that post swinging '60s girl about town, who had a habit of unselfconsciously wandering around the flat semi-clothed, almost an embryonic Patsy from *Absolutely Fabulous*. 'Joanna was great and she became a huge friend,' says Jilly. 'She was wonderful and very disciplined. All she used to have for lunch was a grapefruit.'[93]

Jilly recalls that reviews for the first episode were quite good and then it all went wrong. 'I think I lost heart in it really.'[94] One critic joked about *It's Awfully Bad for Your Eyes, Darling* by saying, 'and absolute hell on the ears'. With this kind of response, it was no surprise that the BBC didn't want a second series. Not that Jilly was bothered:

> During the making of the series there were rows and I was terribly upset that the scripts were messed about with. I was probably an awful nuisance and crying and all that sort of thing and when it just came to an end, we all said, jolly good thing too. I don't think anybody minded at all.[95]

Jilly much preferred going back to working on her own as a journalist and then enjoying a highly successful career as a novelist.

Looking back, perhaps the show was too esoteric. One could even argue for it being a little ahead of time. In some ways the show can be viewed as a forerunner of the Dawn French/Jennifer Saunders/Ruby Wax scripted comedy of the mid-'80s, *Girls on Top*, whose flat share scenario also featured four wildly different women.

December

The year was to end on a bizarre note with a sitcom featuring Mike and Bernie Winters, a popular double act of the late '60s and early '70s. Their appeal was simple: Mike played the straight man to Bernie's daft Jerry Lewis-inspired clown and they toured the variety halls of the UK with great success and landed their own television stand-up and sketch shows.

The established writing partnership of Vince Powell and Harry Driver were behind the show, casting the brothers as a pair of out of work music hall comedians hoping to catch a lucky break in the business. Unfamiliar with the discipline of comedy acting, the pair looked out of their depth and the scripts didn't help. Mike and Bernie later complained that the show gave them little to no scope for characterisation.

Predictably mauled by the critics, only six episodes of *Mike and Bernie* were made by Thames, although the public's viewing pleasure was somewhat enlivened by a cavalcade of guest stars, including Peter Jones, Bill Pertwee, DJ David Hamilton, Fred Emney, Roy Barraclough, Billy Dainty and then current Chelsea footballers Peter Osgood, Ron (chopper) Harris and Charlie Cooke.

Chapter Three

1972

February

To a generation of children Leslie Crowther was the host of the long-running kids show *Crackerjack*, then in 1970 he was lured away from the BBC by London Weekend Television and given his own sketch show. What Crowther really aspired to be was a sort of British Dick Van Dyke, the all-round American entertainer who starred in his own highly successful sitcom in the States. Crowther wanted to come up with a similar vehicle for himself and teamed up with writer Ronnie Taylor to throw a few ideas around. The result was *My Good Woman*.

This genteel and quintessential middle-of-the-road husband-and-wife comedy was an enormous hit and featured Crowther as a hapless husband whose wife was a compulsive charity worker and do-gooder. It was a classic domestic sitcom situation. 'Like all those male characters in those days Leslie was the butt of the jokes,' says William G. Stewart, who produced the series:

In *Bless this House* Sid was the butt of the jokes, Patrick was the butt of the jokes in *Father Dear Father*. The male characters were always the butt of the jokes. But it was good fun, and working with Leslie was sheer joy, we were like brothers. He was a great comedy actor, and nobody worked harder. Leslie was one of the most professional actors I ever worked with.[1]

Cast as Leslie's wife was Sylvia Sims, who had never played comedy before, being previously best known for her dramatic film work, notably *Ice Cold in Alex* (1958) and *Victim* (1961), co-starring with Dirk Bogarde. Someone else making his comedy TV debut was Richard Wilson, playing a vicar and the main benefactor of Sylvia's tireless charity work. 'It was one of the first things he did,' recalls William G. Stewart. 'But you could see that it was only a matter of time before someone would look at him and say, "We just need the right character because this guy's good." I could see it a mile away.'[2]

My Good Woman ran for five series, coming to an end in 1974, much to Crowther's disappointment since it was still enormously popular with the public; Ronnie Taylor simply couldn't come up with any more scripts. Instead, in 1976 Taylor created another sitcom for Crowther, the less successful *Big Boy Now!* in which he played a middle-aged bachelor still living at home.

★★★

One of Britain's most versatile actresses, appearing in everything from West End musicals to kitchen sink drama and Carry On movies, Dora Bryan starred in *Both Ends Meet* for LWT. She plays Dora Page, a working-class widow looking after a teenage son who is constantly short of money. She works at a local sausage factory owned by Julius Cannon, played by Ivor Dean, whose bloodhound features typified the stereotypical notion of Scotland Yard duffers in '60s TV series like *The Saint*.

Wendy Richard, playing a sexy factory girl, noted in her autobiography that *Both Ends Meet*, 'turned out to be not the funniest of sitcoms'. It was all fairly predictable with stock situations such as the episode when Dora's house is nominated as a collection point for jumble and, of course, all her treasured possessions are removed by mistake. But Dora's infectious scattiness just about carried it through two series.

April

Tales from the Lazy Acre was a piece of Irish whimsy that Hugh Leonard wrote as a follow-up of sorts after the success of *Me Mammy*. It teamed once again Milo O'Shea and David Kelly, and consisted of seven comedy playlets, each based on an Irish myth or urban legend. O'Shea took the lead role each week, playing a variety of characters, while Kelly played an old storyteller who narrates the tales on the banks of a canal in Dublin. 'It was a splendid series,' says Kelly, 'again, with the wonderful Yootha Joyce. And Hugh's writing was magic. The wonderful thing about that period was that many of the writers wrote quality dialogue, not just jokes. The language was so good. So many of those sitcoms were beautifully written. And back then the F word was unacceptable.'[3]

***

Bad language was indeed frowned upon in sitcom land, but ITV were about to launch a new sitcom that was to stir up more controversy and notoriety than any other in the whole decade.

Love Thy Neighbour was born innocuously enough. Vince Powell was driving home one evening listening to a news item on the radio about the problems raised in society due to a recent influx of West Indian immigrants; Enoch Powell's inflammatory 'Rivers of Blood' speech was just five years before. One man raised concerns about the price of his house being affected if one of these families moved in next door. Powell thought that such an eventuality had great comedy potential and went to see his writing partner, Harry Driver. Obviously aware of the delicate nature of the idea, Powell was nevertheless surprised when Driver wanted nothing to do with it, fearing a backlash from critics, the Independent Television Authority and, most importantly, the public. Undeterred, Powell arranged a meeting with Philip Jones at Thames, where he got exactly the same reaction: 'It's too controversial luvvie.'[4] Since Powell was under contract to Thames, he was unable to take his idea to another broadcaster.

Less than a year later, Powell was invited to speak at a conference organised by Thames executives for their production staff. Going through his résumé of shows and what he was currently working on, Powell finished with, 'But what I would really like to do is a series about a West Indian family moving to live next door to a white family.' Philip Jones put his head in his hands and groaned, but Howard Thomas, Managing Director at Thames, said, 'That's a very interesting idea. We should do a pilot.' *Love Thy Neighbour* was born.[5]

William G. Stewart, who was asked by Jones to produce the series, has a different take on how the whole thing got started:

We had an away weekend at Brighton for the light entertainment department to talk about possible future shows. And I think it was Jeremy Isaacs, then Controller of Programmes, who said, 'What about a comedy with a black family living next door to a white family?' And I remember Philip saying, 'We'll take that on board,' and he wrote it down. It was only later that he asked Harry and Vince to come up with a script.[6]

Whatever the real story, the premise of *Love Thy Neighbour* was actually quite an interesting one, and handled with a little more political savvy might have served as an insightful and valid commentary on Britain's burgeoning multicultural society. But, heh, this was a sitcom, not *Play for Today*. Factory worker Eddie Booth, played by Jack Smethurst, is your typical working-class little Englander and a staunch Labour supporter, living with wife Joan, played by Kate Williams, in a typical street of terraced houses. When their new neighbours Bill and Barbie Reynolds move in, it marks the end of the world for Eddie when they turn out to be, well, black. While the two wives get on perfectly well, the antagonism between Eddie and Bill is represented by obvious racial name calling.

Predictably the critics despised the show, but Rudolph Walker and Nina Baden-Semper, who'd been cast as the Reynolds, claimed not to be offended by the racial overtones in the scripts. Indeed, the show was watched by many black families simply because there was no other regular black representation on peak-time television. 'I was a black face on the screen, at a time when you didn't see black faces on the screen,' Rudolph Walker was later to say. 'That sort of exposure just hadn't happened before, and it inspired a lot of young, aspiring actors.'[7] Walker even started getting recognised in the streets. 'I remember going to open Vauxhall Motors in Luton. They had to bundle me into a marquee. There were girls screaming everywhere, climbing on top of the marquee.'[8]

Often featuring in the week's top ten ratings, Powell and Driver were asked to write a stage version, which played to packed houses at the Winter Gardens, Blackpool, throughout the summer of 1973, followed by a UK tour the following year. There was also a movie, financed by Hammer, that Powell and Driver wrote in a staggering seven days. And it looks it. *Halliwell's Film Guide* decreed: 'It might have been worse, but not much.' If anything, the film strays even further over the racially offensive line, especially in the scene where Bill and his black co-workers at the factory throw Eddie into a large pot with vegetables as they do some kind of tribal dance in their underwear. Gadzooks!

Midway through the series' run, in November 1973, Harry Driver died suddenly, aged just 43. Devastated, Powell refused all attempts to team him up with another writing partner and continued to work on *Love Thy Neighbour* by himself. Finally, in 1976, after fifty-six episodes over eight series, Philip Jones made the decision that the show had finally run its course, especially in the face of adverse criticism they were receiving from the Race Relations Board.

But that wasn't quite the end. Bizarrely, in 1980 Powell was asked to resurrect the series for Australian television, since the original show had been such a massive success down under. There was only one snag: the Australian producers couldn't afford to pay all four actors so Powell had to come up with a premise featuring just Jack Smethurst. The idea was that Eddie Booth decides to emigrate to Australia and goes on ahead of his wife to set up home in a suburb of Sydney. The twist is that this time Eddie finds himself to be the outsider and the victim of prejudice from lager-swilling Aussies, who refer to the English as 'whinging pommie bastards'. Besides not being the least bit funny (only seven episodes were made), the show simply couldn't function without the other actors' participation.

However distasteful *Love Thy Neighbour* may look to some of us almost fifty years on, there's no denying the fact that Smethurst and Walker did make for a great team on screen. William G. Stewart recalls someone coming up to him once asking if he was ashamed of being associated with the show, and in all honesty, he replied that he wasn't:

> I'm not a great one for political correctness but I do appreci-
> ate that it's a different climate now. But black people didn't
> object. And what's more, the white guy hardly ever came
> out on top. Jack always came unstuck, not only from his
> neighbours but his wife. Jack's character was always the loser.
> I don't think it was as well written as it could have been if
> I'm honest, and I think there were too many personal racial
> insults, but I don't apologise for doing it.[9]

May

Partly inspired by the classic 1937 Will Hay comedy *Oh, Mr Porter!*, *The Train Now Standing* was a pleasing sitcom from LWT revolving around a decrepit and largely forgotten railway station tucked away in a remote spot of the country where modern life scarcely gets a look in. Bill Fraser plays the regimental station master who is equally stuck in the past, even to the extent of continuing to wear the uniform of the long-since-demised Great Western Railway, and spouting dictates to his staff from a rule book that came into force in 1933.

Life at the station is only mildly interrupted by the odd train (just three a day), and the occasional run-in with the area manager, played by Denis Lill in the first series and in the second and final series by Garfield Morgan, later to give John Thaw's Jack Regan a regular hard time in *The Sweeney*.

Among a surprising number of writers who worked on the series (five in all) was Ian La Frenais in a rare excursion away from his regular collaborator Dick Clement. Outdoor scenes were filmed on location at a disused station in Bodiam, East Sussex, that was owned by a local railway preservation society.

June

Alcock and Gander was a Johnnie Mortimer and Brian Cooke creation written especially for Beryl Reid, with whom the writers had recently made the film of *No Sex Please – We're British*. That featured one glorious line delivered by Miss Reid when she brings Arthur Lowe's bank manager back to her apartment and says, 'Do you like herb omelette?' And he replies, 'What the Tijuana Brass fella?' 'We really enjoyed working with Beryl on that film,' remembers Brian, 'and afterwards she said she wanted to make a series with us, so we sat down and wrote, with her, *Alcock and Gander*, and it was quite funny.'[10]

Beryl played Mrs Alcock, who runs a number of highly dubious organisations from two seedy rooms above a Soho strip club. Now very well established, Mortimer and Cooke pretty much had all the power they needed. 'We had complete autonomy,' says Brian. 'Although one time there was a particular producer who didn't like this actress that we liked and wanted to replace her. We said, "Well, you can do that because you're in charge, but what we'll do is we'll have a funeral in episode two and it'll be hers."'[11]

They could also insist that wherever possible it was episode three of any new series that went before the cameras first. In this way they figured that by the time it got to recording the all-important opening episode the cast would have a good handle on the characters. 'Episode three of *Alcock and Gander* went enormously well,' Brian remembers:

> There was a huge audience reaction and we thought, that's it, we're away. Now show two, which was the next one we recorded, wasn't quite so good. Beryl was a bit iffy and wasn't so sure of her lines. And then the pilot was disastrous. The problem was Beryl had been used to appearing in films when she had all the time in the world. On film you can do a line and re-do it until you get it right, on television you're shooting live with an audience and she couldn't handle it. God love her she tried hard but she couldn't do it. So, we just did six episodes and at the end of it we sat and looked at each other and the producer said, 'It's not working is it?' And we said, 'No.' So, that was it.[12]

There was one positive, though. Playing Beryl's young assistant in the show was a certain Richard O'Sullivan. 'We were so impressed with Richard that we were keen to use him again,' recalls Brian. 'And that was what led to *Man About the House*.'[13]

***

One of Ronnie Barker's most treasured comic characters was Lord Rustless, a decrepit cigar-smoking peer with mad bushy eyebrows and sex on the brain who made his first appearance in the 1969/70 ITV series *Hark at Barker*, set in the fictitious Chrome Hall. Conceived by Liverpool-born playwright Alun Owen, who'd written the screenplay for The Beatles' *A Hard Day's Night*, *Hark at Barker* boasted an outstanding writing team that included Alan Ayckbourn, forced to write under a pseudonym because he worked at the BBC at the time, John Junkin, Bill Oddie and Graham Chapman. There was also a certain Gerald Wiley, in reality Ronnie Barker.

The show earned Barker the Variety Club's ITV Personality of the Year award and inevitably led to a sequel, but this time Lord Rustless was to switch channels to BBC 2 in *His Lordship Entertains*. It was Barker's own idea that for the new show Chrome Hall, in order to maintain its upkeep, has been turned into a hotel. This time Barker restricted himself to just appearing as Lord Rustless, having played as many as eight different characters in *Hark at Barker*. He did, however, write all seven episodes, hiding behind yet another pseudonym – Jonathan Cobbald.

Produced by Harold Snoad, many of the original cast made welcome returns, notably David Jason as the impossibly ancient gardener Dithers and Josephine Tewson, whom Snoad would later successfully cast in *Keeping Up Appearances* as Hyacinth Bucket's long-suffering neighbour Elizabeth.

His Lordship Entertains was both inventive and funny and over the next couple of years Barker and Harold Snoad had numerous discussions about making another series. 'However, both of us were busy on other projects,' says Harold. 'And then when we finally thought we would suggest to the BBC that we make a second series, Ronnie rang me to say that he'd just heard that there were plans to make a series called *Fawlty Towers* and that he didn't think the BBC or the public would want two series set in a hotel.'[14]

July

For many who remember *In for a Penny*, this toilet-based sitcom from LWT just about ranks amongst the worst ever made. A shame really because it gave Bob Todd, for years one of Benny Hill's comedy sidekicks, his first starring role as toilet attendant Dan, who has worked for twenty-five years in a large Victorian-era public convenience situated at the Town Hall. Cue a veritable barrage of dodgy lavatorial humour that even the Carry On films might have baulked at perpetrating.

Curiously, the writer behind *In for a Penny* was John Hawkesworth, who had just produced the incredibly popular costume drama *Upstairs, Downstairs*. Luckily this flop did not smear his reputation as he went on to produce the BBC's *Duchess of Duke Street* (1976–77), the bomb disposal drama *Danger UXB* (1979) and Granada's critically lauded Sherlock Holmes series with Jeremy Brett.

***

Another stinker was *Birds in the Bush* from the usually capable hands of David Croft, taking a well-deserved rest from *Dad's Army*. It starred the usually dependable Hugh Lloyd, who travels to Australia with a friend to take possession of an old inherit-ance, which turns out to be a farm in the Outback run, luckily enough, by several beautiful young nieces, including former Miss World Ann Sidney.

Although intended primarily for a UK audience, *Birds in the Bush* was a co-production between the BBC and the Australian network ABC and shot on film in the Outback. It was a tough location. 'We had a loo strike,' observed Croft, 'because the ladies, quite rightly, refused to use the adjacent million square miles of bush as a lavatory and had to be bused every couple of hours to the nearest town.'[15] In the end portable loos were brought in. To complicate matters further, Hugh Lloyd con-tracted jaundice and was unable to work for weeks.

Looking for a suitable ranch to film at, the crew located a run-down house, with a corrugated roof, belonging to a man living on his own; in the backyard was a 10ft pile of discarded beer cans. Croft thought it was perfect, only when they turned up for filming the man had done a spring clean and repaired the whole place.

Aired in Britain as *The Virgin Fellas*, so bad was it that only seven of the thirteen episodes produced were ever shown. It was later voted the worst show of the year by the radio and TV writers' section of the Critic's Circle.[16]

September

Cambridge Footlights alumni Richard Stilgoe was very much a rising star in the early '70s, appearing and writing for numerous revue-type shows on television before making his name on the BBC's *That's Life*, a light-hearted consumer affairs programme for which he wrote comic songs satirising domestic misfortunes.

A Class By Himself turned out to be Richard's only foray into sitcom and came about during a brief stint at HTV, the ITV franchise for Wales and the West of England. Managing director Patrick Dromgoole liked his idea about a student hitchhiker who gets picked up by a mad old lord in a Rolls-Royce and put to work coming up with schemes to raise money for his crumbling stately home. 'It was dreadfully English,' says Richard, 'and not a million miles away from something like *To the Manor Born*. An awful lot of English humour, amazingly still, is class based, and there was a lot of that in it. And I suppose if it had a dad it went back to P.G. Wodehouse.'[17]

Richard wasn't only the writer, he cast himself as the student and thoroughly enjoyed playing the role:

I've always been a show-off, so that was great fun. There are few better feelings than having written a line that's meant to be funny and you say it and the audience laughs. But overall, the show had very little artistic merit.[18]

And for that Richard blames no one but himself:

I was disgracefully late with all of the scripts. The actors don't mind that too much, but the director does because he sort of needs the script so he can build the sets and things like that.[19]

Lasting just the one series, *A Class By Himself* was a bit of a missed opportunity for Richard, but there were compensations, such as the thrill of working with John Le Mesurier, who played Lord Bleasham, pronounced Blessem; his ancestral home being Blessem 'all, of course. Le Mesurier was, of course, currently riding a wave of popular success with *Dad's Army*. 'It was a huge privilege to work with John,' says Richard:

I learnt an awful lot from him. He had this marvellous way of making every line sound like he had just thought of it, which is the primary skill of acting really. He was wonderfully idiosyncratic. He did quite a lot of improvisation too, not asked for by the author, but he always seemed to make the dialogue better.[20]

In one particular episode Richard wrote a part for a young singer, intending it to be filled by a particular young lady, whom he very much fancied. 'There was to be a little recital at the stately home and we needed an opera singer and so I invited this lady to come and be in it and sing a duet with me – and we've been married ever since.'[21]

Never tempted to return to sitcoms, Richard went on to write the lyrics for the musicals *Starlight Express* and *The Phantom of the Opera*. In 2012 he was knighted for his services to charity.

★★★

For a show that became one of the '70s most popular and longest running, it's interesting to note that the origins of *Sykes* go back to 1960 when the dream pairing of Hattie Jacques and Eric Sykes first hit British TV screens. Back then it was called *Sykes and a ...*, the title deliberately left blank so that each programme had a different subject matter around which half an hour of comedy was created. For example, we had 'Sykes and a Stranger' with Leo McKern as a brash ex-prisoner who claims Hattie as his fiancée, 'Sykes and a Golfer' in which Eric beats champion golfer Peter Alliss in a tournament (sadly, it turns out to be a dream), and 'Sykes and a Plank', where Eric and Hattie transport a piece of wood from a timber yard, an idea Sykes later reworked as a short film.

Eric had asked Johnny Speight, whom he rated as one of the best comedy writers in the world, to write the pilot episode. Speight decided to make Eric and Hattie husband and wife; that didn't sit right with Eric. 'Johnny,' he said at the first script meeting. 'I don't want to alter a word of this. It's brilliant. But we're not going to be husband and wife, we're brother and sister. And not only that, we're twins.'

Speight looked incredulously at Sykes. 'Twins!'

'Yes, twins,' replied Eric, and then with a mischievous glint in his eye, 'and further than that, we're identical twins.'

'Why can't they be husband and wife?' asked Speight.

'Well, I'll tell you why, John. Husbands and wives at some time in their relationship are going to have a spat and grow apart, but brother and sister, they seem to be closer than many married couples.'[22] And that's how it was. Indeed, so convincing was their on-screen relationship that many people actually mistook Eric and Hattie for real siblings.

William G. Stewart worked on the show as a floor manager and recalls going out on location to a circus. The idea was for this elephant to step over a prone Hattie Jacques. The elephant they were using was an old trooper called Burma who did this kind of thing all the time, but even so it was a bit nerve-wracking. Stewart saw the animal gently rub its front leg against the side of Hattie's breast and then gently step over her. Everyone was happy with the shot. The producer was Dennis Main Wilson. 'One more take,' he said.

'No, Dennis,' Stewart implored.

'One for safety.'

'Dennis, this is one time we don't need one for safety. It's fine. It's in the can, let's just leave it.' After a slight pause Stewart added, 'Please tell me, Dennis, how many times does Hattie's insurance allow us to do this.'

'What insurance?' Dennis said.

'Dennis, you're not telling me that Hattie's not insured for this?'

'No, I couldn't get insurance, nobody would insure her.'[23]

The show was enormously popular and ran until 1965. Then, after a gap of seven years it returned in the summer of 1972, 'by popular demand,' says Eric. 'And when they asked me to do it again, I was delighted, and so was Hat, because we were a family.'[24] The situation remained very much the same, the couple still lived together in their suburban terraced house, with the snooty interfering next-door neighbour Mr Brown never very far away, played again by Richard Wattis. There was also a new character in the person of a busybody policeman, played by Deryck Guyler.

The intervening years hadn't changed the pair very much; Eric remained as accident prone as ever, and still the eternal child:

> Because we were brother and sister, Hattie looked upon me as in need of protection, so when I said, 'I've got a great idea Hat,' she was, 'Oh, Eric, not another one, no.' In many respects we were both innocents in a very technological world.[25]

Eric had first worked with Hattie on the radio series *Educating Archie* in the 1950s, and theirs was a working relationship based on mutual respect and trust. Indeed, when on the odd occasion Eric arrived for a rehearsal feeling tired or under the weather, it was Hattie who took over the reins; their comedy instincts were so in tune. 'But the strange thing was,' says Eric, 'when we were not doing the shows we never met up. Hattie would be off doing the Carry On films and I would be doing the odd film or stage or some TV. I never met any of the cast in between shows because I'm not gregarious. Hattie was, she was the life and soul of the party, she was a real gem, but in all the years we worked together I only ever visited her house twice, and I think she came to see me maybe three times. So, when we met at the studio after all this parting, it was like the family getting together again.'[26]

Like its 1960s equivalent, *Sykes* was good wholesome family entertainment with nary a swear word or sexual innuendo in sight; a deliberate stance on Eric's part. 'My idea of television is that we are invited into millions of homes and because of that you behave responsibly. That was my philosophy, to get honest laughter because I maintain that a good honest laugh is worth six months on the NHS.'[27]

Eric saw each episode as a little playlet, with a beginning, middle and an end, and he wrote all of them on his own. The beauty of being a single writer was that nobody could say NO! He could put whatever he liked down on the page. 'Look at some of the modern shows, they have about four or five writers on them. Then it's additional dialogue by another twelve writers, so you cannot then have a good situation comedy because you are just littered with jokes that might have no relation to each other.'[28]

Even so, the scripts Eric delivered on the first day of rehearsal usually bore little resemblance to the show that eventually went out to the public. 'Because we were all such mates, I always allowed the cast of *Sykes* to put forward any ideas that they had and I welcomed them. They didn't accept verbatim what I had written because I always said, this is not written in stone.'[29] This collaboration usually meant that by the end of the week everyone knew the script backwards and could have a day off before the recording. 'That way everyone came in much brighter, because you can over-rehearse. And that's one thing you can't do. You over-rehearse a comedy and you're gone because the strength of comedy is its spontaneity.'[30]

Eric had his own way of relaxing before each episode went before the cameras on Saturday. 'On the Friday night I used to take a heavy sleeping pill and sleep like a log. Then I'd get up and still be a bit happy with the pill and just walk through the morning's technical rehearsal till the afternoon when the pill had worn off and then I was ready to work.'[31]

Some of the new episodes turned out to be reworkings of the 1960s scripts – notably the golfing episode, with Tony Jacklin instead of Peter Alliss, and the convict episode with Peter Sellers in place of Leo McKern. 'At that time Peter was one of the most sought-after international stars in the world,' says Eric. 'And he very rarely appeared on television. I rang him up and said, "Peter, I've got a lovely part for you," and he came in and he did every rehearsal beautifully.'[32]

When it came to the day of the recording, Sellers had a surprise up his sleeve. In the scene, Eric was sat on a sofa complaining to Hattie how dull his life was, that nothing exciting ever happens, when there's a knock at the door:

> Hattie opened the door and I could sense that something was going on because I could tell that she'd gone; Hattie was a great giggler you see. I turned round and got the shock of my life. Peter, who had done all the rehearsals with us, was standing at the door and he'd changed completely. He'd blacked out some of his teeth, he'd got a crew cut, he was that prisoner on the run. He grabbed Hat and gave her a big kiss, 'Hello darling.' Poor Hat was gone laughing and when I turned round and saw Peter I went too, so we were off to a good start. Peter was brilliant in that episode, an absolute riot.[33]

What rankled with Eric for years was the lack of any publicity about Sellers' appearance on the show:

> Don't forget we had the most famous comedian in the world doing a guest spot, and in the *Radio Times* all it said was: *Sykes*, episode 'The Stranger' starring Eric Sykes and Hattie Jacques, with Peter Sellers. No picture, no nothing, no pre-publicity, not one thing. They should have had him on the cover. It was totally thrown away. It beggars belief.[34]

Such was the popularity of the series that Eric took one of the episodes and adapted it into a stage show that he intended to take on tour round the world. The regular cast were all involved save for Richard Wattis, who couldn't stand the thought of flying. 'Listen,' said Eric. 'It'll be first class on a 747, glass of champagne, you've got room to stretch, it's just like sitting in a club.' Wattis wasn't convinced. 'No Eric,' he said. 'I can't. I have to take a Librium to cross the road.'[35] The tour included Australia, Hong Kong, Singapore and Kenya. In Salisbury in Rhodesia (as it was called then), they played an old rickety theatre with a tin roof. 'When it rained,' recalls Eric, 'which it did quite frequently, they couldn't hear us speak on the stage.'[36]

After seven series, and still drawing in big audiences, Eric refused to make any more following the tragic early death in October 1980 of Hattie, aged only 58. 'I had so many actresses getting in touch with me to say that they could play Hat's part,' remembers Eric. 'But I said, there's only one Hat. So, I refused to carry on with anyone else but Hat. It was the same when Richard Wattis died in 1975, I didn't have another man living next door, I made it a woman. Again, there was only one Richard Wattis.'[37]

Looking back, Eric was understandably proud of *Sykes*, not only by what he managed to achieve, but the fond memories of working with so many talented individuals:

> There was great camaraderie between us, we were a band together. I can't remember a raised voice between us. I believe that you cannot do a comedy if there's any rancour in the cast, because any rancour comes over, it comes through the screen, it comes across the stage to the audience. A good comedy should always have a nice feeling between the cast, then everybody works for everybody else.[38]

***

The public had only just got used to the controversies stirred up by ITV's *Love Thy Neighbour* when the BBC decided to bring back its own uber bigot, Alf Garnett, in *Till Death Us Do Part*, who'd been off the nation's screens for over four years.

Alf Garnett began life in a single play in the Comedy Playhouse slot back in 1965 and was the creation of Johnny Speight. The show's aim was to highlight the pressures felt by the white working class at a time of great social change in Britain and Alf Garnett was, according to *The Financial Times*, the, 'rampaging, howling embodiment of all the most vulgar and odious prejudices that slop about in the bilges of the national mind'.

Producer Dennis Main Wilson was charged with casting the show and his first choice for Alf was Peter Sellers, having worked together on *The Goon Show*. Sellers was known to be a huge admirer of Speight and after reading the script agreed to do it. Speight knew better, that a film offer would come along and get in the way and that a BBC fee wouldn't be enough for someone who bought an Aston Martin every week.

Next on Wilson's list was Leo McKern. Again, McKern said yes but having just done an American film he'd bought a yacht and was away sailing on the recording dates. Wilson looked at his third choice, it was Warren Mitchell.

The pilot was well received by critics, and Dennis Main Wilson turned up at the BBC bar at Television Centre suitably chuffed with himself. That was until he bumped into Tom Sloan, Head of Light Entertainment, who declared that over his dead body would they make a series out of such subversive muck. Luckily David Attenborough, then Head of BBC 2, was there and said, 'If you don't want it, Tom, I'll have it.' Sloan turned round, 'No, I'm doing it.'[39] A first series went out in 1966 but Sloan never did like the show and really wanted nothing to do with it.

Alf Garnett hailed from solid East End stock, as did Speight, and the show took place within the comparatively realistic setting of working-class family life. There was Alf's long-suf-fering wife Elsie, played by Dandy Nichols, his daughter Rita (Una Stubbs) and her socialist layabout husband Mike (Anthony Booth), who frequently locks horns with Alf.

Till Death Us Do Part quickly caught on with the public, becoming one of those rare shows that used to empty the streets and the pubs because everyone was watching it at home. As for Alf Garnett, he became the most talked about character on television. If there was a problem, it was that Warren Mitchell played the part too well. Speight always said he didn't create Alf, society did and he just reported it. The series was meant to challenge hot topics such as racism, yet certain sections of the viewing public missed the point and took on Alf as their champion. Mitchell would recall an exchange with a football fan who came up to congratulate him on having a go at immi-grants. 'Actually,' Mitchell hit back, 'we're having a go at idiots like you.'

The show broke a number of taboos, especially its use of lan-guage; Alf calls his son-in-law, 'a scouse git' and his wife, 'a silly moo'. Bizarrely as the series went on Michael Mills made a deal with Speight that allowed him twenty-five bloodies per show. Speight never forgot having to go and see Mills in his office after exceeding the quota. 'I've counted them,' said Mills, 'and there are thirty-six in the show. I'm willing to swap you those blood-ies for one tit.' Speight said, 'Look Michael, one tit is not an obscenity, it's a deformity.'[40]

In 1968, after three series, the BBC decided to cancel the show, no doubt fed up of the hundreds of complaints it used to receive, along with various run-ins with Mary Whitehouse. There was also Speight's habit of delivering his scripts late and sometimes unfinished. Its triumphant return wasn't really much of a surprise, the BBC had already brought back one of its successful sitcoms from the 1960s for colour production, *Steptoe and Son*, and planned to do much the same with *The Likely Lads*. Maybe the BBC had also taken stock of the proliferation of working-class-themed sitcoms over on ITV, the likes of *On the Buses*, *Please, Sir!* et al and saw that the likes of Steptoe and Alf might redress the balance.

For the '70s version the old team was reunited, the main cast stayed the same, Speight turned out the scripts and Dennis Main Wilson produced. Wilson has been described as one of the most important and influential of all producers and directors in British comedy: *Hancock's Half Hour* and *The Goon Show* were just two of his credits on the radio before he moved into television. In real life he was a colourful character. His predilection for consuming alcohol led Spike Milligan to affectionately nickname him Dennis Main Drain. 'Dennis was a total shambles,' recalls William G. Stewart, 'except he was very successful. I was told a story when he was doing *Till Death Us Do Part*. One day on the set Warren and Johnny were arguing about a scene or a line and they were getting a bit heated about it and Dennis said, "That's what I like to see, that's what generates talent, my writer and my star arguing – carry on!" Dennis was mad, absolutely mad.'[41]

Alf Garnett also made something of an impression on the nation's cinema screen with two films, produced in 1969 and 1972, as well as the format being successfully transported to the US as *All in the Family* (NBC 1971–79). Here the Garnetts became a working-class family living in Queens, New York, and the patriarch was one Archie Bunker. Carroll O'Connor's performance in the role was to achieve cult status. His chair from the show is actually preserved for posterity in the Smithsonian Museum in Washington DC.

The Alf Garnett of the 1970s was just as opinionated as he was in the '60s and Speight's scripts no less political or controversial. Speight also had time to come up with another sitcom in 1972, very much in the Garnett vein, featuring two vagrants, one Irish, played by Cyril Cusack, the other cockney, played by *Zulu* star James Booth. Entitled *Them*, both men wander the country, sharing adventures and clashing with establishment figures such as policemen and pub landlords.

Sadly, as it went on the new series of *Till Death Us Do Part* suffered due to the noticeable illness of Dandy Nichols, who departed the series in 1974 with her absence explained away by having to go to Australia to look after relatives. Alf's new nemesis instead became his next-door neighbours, played by Patricia Hayes and Alfie Bass. When it was clear Dandy would not be able to film any more episodes, the series was dropped in 1975.

In 1981, Alf made a surprise switch to the opposition when ATV made six episodes under the title *Till Death …* that saw Alf and Elsie move down to Eastbourne and retirement. Because of Dandy Nichols' continued poor health, director/ producer William G. Stewart decided not to film the episodes before a studio audience. Stewart also recalls the moment when Speight was ill in hospital and there was a scene in the script that wasn't working:

> I went to the rehearsals and I said, 'Warren, we've got a prob-
> lem here, I can't get hold of John. The nurse said they'd rather
> he didn't have visitors for a few days. I tell you what I'll do,
> I'll take it home and I'll try and rejig the scene.' And Warren
> looked at me and said, 'What did you say?' I said, 'I'll take
> it home.' He said, 'Bill, you cannot rewrite Johnny Speight.

If it doesn't work take it out.' Nobody had more respect for Johnny than Warren.[42]

Four years later Alf returned to the BBC for *In Sickness and in Health*, which saw the couple stumbling into old age. As Dandy was now suffering from rheumatoid arthritis, Elsie was confined to a wheelchair, her condition cleverly woven into the scripts by Speight. Sadly, Dandy passed away shortly after the first series and subsequent episodes showed Alf having to deal with life as a widower. Not as satirical or vitriolic as its predecessors, *In Sickness and in Health* was a big hit for the BBC, running for six series.

★★★

A sitcom seemed an odd choice for a writer like Brian Clemens, renowned for his work in fantasy and action television shows like *The Persuaders*, *Danger Man* and *The Avengers*. But Brian had written several comedy stage thrillers and two farces, while *The Avengers* always contained heavy doses of sardonic humour.

My Wife Next Door was a romantic comedy that Brian co-wrote for the BBC with Richard Waring, who he remembered fondly. 'Richard was a splendid Falstaff of a man. He loved his creature comforts, especially his wine, and was a thoroughly civilised human being, I liked him a lot – an entertaining dining companion of the old school.'[43]

The new show managed to land two of television's most endearing actors in John Alderton and Hannah Gordon. They play Suzy and George Bassett, a role Brian first thought suitable for Richard Briers, 'but ultimately John was great.'[44] After divorcing each other, they both flee London to start a new life in the country, only to quickly discover, too late of course, that not only have they moved into the same small village, but into adjoining cottages;

the kind of coincidence that only happens in sitcom land. It was
an idea Brian got after watching a revival of Noel Coward's play
Private Lives. 'Two exes in the same hotel – what, I wondered, if
they ended up next door to each other?'[45] This new predicament
allows George plenty of opportunities to win back his wife.

Brian remained very fond of the show. 'It has gentle humour
and was sophisticated, two people still in love but denying it.
It could have gone on much longer.'[46] Brian suspects the reason
why only one series was ever made is because the cast were
unwilling to continue with it. This despite the fact it won the
Society of Film and Television award for the year's best sitcom.
'I was suitably pleased,' says Brian. 'But awards don't fill the
bank balance!'[47]

Perhaps the couple's relationship had been explored about
as far as possible. Just how many times could poor old George
cannily attempt to woo back his wife. This didn't stop CBS,
however, trying to launch a US adaptation, not once, but twice!
The first in 1975 and again in 1980. Brian had nothing to do with
either of them, 'which may be why neither of them succeeded. I
only found out about them after the event. Oh well.'[48]

By then Brian had his hands full anyway writing *The New
Avengers* and creating the hugely popular *The Professionals*. So,
My Wife Next Door remains the one and only sitcom in his highly
impressive CV. Though it wasn't for want of trying. Together
with Dennis Spooner, he wrote a comedy pilot for ATV:

It was about a nouveau riche family, horrified when an out
of the woodwork father turned up. The family were Anton
Rodgers and Vivien Pickles (wonderful). It was called *What
a Turn Up* and aired to at least one terrific notice from *The
Times*, but, inexplicably, did not continue into series. We also
conceived something called, *Which Way Is Tipperary?* that

nearly got made by LWT. It was a World War One series that pre-dated *Blackadder Goes Forth* by some years.[49]

November

Turnbull's Finest Half-Hour lampooned the world of television with its plot of a military man parachuted in to run a failing television company. According to writer Mike Sharland, much of what happened was based on real events:

> There was a famous occasion when, at the start of commercial television, a naval gentleman was put in to run it and set it up. My father, Peter Croft, and my uncle, David Croft, were both there as TV directors and to their surprise all the typewriters were confiscated for some military reason. Then later the chairs went and they all sat on the floor next to the radiators trying to keep warm, and that was the character that interested me.[50]

Having served in the war himself, Michael Bates was perfect casting and brought a lot of military bearing to the role. 'He was very funny and a delight to work with,' recalls Mike. 'No matter how far you went, Michael brought a realism to manic behaviour.'[51] Unfortunately, the scripts by Mike and his writing partner Ken Hoare were viewed as having strayed too far by the powers that be, who didn't exactly find it funny when the laughs were directed at them. As a result, the show was buried in obscure time slots and never found an audience, lasting just six episodes.

Mike and Ken Hoare did write another sitcom together. A couple of pilots were made and it looked all set to go into a series when they were asked to attend a meeting. They walked in, expecting to see just the producer and maybe the Head of

Comedy, but sat round the table was also a comedy consultant, a comedy script editor and a director:

> There began a couple of hours of totally destructive input from all these people who had never written anything. Ken and I left and in the car park I said to Ken, 'I'm never going to let that happen to anyone else. I'm going to become an agent.' And that's exactly what I did and Ken became a client.[52]

Chapter Four

1973

January

Heavily influenced by the kitchen sink dramas of the early '60s such as *Billy Liar* (which featured a young Rodney Bewes), and *Saturday Night and Sunday Morning*, *The Likely Lads* (BBC 1964–66) was a strikingly naturalistic comedy for its time and the first to use the places and people of Tyneside, giving the North-east a real voice on television for perhaps the first time.

Its origin lies in a BBC director's course undertaken by Dick Clement. Tasked with making a short programme on a shoestring budget, he enlisted his drinking buddy Ian La Frenais and together formulated this idea of two working-class lads just out of school employed in a Newcastle electrical components factory. It hung around for a while until both men were called in to a meeting and left the room with a commission to do six episodes; suddenly they were writers. They were also terrified when the reality of what they were being asked to do sunk in. Given an office at BBC Television Centre, with a bit of encouragement the words started to flow. It was life-changing stuff and wildly exciting; Ian recalled having a panic attack the night of the first recording and going to see the BBC nurse.

Shown on BBC 2, *The Likely Lads* was a surprise hit, striking a chord of familiarity with young working-class people up and down the country. It also made household names out of the young leads, James Bolam as the fiercely working-class and irresponsible Terry Collier and Rodney Bewes as the slightly more aspirational and level-headed Bob Ferris. 'We were determined when we first did that show that we wanted to cast actors,' says Dick Clement. 'A lot of sitcoms were built round comedians, ours was not. We never went for that, we wanted to feel that it was as real as it could possibly be.'[1]

After three series and twenty episodes *The Likely Lads* ended in 1966 with the boys joining the army, only Ferris doesn't pass the medical and Collier faces years of military life alone. And that's where they were left until seven years later when both writers, quite independently of one another, decided it was time to resurrect them.

'I was on holiday in Cornwall,' recalls Ian, 'and Dick was on holiday in Italy and we both had this separate thought, I wonder what happened to those guys. And I think before we made a deal, we'd written the whole first series.'[2] As Dick remembers, 'When we started writing it just poured on to the page.'[3]

But how did the two actors feel about coming back? 'Rodney was happy to do it straightaway,' says Dick. 'We had to take Jimmy out for a very boozy lunch because initially he didn't want to do it. Then we started to tell him some of the storylines and what we were going to do and it started to make him laugh and that was what hooked him.'[4]

Meanwhile, negotiations with the BBC had reached a stumbling block, with Dick and Ian holding out for a higher fee. 'And the difference between what the BBC was offering and what we wanted was £100 a script,' says Dick:

> It wasn't a vast gulf but we were pissed off. Come on, we're worth it. But they kept haggling and haggling. So, we went to Thames and they said, 'Yes, we'd love to do it,' so we said, OK, fine. And then just at the last minute they said, 'We'd better check with the BBC first,' and the moment Thames checked with the BBC they agreed to pay our fee. By then we had written the first thirteen episodes. So, the moment the BBC said yes, they received thirteen scripts.[5]

In *Whatever Happened to the Likely Lads?*, we discover that the two men's personalities haven't really changed all that much, and the bond that linked them was curiously as strong as ever, only their circumstances had altered. Collier, back from the army, was as cynical as ever, an unreconstructed working-class man, clinging on for dear life to old-fashioned attitudes. Meanwhile, Ferris has become a success in business and embraced the middle-class life, settling down with his relentlessly bourgeois fiancée Thelma (Brigit Forsyth) in a new suburban housing estate. Naturally, Collier despises his old friend's nouveau riche aspirations, seeing it as a betrayal of his roots, while Ferris looks down on Collier's lack of ambition.

In between the laughs and familiar sitcom situations, Terry Collier's bid to find work and his place in a new society was as powerful a piece of social commentary as any drama from the same period. We watch as both of them react to a different world to the one they inhabited just a few years before, especially Ferris with his house, his white-collar job and his flared trousers and blow-dried hair. 'It was the age of rampant consumerism,' states Ian, 'and Terry had been stranded culturally and had missed out.'⁶ As Dick stresses, 'Terry felt that the '60s had passed him by, that he'd missed everything, topless waitresses and rampant promiscuity.'⁷ The landscape around them was changing too. Gone are the streets where they both grew up, their past erased, and old haunts knocked down and reduced to piles of bricks or turned into nondescript '70s concrete.

Whatever Happened to the Likely Lads? is a melancholic master-piece, among the best sitcoms ever made, and one of the most poignant comedies written about friendship. Jimmy Gilbert, who had just been made Head of Comedy at the BBC, produced and directed the series and barely had to alter one word, the scripts were that perfect.

They fulfilled a couple of other purposes, too. Gilbert felt there wasn't enough reality in comedy and that too many shows were based in London and the South-east. Another bug bear was that most sitcoms were studio-bound with exterior filming used only sparingly. On Gilbert's urging, the cast and crew went up to Newcastle and did an extensive location shoot in order to get a feeling of the location in the same way Gilbert later did with *Last of the Summer Wine* in Yorkshire.

After two series of thirteen episodes each, unusual since most sitcoms ran for either six or seven episodes, and a Christmas spe-cial in 1974, the writers put an end to the series. 'I don't think there was any question,' says Ian. 'We thought, that's it.'⁸ James Bolam didn't want to do any more either, keen to embrace new challenges. 'Jimmy was always a very serious actor,' says Dick. 'And his relationship with Rodney was tricky. They were very different people.'⁹ Working together there had never really been any problems. Dick was standing on the studio floor once watching a scene the pair of them were doing together. 'It was one of those moments when every line was perfect, every line was perfectly timed, and at the end of it Jimmy just said, 'Well done, Rod.' He respected the fact that it had gone so well and it was a perfect piece of acting.'[10]

In 1976 the British film company EMI asked the writers to turn the show into a feature. At the time they were in Los Angeles trying to get green cards, which meant neither of them could leave America and so they weren't around for any of the filming, mostly done on location around rural Northumberland thanks to a plot that saw Terry and his new girlfriend join Thelma and Bob on a caravan holiday.

When it came to writing *The Likely Lads* screenplay, Dick and Ian were in the favourable position of having already worked on films, including the Oliver Reed/Michael Crawford comedy *The Jokers* (1967) and the Richard Burton East End gangster flick *Villain* (1971). This put them at a distinct advantage over most other sitcom writers, who when faced with turning their shows into a ninety-minute film invariably strung three episodes together and hoped for the best. 'Because we had written movies,' says Ian, 'we knew how to create a ninety-minute narrative and I'd argue that made our film a little better than some of the others.'[11]

By the time the film received its world premiere in Newcastle, the writers were allowed back in the country. It was scarcely a glitzy opening, with its football star guests and a nosh up of chicken and coleslaw at a reception afterwards. 'That was held in a place called the Assembly Rooms,' recalls Ian, 'an old Victorian building that was cold and draughty. It was quite awful, but everyone was so drunk after an hour it didn't matter.'[12]

Whatever Happened to the Likely Lads? was a watershed moment for Dick Clement and Ian La Frenais. Both of them were nervous about returning to television and sitcom after being away for several years, especially since after the original *Likely Lads* they'd worked with Harry H. Corbett on a 1967 sitcom called *Mr Aitch* that was viewed as a failure. 'So, for me *Whatever Happened to the*

Likely Lads? validated us,' confirms Ian. 'It said, they're not a fluke, they didn't have this one-hit wonder, and that's why to me that show is a landmark for us both.'[13]

***

When the BBC requested a third series of *Up Pompeii* from Talbot Rothwell the writer complained that his inferior health meant he wasn't up to the job. This necessitated a rethink and so Ancient Rome was dropped and it was decided to rework the format to medieval Baghdad. In other words, *Whoops Baghdad*, with the ever-present Frankie Howerd, was *Up Pompeii* in all but name.

For producer John Howard Davies, the show never worked. 'Frankie was the most appallingly difficult person to work with because if the script didn't immediately work, he would throw it out. And so, we went through a raft of writers, all chomping at the bit, writing this and writing that. It was not a very happy show.'[14]

David Nobbs was one of the writers brought in and remembers the legendary comic as, 'immensely neurotic and difficult',[15] but also extremely generous in spirit. What was perhaps the most difficult aspect of writing for Howerd was his peculiar asides, the ohh, yes, no, no, yes, all that stuff. 'He was very odd, Frankie,' says David:

> If you didn't put in any of his asides, he would say, 'Where are my asides? That's what I do.' Then if you put them in, he moved them around and ignored them, but he had to have them there.[16]

Because much of that stuff had its own special rhythm, David found it sometimes easier to just speak it through as he was writing it:

I remember on one occasion I was in the study at home doing Frankie's stuff out loud and my stepchildren brought some friends back from school and they came in and said, 'You're really embarrassing us, our friends think you're a nutter.' So, I went outside and walked along the common near our house doing all of Frankie's asides out loud. I saw this police car following me up the road. It stopped and these policemen came over and asked me what the hell I thought I was doing. I said, 'I'm writing for Frankie Howerd.' I showed them a membership card of the Writers Guild of Great Britain and they believed my explanation and said, 'I'm terribly sorry, sir, but we have had rumours of an escaped lunatic in the area.'[17]

Brian Cooke also has fond memories of writing for Howerd, especially how personally 'involved' the comedian liked to get with his writers. If you hadn't been chased round his dressing room, you hadn't served your apprentice:

I remember when Johnnie Mortimer and myself were working with him the tannoy came on in the studio, 'Could Mr Cooke please join Mr Howerd in his dressing room.' And I'm sitting there and John said, 'Lie back and think of England.' I got to his dressing room, and to Frankie it was just like chasing up a young girl. I produced photographs of the family but to no avail and we ran around until he gave up in the end. But he was alright Frankie, he meant no harm.[18]

It's hardly a surprise to learn that many of the scenes in *Whoops Baghdad* feature scantily clad harem girls and people called Mustapha. No longer playing Lurcio, but giving exactly the same performance, Howerd is this time Ali Oopla, constantly at the beck and call of the Wazir of Baghdad. The saucy antics were given a late-night slot but never found the mass audience of its predecessor. As a result, only six episodes were made.

February

Frank Spencer must rank amongst the most popular comedy characters in British television history, and a boon for count-less impersonators with a brown raincoat and a beret. *Some Mothers Do 'Ave 'Em* may not be the funniest sitcom ever made but quite possibly contains the genre's standout performance. Michael Crawford turned the well-intentioned but appall-ingly accident prone innocent Frank Spencer into a totally believable character.

Spencer might easily have grated on audiences, but Crawford imbued him with an almost childlike quality that won their sympathy. Each episode saw the well-meaning but clueless Frank reap some unlikely destructive catastrophe or reduce rational folk into quivering wrecks within ten minutes. One wonders how his long-suffering wife Betty, played by Michele Dotrice, avoided a nervous breakdown.

Frank Spencer was the creation of writer Raymond Allen, who'd been sending in material to television without success since he was 12 years old. Rejection letter followed rejection letter, 'But at least in those days they seemed to have more time for you,' he says. 'If you wrote a script and sent it to television you usually got a reader assigned to it and they would spend two or three pages giving you advice.'[19] Raymond remembers an early trip to the BBC and passing an office with two readers sat at a desk with piles of scripts in front of them.

Undeterred, Raymond continued sending in material, something like forty-five scripts over the years, all the time working odd jobs. 'People say, how on earth did you keep going, but you always think something's going to happen. And all you need is that one breakthrough.'[20]

That breakthrough finally came when Raymond was in his early thirties. Desperate to try and sell something, he read an article in a newspaper by an actress complaining about the lack of leading roles for women in situation comedy. 'I thought, that's a chance for me, I'll write a comedy for a woman.'[21] The idea came to him of a struggling married couple, and in the beginning, Raymond intended the wife Betty to be the main character, for whom all the best lines and situations were written; Frank was to be much more in the background. 'But then I found that the character of Frank took over.'[22]

As he'd done for years, Raymond sent the script in but this time the reaction of the readers was positive and it fell on the desk of Michael Mills. Raymond was asked to come and see him:

> They were worried because a lot of people can write one script, but when they're asked to write a whole series, they just can't do it. So, Michael Mills said to me, 'I'll tell you what, we'll give you three weeks to write a second episode and if we like it, then you'll get a series, and if we don't like it, you'll never hear from us again.'[23]

It was make or break time.

That first script took Raymond something like three months to write and here he was being asked to come up with another one in just three weeks:

> But I did it, I put something together in about two weeks and I was really pleased with it. Then I went to see Michael

Mills again and he said, 'I'm sorry, this second script is terrible, totally unfunny,' and he just threw it in the wastepaper
basket. But he said, 'Don't worry, you've got another week
left.' So, in desperation I quickly wrote another script and
luckily they liked that one.[24]

Success or failure clearly depended on getting the right actor
to play Frank Spencer and the BBC's first choice was Norman
Wisdom, which made sense given his mastery of physical
comedy and innocent clown persona. Mills asked Raymond to
send Wisdom what he considered to be his best script. 'Wisdom
didn't see any humour in it at all,' remembers Raymond, 'and he
wrote back to the BBC saying, "I like the story but I suppose he
puts the funny lines in later?"'[25] Then Michael Crawford became
interested. Although he was already fairly well known, *Some
Mothers Do 'Ave 'Em* was to turn Crawford into a major TV star.
And just like Arthur Lowe as Captain Mainwaring or Leonard
Rossiter as Rigsby, today it's impossible to visualise anybody
else playing that part.

According to Raymond, it was Crawford who came up with
Frank's voice and mannerisms. The beret, too, was his idea. As
for the character's trademark raincoat, Raymond had long been
a fan of Humphrey Bogart and treated himself to a raincoat that
looked like the one the star wore in films like *Casablanca*. Proudly
wearing it to the BBC one day, the reaction was somewhat of a
disappointment: 'People thought I looked ridiculous.'[26] It was
the show's costume designer who took inspiration from it and
went out to buy the exact same raincoat for Frank Spencer. 'I
never wore it again,' says Raymond.[27]

Audience response to the very early episodes was lukewarm
at best. Raymond recalls Bill Cotton, then Head of Light
Entertainment, coming up to him at rehearsals and saying,
'Don't get too depressed about it, just think of going on to better

things.'[28] Pretty soon though Frank's antics caught on with the public and a second series was hurriedly mounted for the end of the year, during which Frank and Betty welcomed a baby girl to their household.

Raymond had an excellent relationship with Crawford, indeed as the actor developed the character, Raymond began to write for Michael's strengths and the whole thing came alive. 'I was amazed by its popularity,' says Raymond. 'But then I suppose the character of Frank Spencer was instantly recognizable.'[29] It also helped that there was a lovely chemistry between Crawford and Michele Dotrice as Betty, audiences really did warm to them as a television couple.

Most spectacularly of all, Crawford flung himself into the physical aspects of the role, performing many of the hair-raising stunts that became a feature of the show, whether dangling from a car hanging over a cliff, being air-lifted off the roof of a church by a helicopter or roller-skating underneath a moving articulated lorry. As the series went on these stunts became increasingly more elaborate. 'That became a bit of a worry,' admits Raymond. 'Michael used to think up the stunts and I always had a dread that he was going to break a leg or something. But he loved doing them. Some of the stunts were really quite dangerous. I don't know how he was allowed to get away with it.'[30]

After two Christmas specials in 1974 and 1975, Crawford decided to hang up his beret and move on to other projects, fearing that the role threatened to permanently typecast him. In 1978 he was tempted back for one more series and a final Christmas special, refusing all offers from the BBC to continue in the role afterwards. There had been talk of a film and Crawford even rejected a five-year contract to play a similarly themed American version of Frank Spencer set in New York.

Instead, Crawford gravitated towards musical stage shows such as *Barnum* and *Phantom of the Opera* and became an international star. He did, however, resurrect the character one last time for a sketch as part of the BBC's Sports Relief charity show in 2016. It was the first time Raymond had met Crawford since 1978.

Raymond Allen continued to write the odd thing for television but never again achieved anything like the success *Some Mothers Do 'Ave 'Em* brought him. To some extent it became just as much of a millstone round his neck as it did for Crawford. Handing in a comedy script, they'd be rejected by producers saying, 'It's quite funny but it's not as good as *Some Mothers* …'[31]

★★★

Following the end of *Queenie's Castle*, Diana Dors returned as the equally blousy and no-nonsense Di Dorkins – known as 'Big D' – the owner of Garsley Garments, a large textile company, in Yorkshire Television's *All Our Saturdays*. She also finds time to manage the firm's unsuccessful amateur rugby team, which is regularly rooted at the bottom of the league table, and is determined to turn their fortunes around, through any means necessary.

Tony Caunter, another exile from *Queenie's Castle*, was among the supporting cast. Later to find fame as *EastEnders'* regular Roy Evans, Tony feels that although the premise of the show was good it just didn't work, largely due to a lack of care and attention being spent on the scripts. 'They were rather cobbled together,'[32] he admits, and going into it the cast did rather have a sense of foreboding:

> Then we did the first episode and the studio audience loved it. But you can get a false impression from studio audiences.

You think, heh this really is much better than we thought it was, because they laugh and they clap and they cheer, but really, they're just out to have a good time frankly. And when we all watched it on television, we looked at each other and said, we were right, weren't we, it's not as good as we would like it to be.[33]

What did surprise Tony more than anything else was the seeming lack of interest shown by Diana Dors, who didn't use her undoubted clout as the star to get things improved. 'But I did enjoy very much working with her again. She was a very good actress actually and had a great sense of humour, very self-deprecating. She was such fun and very raucous. She would tell me outrageous stories about her time in Hollywood that I daren't repeat to anyone.'[34]

By this time Diana's husband, Alan Lake, had been released from prison and from what Tony was able to observe, theirs was very much a love/hate relationship:

It was terribly volatile. But Diana seemed to be attracted to these kinds of people. She also had a great penchant for the underworld side of life, she had a lot of friends who were gangsters and such like. She admitted to me that she liked that excitement. She also told me once, 'People think I'm this wild thing, and yes I can be and I have been, but I like nothing better than being at home with the kids, feet in front of the fire watching a bit of television.' She had that domesticity thing about her.[35]

***

When Lord Seacroft Sr loses the family fortune in a card game, topping off his run of bad luck by being shot dead in a hunting accident, Lord and Lady Seacroft are forced to auction the family heirlooms and face up to a new life of roughing it in a council flat. That's the interesting premise of LWT's *The Upper Crusts*.

The well-known British film actors Charles Gray and Margaret Leighton made for unlikely sitcom stars, but were perfectly cast as the Lord and Lady, while Lalla Ward, soon to become a household name as Romana in *Doctor Who*, scored as one of their spoilt-rotten children.

Much of the show's humour arose from the family's efforts to keep up appearances in their sordid new surroundings. There's one amusing scene where Margaret Leighton decides to give guided tours of her modest new abode, stating grandly, '... and this is the west wing.'

Despite the high-calibre cast and writing prowess of Keith Waterhouse and Willis Hall, *The Upper Crusts* lasted just the one series.

March

Jeremy Lloyd once suggested he might never have been fortunate enough to have become a writer had he not been lucky enough to be such a failure at everything else. And it was with David Croft that he achieved his greatest successes, as co-creator of two of the longest-running sitcoms in British TV history: *Are You Being Served?* and *'Allo 'Allo!*

Are You Being Served? was based on Lloyd's own experiences in the late 1940s as a junior sales assistant for the prestigious Simpson's department store in Piccadilly. He took the idea to Croft, who immediately recognised its potential and suggested they work on it together. Within four days they'd finished a pilot, with one important change. Lloyd's original idea was to have the action take place solely in the men's department, while Croft believed there would be more conflict and comedy mileage if the management forced them to share the same floor as the ladies' outfitting department.

The fictitious and past-its-prime London department store of Grace Brothers was born and together Lloyd and Croft peopled it with one of sitcom's most beloved cast of characters. There was Captain Peacock, played by Frank Thornton, the epitome of the type of floorwalker who patrolled department stores in those days, overly officious with a military bearing and a penchant for treating the staff like unruly children. Mrs Slocombe, head of ladies' fashion, was played to perfection by Mollie Sugden, with her outrageously dyed bouffant hairstyles and endless supply of tales about her 'pussy', a running gag that never wore out its welcome and typified the Carry On style humour the show excelled in.

Mrs Slocombe's assistant, Miss Brahms, was originally conceived as Jewish, but when the producer's first choice, comedy actress Sheila Steafel, proved unavailable Croft went to the other extreme by casting Wendy Richard. The future soap star played Miss Brahms as a typical Essex girl, a bit ditzy and the target for numerous sexist comments from sales assistant Mr Lucas, played by Trevor Bannister, a character based very much on Jeremy Lloyd himself.

The rest of the cast was made up of the stuffy Mr Rumbold (Nicholas Smith), the grouchy Mr Grainger (Arthur Brough) and the store's owner, Young Mr Grace (Harold Bennett), a decrepit invalid fawned over by buxom secretaries. But undoubtedly the character that made the biggest impact was Mr Humphries. This was another example of supreme casting by Croft, who hired the largely unknown John Inman. Unlike the rest of the cast, Inman came from the world of variety and pantomime and had struggled for years to find a niche for himself on television. 'John was a very camp person,' remembers Trevor Bannister. 'He was what he was, and eventually a part came round that suited him down to the ground, he put it on like a glove. Mr Humphries and John were one of the same really.'[36]

The role of Mr Humphries took off almost immediately and after a couple of years Inman was one of the most recognised faces on television; declared BBC TV's Personality of the Year in 1976. But there were some who took enormous offence at what they saw as a gross stereotypical portrayal of a gay man. 'John got a lot of flak over that character from the gay lobby,' reveals Bannister. 'They thought they were having the piss taken out of them. By the third series he was actually getting some active hate mail and all sorts of stuff.'[37]

With the cast in place, the pilot episode was recorded and as Croft and Lloyd waited for the executives to make a decision whether to put it out or not, tragedy struck on 6 September 1972 at the Munich Olympics with the murder of Israeli athletes by Palestinian terrorists. As the world watched in horror, the games were temporarily shut down, resulting in major scheduling problems for the BBC. 'They were desperately looking for stuff to put on,' says Bannister. 'And it just happened that somebody pulled our show off the shelf and that was it. If it hadn't been for the Munich disaster, we might never have seen the light of day.'[38]

With a largely captive audience, the ratings were high but the general consensus within the upper echelons of the BBC was that *Are You Being Served?* was a bit, well, common. It now seemed unlikely that a full series would be commissioned. Luck, however, was about to play a spectacular hand. One afternoon Croft was passing the office of Bill Cotton, the new Head of Light Entertainment, when he overheard that the next series of

Till Death Us Do Part couldn't be delivered, thus leaving a sizeable gap in the schedules. Croft poked his head inside the door to enquire why they didn't give *Are You Being Served?* a try; it was cheap and he and Lloyd could deliver the scripts quickly. 'OK,' said Cotton. 'But do we have to have the poof?' Croft protested, 'He isn't a poof. He's a mother's boy and he hasn't made up his mind yet. And without him, bang goes half the comedy.' Croft won the day. 'And that was how a programme's future was determined in those days,' he recalled years later. 'There were no big committees to convince, it was all about one person's hunch; if they felt it seemed right, you got the go ahead.'[39]

Are You Being Served? began in earnest in March 1973, with Croft not only producing but also directing the first batch. 'He had a very strong hand on the wheel,' confirms Bannister. 'Complete control over it, which made a real difference.'[40] However, the first series received a slightly mixed reaction from the public. 'This is often the case with a new series,' states Harold Snoad, who replaced Croft as director on series two because he was too busy on *Dad's Army*. 'Because it takes time for the audience to become aware of the relationship between the various characters and their likely reaction to what has happened or is about to happen.'[41] As it turned out, the viewing figures shot up for series two and Snoad recalls that Croft came into his office after the last episode had been transmitted and said, 'Thanks, Harold, well done. I'll have it back now!'[42]

With its bawdy humour, *Are You Being Served?* was never going to be a critics favourite, but viewing the early episodes in particular is to be present at a master class in comedy acting. Everyone got on, too, with Sugden acting very much as mother hen to the whole cast. 'She was a sweet lady,' remembers Trevor.[43] It was very much a team effort, with both Croft and Lloyd open to ideas. 'One of the good things about that show

was a lot of us had already worked together or knew each other,'
says Trevor:

Naturally there's always a honeymoon period when you put
together a cast for a new show and people have to get to know
each other and so on, and that's very evident from most sitcoms. But in our particular case, Frank Thornton and I knew
each other and I had worked with Wendy and Mollie before.
And Arthur Brough, who played Mr Grainger, gave me my
very first job in the theatre, so I knew him from way back.
It was extraordinary that we ended up working together. He
was a delightful man.[44]

Each episode was recorded at the BBC Television Centre in front
of a live audience, something Trevor never really got used to:

I hated studio audiences for the very simple reason that your
instinct as an actor is to respond to an audience and your
performance can alter according to the way they're receiving what you're doing. But you can't do that in a studio
because you're restricted and confined. If you had something
which was mildly amusing and the audience found it so in
the theatre you probably think, I can embellish that into a
bigger laugh, but you can't do that in television. I found it
very frustrating.[45]

With *Are You Being Served?* riding high in the ratings, Bernard
Delfont approached Croft and Lloyd to adapt the show into
a stage play. The plot had everyone at Grace Brothers going
off on a staff holiday to that most '70s of destinations, the
half-built Spanish hotel. Opening in June 1976 at the Winter
Gardens, Blackpool, the show was a huge success, playing to

capacity audiences right through the busy summer season. The following year the play was turned into a feature film, shot on a penury budget with the Spanish locations replicated on a sound stage at Elstree. 'When we heard that the story took place in Spain, we all thought, oh lovely, we're all going to go to Spain and do some filming,' recalls Trevor. 'Did we hell. But it was a lot of fun.'[46]

Shot in a rapid six weeks, the only location filming was a day's shoot at Gatwick Airport. Trevor recalls the cast attending a gala premiere over in Holland where the show was hugely popular. 'All the bars used to be empty when it was shown on the television. We used to go over there to open a store or something and there'd be a crowd of 20,000 people waiting for us.'[47]

By the late '70s the show was attracting interest from foreign networks. Garry Marshall, who'd written and produced *Happy Days* and would later direct *Pretty Woman*, brought Croft and Lloyd over to the States to help with the writing and casting of a US version. Croft remembers one young actor, then a huge success at LA's Comedy Store, coming in to read for Mr Humphries. His name was Robin Williams. While Croft thought Williams was very funny, his personality was so over the top that he convinced himself that the comic would sabotage the whole production. 'I turned him down and thus prevented myself from becoming a millionaire.'[48] It didn't matter anyway; the pilot was not picked up for a series.

Back in Blighty the show had taken a break, with the cast unsure when or if it would return. According to Trevor Bannister, this state of affairs pretty much happened after each series, leaving the actors totally in the dark. More than a little fed up, Trevor agreed to join a play due to tour the country for six months. Just days later the BBC got in touch to say they were indeed going to do another series:

I told them that I'd already committed to another job. Their reply was, 'Well you'll have to give it up.' I said, 'Don't talk to me like that, telling me what I'll do and what I won't do. I'm doing the play and if that means I'll have to give up the series, so be it.' And that's the reason I left.[49]

By then Trevor had done seven series and frankly he'd had enough of it. When you have to say a joke that you remember saying five years previously it's really time to call it a day:

In fairness, as much as I loved the show and loved everybody, it had spread its wings in rather broad directions. I mean, we were forever doing songs and dances and having people getting out of the lift in a frogman's outfit saying the traffic was terrible so I had to swim up the Thames, all that sort of stuff, and it began to get a bit silly. I think it lost direction a bit.[50]

In Trevor's opinion *Are You Being Served?* was not true situation comedy, more sketch comedy, end of pier stuff; it bore no relation to reality or truth. 'Something like *Dad's Army* had more depth to it because the characters had a life outside the platoon. With our characters, you never saw them outside of the store, you never knew what their backgrounds were.'[51]

By series ten, in 1985, the writers had reached pretty much the same conclusion, that the show was running out of steam. Still pulling in good ratings, the BBC were keen for another series but Croft was adamant that it should end.

In 1992 many of the cast were reunited for a spin-off show, *Grace and Favour*, set in a country mansion hotel they've inherited from Mr Grace. While it was fun to see such endearing characters return to our screens, the old magic just wasn't there and the show petered out after two series. Something else was missing, too: satire. The entire floor of Grace Brothers was a microcosm of the English class system, especially evident in the barbed interaction and conversations between the maintenance men and the higher-class store personnel. 'That's where I always felt *Grace and Favour* didn't work quite the same,' says Bannister. 'You're not in the store, you're all the owners of this hotel that you've been given and there's no boss any more, everybody was equal, and that's what didn't work. A lot of the fun of *Are You Being Served?* was the pecking order.'[52]

Perhaps strangest of all was how the show became a cult success in America when it was shown there on cable during the 1990s. 'I think it has endured for so long because it's still funny,' claims Trevor. 'And it was never meant to be offensive. There was never any bad language or anything overtly sexual; it was all a bit schoolboy humour. Innuendo played its prime part, but as we always used to say, innuendo is in your mind. The humour went back to the Brighton seaside postcards, ladies with big boobs, it was that sort of humour. And that's timeless – and very English.'[53]

April

Our Kid was an odd slice of northern life from the prolific duo of Keith Waterhouse and Willis Hall. Set in Halifax, Ben Buslingthorpe (Ken Platt), vows on his mother's death bed to look after his baby brother Bob (Barrie Rutter). Now middle-aged, Ben still looks after 'our kid', even though Bob is perfectly capable of looking after himself.

Busy on other projects, Hall and Waterhouse only wrote the first episode, with the rest of the writing chores farmed out to other people, including David Nobbs, who approached the assignment in a most logical way. 'I watched the first episode and deliberately wrote my episode in a way that was consistent with what I had seen. I loved the work of Hall and Waterhouse and I think I managed to capture the same spirit.'[54]

Nevertheless, this series from Yorkshire Television lasted just six episodes.

★★★

The Gordon Peters Show fell flat, too. Gordon Peters was an actor who'd learnt his trade in provincial theatres, summer season, pantomimes and cabaret. He'd even appeared in the very first episode of *Dad's Army* as an accident-prone fireman, or rather he didn't; his Chaplin-esque antics were edited out prior to transmission. Finally, he got his big break, his own show, which grew out of a Comedy Playhouse pilot called *The Birthday*, in which his character, a lone figure that bore his own name, throws a party but ends up hiring a bunch of young girls when no one turns up.

With a total unknown in the lead, producer Dennis Main Wilson filled every episode with a familiar TV face, from Bill Pertwee and Frank Thornton, to Tony Booth and Henry McGee. It didn't work. Peters was to call his show, 'a superb flop' when it was pulled after just six episodes.

May

For every *Fawlty Towers*, sadly we must endure a *Romany Jones*, thus the balance of the Universe is kept in order. Created by the *On the Buses* team of Ronald Wolfe and Ronald Chesney, the public nevertheless lapped it up and LWT ended up making four series out of it, despite its star dying half way through.

Romany Jones was designed as a vehicle for James Beck, the popular Private Walker in *Dad's Army*. Beck plays layabout Bert Jones, who lives on a rundown caravan site with his much-put-upon wife Betty (Jo Rowbottom). Their neighbours the Briggs, Wally and Lily, are an uncouth cockney couple, played by Arthur Mullard and Queenie Watts, from the Albert Steptoe school of hygiene; dropping fag ash on to bread as its being buttered etc.

Tragically, after completing the second series the talented and likeable Beck died. Wolfe and Chesney couldn't think of anyone to take over the role and so the caravan was re-let to two entirely different characters – Jeremy and Susan Crichton-Jones. Rather posh and less worldly, this new couple end up easy prey to the various nefarious schemes of Lily and Wally. Without the presence of Beck, Mullard and Queenie Watts inevitably became the focal point of the new stories and were later rewarded with their own spin-off show, *Yus My Dear* in 1976, which, if you can credit it, was even worse.

June

John Kane had always enjoyed writing, going back to his amateur dramatic days growing up in Arbroath when he wrote sketches for the annual panto. At drama school he wrote a Christmas play that was put on at the King's Theatre in Edinburgh in 1965. Even when his acting career took off, when he was asked to join the Royal Shakespeare Company at Stratford, he continued to write. Then in 1970 he played Puck in Peter Brooks' celebrated production of *A Midsummer Night's Dream*.

Around this time John had appeared in a couple of RSC productions with Roy Kinnear, 'and he was such an adorable, funny,
lovely man that I wanted to write a sitcom for him'.[55] Entitled
'Leggit's Choice', it was about a middle-aged man called Neville
Leggitt who still lives with his mother, partly as a repellent to
getting hitched himself. But when his mother decides to get married again, Neville does everything he can think of to sabotage
the wedding. John's agent sent it to the BBC, they liked it and he
was asked to go and meet with comedy producer Duncan Wood:

> But when I said it was for Roy Kinnear, Duncan Wood said,
> 'I'm afraid not, Roy's not sexy, women don't like him,' which
> surprised me. 'But we have other ideas for it.'[56]

More meetings followed, including one with Ronnie Barker,
who at one point was interested in doing it. All the while John
was appearing in *A Midsummer Night's Dream*, which by 1971 had
moved into the West End. Some of his afternoons were spent
over at Elstree studios to work with David Pursall and Jack
Seddon, who among other credits had written some of Margaret
Rutherford's Miss Marple films back in the early and mid-'60s.
They had been hired by the BBC to coach young writers like
John. 'But mainly we would have boozy lunches in the studio
bar, it was very pleasant.'[57]

While continuing with *Midsummer Night's Dream* in the West
End, John got a call saying that Terry Scott had read his sitcom,
now called *Son of the Bride*, and liked it. Scott was then appearing as an ugly sister in the London Palladium pantomime. 'And
I met him in his dressing room,' recalls John. 'And the first
thing he said to me was, "First of all, you understand I'm not
a poof." He was sitting there in make-up, vast eyelashes and
full costume.'[58] Scott said he was interested but wanted John to

make a few changes. This he did and when he came back Scott agreed to make it. He also wanted John to work on his long-running sketch show *Scott On ...*, so to his astonishment John found himself with two contracts, one with BBC 1 and one with BBC 2.

Originally *Son of the Bride* was going to be made in 1972 but Scott suffered an aneurysm and had to have a period of rest, so it was pushed back. Hopes were high for the show when it did go into production. At the recordings the studio audience loved it and Scott told John that the scripts were the best he'd had in years and that it was going to run and run. When the series went out it got respectable notices, with one critic calling it an 'oedipal comedy', but somehow it just didn't connect with the public and no second series was made.

Even so, John enjoyed working on it. The process for each episode, be it *Son of the Bride* or *Scott On ...*, was always the same. After finishing a script John would send it to producer Peter Whitmore, who'd read it, maybe make suggestions, and then John would make any changes required:

> Then we would go to Terry's house and we would sit, Peter, Terry and myself, and we would read the scripts aloud, usually about three at a time, and Terry would say, 'Mmm, need a change there, that doesn't quite work.' I'd say 'Fine' and make a note of it. Or he would say, 'Yeah, that's fine,' and put it aside and we didn't see that script again until we got to rehearsals. It was like a kind of cottage industry. There were no executive producers. There was no script editor. It was such a simple business then.[59]

★★★

Six feet under was the destination for *Nobody is Norman Wisdom*. With his film career now well and truly over, Wisdom had another stab at the sitcom genre, three years after his debut met with disappointing results. Sadly, this met with a very similar fate. This time he portrays a nondescript character who is completely under the thumb of his domineering mother and deals with life's problems by flitting in and out of a fantasy world. Seemingly with no personality of his own, all he needs is the dress or a uniform of a profession to give him confidence and power. For example, dressed as a barrister he successfully defends an elderly war hero accused of theft.

Wisdom dispensed with the usual practice of recording before a live audience or using canned laughter, believing that the series would stand or fall on its own merits. It was a decision he later came to regret:

> I'm beginning to wonder whether hearing others laugh does have an effect on viewers, even if it's only subconscious. Laughter is very catching after all.[60]

In a bid to escape his slapstick image, the humour Wisdom employed this time was much more low key and although the first episode scored high in the TV charts, the ratings tumbled afterwards and only six episodes were made.

July

Hailing from the assured pen of John Esmonde and Bob Larbey, *Bowler* was that most rare of animals, a spin-off show that derived from another spin-off. Stanley Bowler, played by

George Baker, is a wealthy wide-boy villain with fingers in a whole range of extremely shady pies. He first appeared in several episodes of *The Fenn Street Gang*, 'and the character worked so well we thought it might be fun to give him his own series,' remembers Bob Larbey.[61]

Just out of jail, with tons of cash, Bowler decides he wants the one thing he can never have – class. To this end he embarks upon a series of ill-fated schemes to become accepted among the upper crust of society, including opening his very own gentlemen's club and attempting to set himself up as a laird.

Sadly, *Bowler* never progressed beyond its inaugural thirteen episodes on LWT. 'Despite a fine performance from George Baker, it just didn't work,' confesses Bob. 'We hoped it would but you always hope. If any writer knew the secret of success, he'd be very clever and very rich.'[62]

Despite this failure, Esmonde and Larbey were still considered two of the best comedy writers in the business. Like a lot of writers at the time, they wrote in long hand rather than using a typewriter:

> And we were always together physically when we wrote. And we tried to write fairly detailed storylines, which was always the hard part. When we came to the script, we played all the characters (badly) and improvised dialogue. The only hard part of that was trying to remember what we had just said so we could get it down on paper. At one stage we had an office over a greengrocer's and often wondered what the customers thought, hearing all those bad impersonations and hoots of laughter from upstairs.[63]

★★★

Hoping to emulate the success of such period romps as *Up Pompeii*, the medieval-set *Sir Yellow* falls desperately short, despite the giant comedy presence of Jimmy Edwards. It failed basically because it just wasn't funny enough. Paul Fox, who'd left a top position at the BBC to become Head of Programmes at Yorkshire Television, went on record as saying it was the worst programme he was ever involved with.

Set in the thirteenth century, Jimmy Edwards plays the cowardly knight of the title, galivanting about the countryside with his trusty squire, played by Melvyn Hayes, visiting ale houses and chasing wenches rather than doing battle with his arch foe, Sir Griswold.

Everyone working on the show knew it was rotten. So, what does an actor do when he is faced with such a predicament. 'I suppose it's a bit like a defence lawyer who knows that his client is guilty,' offers Melvyn Hayes, 'but he has to win the case.'[64] In a bid to salvage the thing, David Nobbs was brought in as script editor. 'I didn't think it was that bad actually. It was a romp, perhaps a little bit childish. Maybe it fell between the stools of an adult show and a children's show.'[65]

Staring disaster in the face, Jimmy Edwards hatched a crafty plan. 'We must try and get a second series in the can before this one hits the airwaves,' he told Hayes one afternoon. 'Because they're going to destroy it.' John Duncan was the Head of Light Entertainment at Yorkshire and used to play chess by himself in the canteen every lunchtime. Melvyn, who represented his school at chess, was given the task of getting him involved in a game and then broaching the subject of a second series. 'Look John,' said Melvyn. 'Jimmy's off to Australia to do a tour and I'm doing a play, we've got a two-month gap, so unless we go ahead now with a new series it's going to be next year but by that time, we'll have lost it.' Duncan saw the logic of this and promised to sort it out. And lo and behold the contracts were sent out. 'Sign them as quickly as you can,' Jimmy urged Melvyn. 'And run to the post office to send them back.' The contract was for another six episodes and a month of filming. 'The first show went out on the Friday,' recalls Melvyn. 'And sure enough, everybody hated it. We were due to start filming on the Monday and we all had a phone call telling us not to come into Yorkshire Television. The second series was cancelled. But because Jimmy and I had this contract, they paid us out in full.'[66]

So bad was the reaction to *Sir Yellow* that after just three episodes the series was dropped from its prime-time slot to midnight on Sunday. So, there was to be no second series, but at least there was an end of filming party held in a very posh restaurant that David Nobbs has never forgotten:

> There was this huge table for everybody, I think around thirty people, but there were two people too many, so these two chaps had to sit alone at a smaller table. And one of these actors, who had a tiny part in the show, maybe two lines, said, 'Well, it's easy to see who are the least f*cking important people around here, isn't it?' That was Bob Hoskins.[67]

★★★

Spring and Autumn proved to be another hit for the writing duo of Vince Powell and Harry Driver. This pleasingly gentle comedy from Thames first saw life as a pilot in October 1972 before getting its first full series ten months later. It starred veteran comedy actor Jimmy Jewel, who Powell and Driver had used in *Nearest and Dearest*. The writers so enjoyed working with Jewel on that show they promised to write another sitcom for him.

Jewel stars as widowed pensioner Tommy Butler, who is forced to leave the crumbling northern slum that has been his home for forty years when it's demolished by the local council. He moves into a flat in a high-rise building down south with his daughter, much to the annoyance of her husband.

Feeling somewhat of a misfit, Butler befriends Charlie, a young tearaway whose single mum is too busy to look after him. Butler becomes something of a father figure to the boy as they go fishing and walking together, sharing their differing views on life. As the series progresses so the relationship develops and deepens with the boy becoming a teenager and, by the end of the fourth and final series, leaving school to begin his life as an adult.

August

Man About the House, which became one of ITV's biggest TV hits of the decade, began life as a vehicle for Richard O'Sullivan. Writers Brian Cooke and Johnnie Mortimer had worked with him before, liked him and knew he was a highly talented performer. That only left the right situation to place him into. 'We noticed that in the Evening Standard there were ads from boys and girls asking for a third person to share a flat and we thought this was unusual,' recalls Brian. 'They'd done shows with girls sharing, but no one had done a show about mixed flat sharing. And we thought, that's going to be interesting.'[68]

When they took the idea to Thames' Head of Programmes, Jeremy Isaacs, he wasn't keen, sensing they might have problems with it. 'But it's in the newspapers,' said the writers, 'so it must be harmless. And we'll make sure it's tastefully done.'[69] That's why O'Sullivan suited the premise perfectly. 'He wasn't sexually threatening,' says Brian. 'We had this girl in one of the episodes confess to Richard that she was a virgin and she was prepared to give it up for him, and he backed off so fast.'[70]

O'Sullivan plays Robin Tripp, a trainee chef, who ends up sharing a flat in the Earl's Court district of London with two extremely attractive young women: Chrissy, played by Paula Wilcox of *The Lovers* fame, and Sally Thomsett, who'd been one of *The Railway Children*. Despite the modern premise, with its sexual politics and endless flirting, nothing sexually substantial takes place, with the comedy very much in the ribald tradition of the British seaside postcard.

What raised the series above the average was the introduction of the landlords, a middle-aged married couple living down-stairs. 'OK,' said the writers. 'We've got the upstairs flat, now downstairs there's got to be someone that we can give parental authority to.' Step forward George and Mildred. These two roles were chosen with the same keen eye as the other cast members. For Mildred the writers set their sights on comedy actress Sheila Steafel, who they'd just done a sketch show with and come away from the experience highly impressed. 'We thought she'd be great as Mildred,' says Brian. 'And we actually got hold of her and said, "We've got this new series coming up and we'd like you to play this landlady.' And she said, 'I can do the pilot, but I'm going to South Africa to see my parents who aren't very well and I can't do the series." In the end, our producer, Peter Frazer-Jones, brought in Yootha Joyce and she absolutely made the part her own.'[71] Cast in the role of George was Brian Murphy, who Cooke remembered playing a rather seedy char-acter in *Alcock and Gander* superbly well. 'He was a very good actor and had appeared on stage with Yootha Joyce at the Joan Littlewood Company, but at the time of *Man About the House* he was selling tickets at the Roundhouse theatre.'[72]

George and Mildred were really only intended to be subsidiary characters to begin with, indeed Brian Murphy recalls being told they might not even feature in some episodes. But he and Yootha formed a wonderfully natural partnership and they caught on with the public. Cooke and Mortimer also recognised their potential and started to develop the characters until entire storylines were sometimes built around them. 'Good writers,' says Brian Murphy, 'who are watching and not just precious about their dialogue, started to see what we were capable of and things we could do.'[73]

Fully in favour of the permissive society, Mildred has the misfortune to be married to the most sexless and uncouth individual in the western hemisphere. 'Their relationship was, she liked sex and he didn't,' says Brian Cooke. 'In fact, all she wanted really was comfort, hugs and things like that, but George didn't go in for any of that. And the number of people who wrote to us about that sort of relationship was surprisingly high.'[74]

Right from the start everyone sensed they were on to a winner, that this was something special. 'When we performed it,' recalls Brian Murphy, 'the audience reaction was so good and so warm that we thought, well, that's it, this is a hit.'[75]

The cast just seemed to click and everyone always had a good time making the show.

'It was exciting,' Brian Murphy remembers:

You looked forward to going to work. And because after a period you get to know all the cameramen and the lighting people, it did feel like a family, we would go out and have meals together. And Philip Jones was always there, like a general on the battlefield, he came down on to the studio floor and wished us luck, and sent us all letters at the end of each episode; well done, great show, you'll be pleased to know it's number one again.[76]

Murphy also has fond memories of Richard O'Sullivan:

> He was an excellent light comedian. And perfect for the role.
> Sometimes Richard would blow a scene at the early stages
> just to relax us because we'd all be a bit tense at the beginning.
> He always said that he didn't do it deliberately but it always
> brought the audience on side and relaxed all of us; thank God
> he's gone first, not me. [77]

Besides its enormous success, the show also managed to
break a few taboos. 'It was ground-breaking in its own small
way,' says Brian Cooke. 'I doubt that some of the shows that
came after would have been possible without *Man About the
House*.' [78] It was certainly of its time, especially in the youth-
fulness of the central characters. 'When you look at it now,
Richard's long hair, the outfits he wore, never mind the girls,'
says Brian. 'The only people that were normal in the show
were George and Mildred.' [79]

Inevitably a movie version arrived in 1974, made by
Hammer and featuring the regular cast. Written by Cooke and
Mortimer, the plot was a little hackneyed, revolving as it did
around an unscrupulous property developer who wants to flatten the street to make way for new buildings. 'It is difficult to
expand a sitcom into a movie format,' admits Brian. 'In the
end we did decide that films weren't for us. We're sprinters,
not marathon runners, and stuck with the half-hour format.
And I have to admit that I don't think the film version of
Man About the House really worked. It had its moments. It had
Spike Milligan in it for a start, who made his lines up as he
went along.' [80]

Just as successful was an American version, renamed *Three's
Company*, which ran for 169 episodes from 1977 to 1984. 'ABC

came to us and said they'd like to do the show in America,' recalls Brian. 'We said, wow, great. We knew that the odds were very much against it, there's only been a few British shows that have ever made the transition to America.'[81] Just to make sure they got it right, three pilots were made, with a separate producer attached to each one. Two of the producers made a complete hash of it, with one of them introducing the idea of the guy being a pilot and the two girls as air hostesses. 'Then the third producer said, hang on a minute, if it worked in Britain why wouldn't it work here, and for something like the first thirty or so episodes they stuck with exactly what we did, word for word,' says Brian. 'They put *Three's Company* up against *M*A*S*H* and it beat it, it actually beat *M*A*S*H*.'[82]

On both sides of the Atlantic the ratings were exceptional. Brian recalls that at one point the show topped both the American and British charts simultaneously. The writers also managed to keep it fresh, and most importantly, funny. But by 1976 Cooke and Mortimer arrived at the conclusion that the format had finally run out of steam. Not the characters, though, which the writers believed still had life in them and they went on to create two equally popular spin-offs in *George and Mildred* and *Robin's Nest*.

That still left the problem of coming up with a suitable resolution to *Man About the House*. The writers knew that audiences wanted Richard and Paula Wilcox's Chrissy to end up together. 'What we did, which is often what you do, is to confound them,' explains Brian. 'In the penultimate shows we brought in Richard's smarter brother and he hit it off with Chrissy and they got married. For the actual wedding there was a gag in there that actually happened to me, that somebody had taken a car and covered it in paint and tin cans and everything, but it was the wrong car, and that was in the show.

Very occasionally you can use real-life incidents that have happened to you that work.'[83]

September

Derek Nimmo seemed to make a habit of appearing in ecclesi-
astical garments. It was *All Gas and Gaiters* that first made a star
out of him, playing an accident-prone cleric. Running for five
series between 1967 and 1971, it was the first time that television
situation comedy had taken a swipe at the clergy, albeit gently.
Created by husband-and-wife team Edwin Apps and Pauline
Devaney, the couple purposely chose a religious subject as their
target. And for one very simple reason, in the mid-'60s there
were no rules left to break, and so the Church was in every sense
a godsend!

Bizarrely, the BBC was still making *All Gas and Gaiters* when
writers David Climie and Austin Steele took Nimmo out of his
clerical collar and into a monk's habit. In *Oh Brother!* Nimmo
played the well-meaning and no less accident-prone Brother
Dominic. Launched on the BBC in 1968, it was another ecclesi-
astical hit, running until 1970. In the belated sequel, *Oh Father!*
arriving three years later, Nimmo saw himself promoted to the
position of Father Dominic, though his penchant for disaster
and causing problems for everyone around him remains much as
before, as do the comedy situations.

Among the cast in *Oh Father!* was David Kelly, who thoroughly enjoyed working with Nimmo. 'He was totally unique.
I don't think he was the best actor in the world but he was a
genuinely funny person. And lovely and generous to play
with.'[84] Kelly recalls shooting one exterior scene in a big supermarket in Ealing:

I think anytime you went filming outside the studios of the BBC it was always Ealing. And we were greeted with open arms and we filmed there all day, but the owners had no idea of the amount of electricity used by a film crew and I'm afraid we buggered up all the food.[85]

Sadly, it did appear that the British public had seen quite enough of Nimmo in a smock and *Oh Father!* ended after just seven episodes.

***

In countless British film comedies of the '50s and '60s, Leslie Phillips was the smooth-talking philanderer and the Galton and Simpson-scripted *Casanova '73* was no real departure, 'but I thought the quality of the writing lifted it into a higher bracket,' said the actor.[86] Phillips plays Henry Newhouse, a happily married and wealthy businessman who can't keep his trousers up. Unsurprisingly, his extra-marital affairs land him in farcical situations, such as when he spends three days in a wardrobe after the husband of his latest conquest returns home unexpectedly.

It was all terribly '70s and politically incorrect. Just take the opening titles with Henry in an open-top Mercedes (the actor's own) eyeing up birds in minimal frocks, in particular a sexy garage attendant who inserts her pump into his fuel tank: 'Oh, hello.'

Ironically, Galton and Simpson intended the show to be a humorous comment on the so-called permissive society, but the nation's moral crusader Mary Whitehouse didn't appreciate the joke and complained bitterly to the BBC. There was moral outrage from other quarters, too, as Ray Galton remembers:

We invited all the TV critics of the land to come and watch a preview of the first episode. The critic from *The Guardian*, Nancy Banks-Smith – a very good critic, I used to like reading her until *Casanova '73* – she got up and walked out, and slammed the door behind her. And every week for the whole series she bashed the show. She crucified it every week.[87]

What Miss Smith and others objected to was Henry bedding a new girl every week, including a young Maureen Lipman, Madeline Smith and Peter Finch's ex-wife, Yolande Turner. They chose to ignore what the writers were trying to say about the morals of the times. 'Henry got his comeuppance every week,' says Ray. 'But that wasn't enough for Nancy Banks-Smith.'[88]

To appease the dissenters, the show was moved from its 8 p.m. family viewing slot to 9.25 p.m. This, of course, left a gap in the schedule that some bright spark suggested could be filled by a new quiz show that was going out late at night and watched mainly by insomniac academics. The show in question was *Mastermind*, which went on to become one of the BBC's most popular and longest-running programmes. 'The next time I saw Magnus Magnusson at a party,' said Phillips, 'he expressed his great gratitude for our unseemly behaviour on *Casanova*.'[89]

As for another series of *Casanova '73*, Alan Simpson recalls that it was Alasdair Milne, then Director of Programmes, who put the mockers on that happening when he spoke at a BBC convention:

He said something to the effect that producers have to take more responsibility and the example he used was *Casanova '73*, where he said they made the mistake of indulging successful scriptwriters by allowing them to do things against public taste. So, there was no way we were going to get a second series. He completely stabbed us in the back. But it was such an innocent show, really. It was about adultery, so what. It was never salacious. It was no more salacious than a Whitehall farce. Funnily enough we never worked for the BBC again, not deliberately, it's just the way things worked out.[90]

October

Men of Affairs was a rather coarse sitcom based on Michael Pertwee's London stage farce *Don't Just Lie There, Say Something*, which ran for more than 600 performances in the West End. It starred Alfred Marks as a randy MP and Brian Rix as his hapless Parliamentary Private Secretary tasked with covering up his minister's indiscretions.

Rix also appeared in the 1973 movie version alongside Leslie Phillips. However, when Harlech Television, the ITV franchise holder for Wales and the West of England, made the decision to adapt the story into a sitcom format Phillips was busy making *Casanova '73*. His unlikely replacement was Warren Mitchell, no doubt keen to present to the public another face other than Alf Garnett.

The weekly storylines scarcely strayed from its Whitehall farce antecedent, with lots of dolly birds in various stages of undress scampering around bedrooms and hiding in wardrobes. Joan Sims provided welcome support as the MP's wife.

The series greatly benefitted from a host of guest stars including Alfie Bass, Geoffrey Bayldon, Kate O'Mara (as a KGB agent), Alexandra Bastedo and Bernard Bresslaw. Though seventeen episodes were written, only thirteen ever made it to the screen.

November

Jeff Rawle had only recently left drama school when he came down to London for a general audition at London Weekend Television, which is something that used to happen in those days. 'When kids came out of drama school,' says Jeff, 'wise agents got them in to see the casting department just for a casual interview to see what you might be capable of doing at some point.'[91] Something did indeed turn up, it was called *Billy Liar*.

Created by Keith Waterhouse in his 1959 novel, Billy Fisher, aka Billy Liar, is a working-class 19-year-old living with his parents in a fictional Yorkshire town. Bored by his job as a lowly clerk for an undertaker, Billy spends his time indulging in Walter Mitty-like fantasies. When Jeff read the script he immediately identified with the character:

> I <u>was</u> Billy Liar. I lived in Sheffield and had dreams of becoming a scriptwriter. I used to sit up with a friend every night writing TV scripts that we never showed to anybody. So that idea of going down to London and making it, the determination to try to get out of your rather parochial background, was a massive thing then.[92]

In 1960 Waterhouse's novel was turned into a stage play featuring a young Albert Finney. It was followed a year later by a celebrated film starring Tom Courtenay. The character was then laid to rest for the remainder of the decade, until Michael Grade made it his first commission as the new Head of Light Entertainment at LWT.

Grade started his career as a sports columnist on the *Daily Mirror* from 1960 through to 1966, then moved into showbusiness as an agent. He eventually became joint Managing Director of London Management (Talent Agency), working alongside Billy Marsh, who had discovered, among others, Bruce Forsyth, Morecambe and Wise and Norman Wisdom. Michael learned to put together variety shows and to manage the finances. Gradually, Michael built a talent list that was to prove useful when he was tempted into the medium of television by LWT. It didn't take him long to make an impression on his new work colleagues, Humphrey Barclay included:

> He was youthful and exciting and he came walloping into my office on his first morning saying, 'I've read thirteen scripts of *Doctor at Sea*, they're wonderful.' To have actually put himself out to that extent. I loved working with Michael. We really saw eye to eye. [93]

Billy Liar adapted itself perfectly for sitcom; each episode had its own theme, whether it was Billy being into Kung Fu that week or wanting to be a French painter, wherever his flights of fantasy took him. The audition process to find the right actor to play the part was fairly intensive, with a shortlist of ten. One by one they were called into a room to perform a speech in front of the director, a whole phalanx of executives and Frank Muir and Denis Norden, who were comedy advisors to LWT at the time. 'Each person went in,' recalls Jeff, 'and if they liked you, they asked you to stay and gradually it whittled down until I was the only one left sitting in the room.' [94] Travelling home on the train, Jeff hadn't been back long when the phone rang with his agent confirming he'd got the job.

It was an amazing opportunity. 'But a real baptism by fire,' says Jeff, 'because I had no experience doing any television what-soever and that was frightening.'[95] He was raw, that's for sure, but desperately keen and had the support of an experienced cast that included George A. Cooper as Billy's father. 'George was very un-actorly,' Jeff remembers:

> He came into acting quite late having been a draughtsman previously. He didn't have all those airs and graces. And we had May Warden as Billy's grandmother, who was in her '80s then. She'd worked in music hall. Then there was Colin Jeavons as my boss. They were all very supportive of me. It did feel like a real family.[96]

Billy Liar was launched in a blaze of publicity, with Jeff as the cover star of that week's *TV Times*; he even featured in teen magazines:

> In my whole career I've never known a response in the street like it. I remember getting mobbed outside a school where we were filming one day in Kentish Town. The crew had to liter-ally pick me up off the floor. They were banging on the side of the van and shouting and screaming.[97]

This kind of fame did not sit very easily with Jeff, who also feared being typecast or not being taken seriously as an actor. Fresh from drama school, filled with Stanislavsky, here he was doing something that might be considered a bit frivolous. Was this the kind of acting he wanted to do? As a result, he couldn't really enjoy the experience and was perhaps too self-critical. 'I think I struggled with it in a way that I needn't have done. I should have just relaxed and enjoyed it as being an absolutely brilliant job.'[98]

Each episode was recorded at the LWT studios in front of a live audience. One particular evening they weren't getting any laughs at all after the first three or four scenes. 'George Cooper looked across at me,' recalls Jeff, 'and said, "Oh Christ, just drop your trousers, anything to get a laugh." It was just appalling. And then the assistant director came up to us saying there'd been a mix-up with the tickets. Apparently, our audience was full of disgruntled people who had come down on a coach all the way from Harrogate to see Russell Harty interviewing Dirk Bogarde and they were lumped with us.'[99]

Thanks to superb scripts by Waterhouse and Willis Hall, *Billy Liar* was hugely popular and ran for two series. There were plans for a third but it never materialised. It was remade in the States, running to nineteen episodes during 1979 and starring Steve Guttenberg as Billy, later the star of the *Police Academy* films and *Three Men and a Baby*.

Jeff Rawle was to return triumphantly to the world of sitcom as the perpetually harassed George in the 1990s newsroom satire *Drop the Dead Donkey*.

***

In the early '70s the role of women was changing in British society. Many middle-aged married women began to think there was more to life than running the family home, being a mother and tidying up after their husband. Yorkshire Television's *Beryl's Lot* tapped into this new spirit in its story of a housewife and mother whose perspective on life is transformed on the eve of her 40th birthday when she takes an evening course in philosophy.

Kevin Laffan, who had recently created the rural soap *Emmerdale Farm*, was inspired to write this comedy that blended elements of drama after hearing the real-life story of Margaret Powell. Approaching her 60s, Margaret underwent a similar journey of self-discovery when she left domestic service to go back into education, eventually writing her memoirs and finding success as a novelist. She served as script consultant during the first series.

Carmel McSharry was a familiar face in comedy and drama series on television but *Beryl's Lot* was her finest hour playing a woman determined to break her conventions. Her warm and witty performance arguably created the template for Willy Russell's *Educating Rita* (1980) and *Shirley Valentine* (1986). Interestingly, for the first two series each episode ran for an hour. It was only in the third and final series that it reverted to the sitcom standard of half an hour.

***

Last of The Summer Wine holds the record as the longest-running British TV sitcom of all time, from its debut in 1973 until it was cancelled by the BBC in 2010. It was also reputed to be among Her Majesty the Queen's favourite shows. All of which seems astonishing when one considers it's just about three old Yorkshire duffers getting up to all sorts of mischief as they enjoy a carefree second childhood.

What's even more remarkable is the fact that all 295 episodes were scripted by just one man, Roy Clarke, who also found time to create and write other successful shows for the BBC including *Open All Hours* and *Keeping Up Appearances*.

Clarke fell in love with writing at an early age, but came to the business late after stints working as a policeman, teacher, salesman and taxi driver. He continued to write in his spare time and eventually had several plays accepted by BBC radio. By the late

1960s he was writing drama series on television. His first shot at comedy was *The Misfit* (ITV, 1970–71) starring Ronald Fraser as a rubber plantation owner who returns to England after decades abroad. Its success came to the attention of Duncan Wood, the BBC's new Head of Comedy, who asked Roy if he'd thought about doing sitcom. 'I was given the shortest brief in history,' Roy recalls:

> Duncan told me he was looking for something for three old men, which sounded like the world's worst idea to me. I still wanted to try my hand at sitcom, only I had a heck of a job getting myself interested in the idea until it occurred to me that if they were footloose and free, they could do as they pleased, just like kids. The minute I saw them as children the whole thing just clicked and I wrote them as kids ever since.[100]

Roy was asked to write a pilot and was given James Gilbert as his producer. 'He gave the show its flavour,' says Roy, not least his insistence on extensive location filming. Most sitcoms at the time were studio bound and any film inserts were quite short and functional. 'When Jimmy Gilbert got my pilot and saw the countryside element, he was absolutely determined that he was going to get it on film,' says Roy. 'It was very much new ground for sitcom.'[101]

Casting was important too. Roy had created wonderfully colourful characters and it was a wise decision to cast comedy actors rather than straight comedians. Blamire, the leader in all but name and chief instigator of their misadventures, was played by Michael Bates. Clegg, a widower, and the most reserved and cautious of the gang, was Peter Sallis. Finally, Bill Owen was Compo, the scruffy and perennial adolescent. Sallis had worked for Clarke before and knew largely what to expect.

'When that first script arrived, Bill thought it was gold dust, Michael Bates thought it was a very good part for him and I just knew how good Roy Clarke was, and he didn't let me down.'[102]

There was, however, tension between Bates and Owen when the production team went up to Holmfirth, a small town in West Yorkshire, to start filming. After the first day was completed the cast returned to their hotel for dinner. 'Michael Bates was slightly to the right of Margaret Thatcher,' recalls Peter Sallis:

> And Bill was slightly to the left of Lenin. We hadn't got through our soup before they were at it hammer and tongs. They were actually shouting at each other in the dining room, and Jimmy Gilbert got to his feet and said, 'Outside you two,' and he took them into the corridor and said, 'We've got a great script on our hands, we're on the brink of something, and if I get one more squeak out of either of you about politics, I'm going to take the whole lot of you back to London and recast it.' That shut them up. They never talked politics again.[103]

In spite of those tensions, the actors worked brilliantly as a team. On that very first day of shooting, there was a long shot of the three of them meandering across a field, and Bill Owen said, 'Who's going to tread in the cow pat,' and Bates went, 'Oh, well, yes, I thought I'll do that,' and he did. 'And I thought to myself,' recalls Peter, 'this is very interesting. There was no creative friction at all and that was indicative of the way we worked together pretty much for the whole of the series, all helping each other out.'[104]

The pilot went out early in January 1973 and the first series was launched that November. Roy Clarke didn't give it much of a chance of running for long. 'It was a slow starter,' he says. 'It got a good critical response and no audience for about two series. The BBC in those days used to persevere with some of their shows. They take time to settle in sometimes, and if they get the time they do settle in and then they win their audience. And this was very much the case with *Last of the Summer Wine*. Funnily enough, the minute it got a big audience and became popular, the critics dropped off just like that.'[105]

By the end of the second series in 1975 Bates was struck down by cancer and it was clear he would be unable to continue the strenuous location filming. He died three years later. Sallis was at home one day when there was a knock at his door, it was Jimmy Gilbert. 'I think we've found a replacement for Michael. The character's name is Foggy Dewhurst. Now, who would you cast to play Foggy Dewhurst?' Without hesitation Peter said, 'Brian Wilde.' Gilbert said, 'Well, that's a bit of luck because we've already cast him.'[106] Wilde was to form the classic *Summer Wine* triumvirate, with Foggy bringing more military bearing and precision to their antics.

In 1985, Wilde, tiring of the show, left to be replaced by the rather aristocratic Seymour Utterthwaite, played by Michael Aldridge. As for Peter Sallis, it never for a moment ever crossed his mind to leave the show. 'I was bloody lucky to be doing it. It was my cornerstone, my bridge, my scaffolding, everything.'[107] Nor was he worried about typecasting:

It didn't stop people asking me to do other things. Maybe it was a slight reflection on the fact that Clegg is a sort of a nobody, an everyman, whereas Bill was much more blatantly Compo with the way that he behaved, the way he chased Nora Batty and all that sort of thing. Clegg is a sort of philosopher, really, he's more of a spectator than a participant.[108]

When Aldridge left the series in 1990, Brian Wilde returned and the classic line-up was reunited. By this time the show was almost twenty years old, but Roy Clarke kept it fresh by introducing a huge supporting cast of bossy wives, henpecked husbands and the like, while cleverly never straying too far from its formula of almost knockabout farce. 'When it first started it was all talking heads, but I learnt very quickly from watching the shows that people liked the visuals, that if you can pull off a visual gag you get a much better laugh than a verbal one.'[109]

Tragedy struck in 1999 when Bill Owen died during the filming of season twenty-one. Had his passing taken place in between series, Clarke is convinced the show would have come to an end. As it was, a solution needed to be found and it was decided that the character of Compo should also die and a replacement found in the unusual person of the actor's real-life son Tom.

There were many reasons why *Last of the Summer Wine* endured for so long; the theme of being young at heart, for instance. It also had a timeless quality, it never belonged to any one period, it existed in its own time and its own space, a fantasy land of its own. 'There's something very comfortable about *Last of the Summer Wine*,' says Peter Sallis. 'I always likened it to *Wind in the Willows*.'[110] The actor's favourite joke from all the episodes was typical of the gentle yet almost surreal humour Roy Clarke imbued into his scripts. Foggy produces a dart from a bow and arrow and explains, 'I've put a poisoned head on it so that when it strikes anybody they will go to sleep.' Compo asks, 'What is in the poison dart?' Foggy says, 'Horlicks.'

Wilfrid Brambell and Harry H. Corbett in the iconic *Steptoe and Son*. (Shutterstock)

The Home Guard platoon are ready for action in Dad's Army. (Shutterstock)

Frankie Howerd as the Roman slave Lurcio in *Up Pompeii*, his most famous comedy character. (Shutterstock)

James Bolam and Rodney Bewes contemplating life over a drink in *The Likely Lads*. (Shutterstock)

Sid James brought some of his *Carry On* charm to TV in *Bless This House*. (Rex)

John Inman and Frank Thornton in *Are You Being Served?* (Shutterstock)

One of the most popular sitcoms of the decade, *Man About the House* spawned two spin-offs, *George and Mildred* and *Robin's Nest*. (Rex)

The incomparable Ronnie Barker as Norman Stanley Fletcher in *Porridge*.
(Shutterstock)

Frances de la Tour and Leonard Rossiter (plus cat) in *Rising Damp*. (Shutterstock)

Paul Eddington, Penelope Keith, Felicity Kendal and Richard Briers in *The Good Life*. (Author's collection)

Barry Evans and Francoise Pascal in *Mind Your Language*. (Shutterstock)

The legendary cast of *Fawlty Towers*. (Shutterstock)

Penelope Keith and Peter Bowles in *To the Manor Born*. (Shutterstock)

Chapter Five

1974

January

Following the enormous success of *Dad's Army*, David Croft and Jimmy Perry decided to try their luck with another military topic, this time drawing on Perry's experiences serving with the Royal Artillery in colonial India towards the end of the Second World War, where he ran the concert party and put on shows for the troops. The result was *It Ain't Half Hot Mum*, another ratings winner for the BBC, and Perry's favourite of all the programmes he and David Croft made together.

As with Walmington-on-Sea's home guard, many of these new characters were also based on real people Perry had known, such as the rough and ready Sergeant Major Williams. Determined to instil a modicum of discipline into the camp, much of the drama and humour of the show derives from Williams' exasperation at being put in charge of, 'A bunch of pooftahs', as he refers to them, desperate not to be sent to the front line. First choice for the role was actually Leonard Rossiter. After reading the pilot episode, Rossiter found the part too much of a caricature and, according to Perry, proceeded to demolish the entire script from start to finish. Needless to say, he was not cast.

Next on the list was Windsor Davies, who made the part his own almost immediately. So much so that the writers decided to change the nationality of the sergeant major from cockney to Welsh; Davies had been born in east London to Welsh-speaking parents. As the show grew in popularity, Davies became indistinguishable from the character in the public's mind, but according to Melvyn Hayes he was nothing like that in real life, 'Windsor was a most gentle man. There was one episode where he barked so much during rehearsals that on the night of the recording his voice had gone!'[1]

Leading lights in the concert party included Bombardier Solomons, played by George Layton, who left the show after series two, and Bombardier Beaumont, affectionately called Gloria, played by Melvyn Hayes. At the time Melvyn was unemployed and teaching at the Italia Conti Academy of Theatre Arts in London. One of the teachers told him about this new series and to get in touch with David Croft. He was interviewed and got the part. After four weeks Croft pulled Melvyn aside and said, 'Melvyn, we're going to find it very difficult to write for you.'

'Why is that?'

'Well, you're playing it very effeminately.'

'Just a minute,' said Melvyn. 'The character is called Gloria, spends half the series dressed up in women's clothes and make-up, screams like an idiot, and is outrageously camp, you've written him like that!'

'Yeah, I see what you mean. Alright, carry on then.'[2]

Then there was the diminutive Gunner 'Lofty' Sugden, he of the oversized pith helmet, a role that made an unexpected star out of Don Estelle. Amusingly, Estelle was a discovery, of sorts, of Arthur Lowe. Appearing in a show together, Estelle approached Lowe for tips on getting into situation comedy. Lowe suggested he contact Croft and mention his name. After using Estelle in a small part on *Dad's Army*, Croft saw him as ideal for 'Lofty'.

Other roles were filled by Kenneth MacDonald, who later popped up as the pub landlord in *Only Fools and Horses*, and John Clegg as Gunner Graham, the concert party's pianist, even though in real life Clegg couldn't play a note. When it came time for the show to go out on a summer season tour, they couldn't use Clegg and instead brought in an actor who could play the piano. 'We opened in Bournemouth on the pier,' remembers Melvyn. 'We did the opening number and Windsor walked down front to talk to the audience and this woman on the front row grabbed hold of his leg and said, "Where's our lovely John Clegg," then pointing to this intruder on the piano, "Who's he?"'[3]

The most controversial piece of casting was that of Michael Bates, who wore brown make-up in order to play Indian servant Rangi Ram. However distasteful this may look in today's 'enlightened' times, the simple fact was that back in the mid-'70s there was a paucity of experienced Indian actors who could play a lead comedy role. In his defence, Bates was actually born in India, where his father worked for the Indian civil service, spoke the language and served in the Burma campaign as a major with the Gurkhas. All that made him an excellent choice and his performance manages to steer clear of any kind of crude stereotyping.

However, accusations of racism were levelled at the show. This upset both writers, especially since the idea behind the series was to cover an important part of Britain's imperial history, a period rarely touched upon in drama or comedy. In their own way Perry and Croft wanted to try to explain the presence of the Indian community in Britain and how the country became a multi-racial society; that it was the effect of the aftermath of empire. As it happened, the show was popular within the Indian community in Britain. Melvyn Hayes used to go into his local Indian-run newsagent and they would say, 'When is *our* show coming back?'[4]

Melvyn recalls that before the pilot episode was recorded David Croft gave out instructions to the cast: 'Say the lines as we've rehearsed them. And don't play it for laughs. If it dies on its arse or doesn't get laughs, it's our fault not yours.' The pilot turned out to be a success and a full series was commissioned.

Soon audiences were reaching 15 million at their peak and Windsor Davies and Don Estelle created an unlikely double act that resulted in a number one hit single in 1975 with their rendition of the evergreen tune 'Whispering Grass'. People used to stop Melvyn in the streets, as he was recognised everywhere:

> There was this one guy who came up to me and said, 'Hello, I'm from Australia, we love the show there. Do you know what you're known as down under?' I said, 'No.' He said, 'The number one poofta.' I said, 'Well, that's nice, thank you very much.'[5]

Much of the action was set around a studio-bound army depot, where British soldiers stayed before being posted up the jungle. For exterior filming, Croft first thought about using Kew Gardens but instead opted for some woods near King's Lynn, heightening the feeling of a jungle with a few carefully placed potted palms. And following the same pattern as *Dad's Army*, Croft helmed a few episodes himself before stepping aside to focus on producing and writing, leaving other directors to take over. During one episode this director was lining up a scene between Melvyn and Windsor, deciding to do it as a pair of close-ups. Croft sidled over to him and said, 'No, it's a two shot.' The director wasn't having it, 'No, it's definitely two close-ups.' But Croft insisted. 'How do you know?' asked the director. 'Why are you so certain it's a two shot?' David said, 'I've got a swimming pool that says it's a two shot.'[6]

As with all BBC shows, rehearsals took place at the corporation's own rehearsal rooms in North Acton, a place Melvyn remembers well:

> It was on seven floors and on each floor there were three rehearsal rooms, and on the top floor was the canteen. You'd meet up with the actors from all the other shows. I remember standing in line once at the canteen and in front of me was John Gielgud and I thought, this is one of the greatest actors in the world and what are we talking about, could you pass the butter please, and is that jam over there?[7]

Tragedy was to befall the show when news reached everyone that Michael Bates had been diagnosed with cancer. Entering its fifth series, Croft and Perry couldn't see how the actor could continue, especially seeing how his character was so integral to many of the plotlines. Bates, however, insisted on carrying on. Perry never forgot when Bates threw a party in his dressing room and everyone was greeted with, 'There's white wine, gin and tonic or plasma.'[8]

Now very ill indeed, Bates refused to take painkillers because they left him too dizzy to work. 'It was heart-breaking,' says Melvyn, 'because it got to a point where you could see the pain in his face. But once they said action, the pain seemed to disappear until they said cut. To still give a performance being that ill was remarkable.'[9] It was only after the recording was over that Bates took a couple of tablets and slumped into a chair. When he died the decision was taken not to replace him. 'We carried on for several more years without him,' said Croft. 'But to us the series was never quite the same.'[10]

It Ain't Half Hot Mum finally came to an end after fifty-six episodes in 1981. In the poignant final episode, the team get demobbed and make their way home.

A few years later Croft and Perry came up with an idea for a sequel that involved the concert party running their own theatre after the war. Sadly, nothing came of it.

March

ITV's first new sitcom of the year featured two performers with an old-fashioned appeal in Hylda Baker and Jack Douglas. *Not on Your Nellie* saw the veteran actress channelling the no-nonsense northerner role she perfected in *Nearest and Dearest*, this time as Nellie Pickersgill, summoned down South from Bolton to help run her ailing father's Chelsea pub. Nellie turns out to be tee-total and brings a dictatorial approach to maintaining order by keeping a watchful eye on the regulars, along with the flirty bar maids and her wayward father. Jack Douglas later appeared as Nellie's cousin and in one episode even turned up in a dual role as his famous character Alf Ippititimus, he of the nervous tics and 'phwaay!' catchphrase that had served him well for years in panto and several Carry On films.

The show was created by Roy Bottomley and Tom Brennand, two of the regular writers for *Nearest and Dearest*, who weren't averse to recycling some of their old gags and routines. They also indulge in some crude stereotyping. There is a gay couple, who hail from the fashion world, who are subjected to regular taunts and coarse jokes, while Sue Nicholls plays a barmaid called Big Brenda. The actress suffered the indignity of having to wear a large false bosom, no doubt because her own weren't deemed to be 'comedically' adequate.

By the end, tragically, Hylda's memory began to fail, making it harder to learn lines. She was also refusing to attend some rehearsals. No one knew it at the time but she was suffering from the early onset of Alzheimer's.

Following an accident on the set, when Hylda slipped and broke her ankle, the show finished prematurely after just four episodes of series three. It also marked the end of Hylda's regular television career; after that her appearances on TV became increasingly rare.

April

William G. Stewart was in his office at Thames one day when Philip Jones came in and said, 'We're going to get Harry Worth.' In the mid to late 1960s Harry Worth was a big comedy star at the BBC, appearing in a series of sitcoms that saw him playing pretty much the same kind of character, a bumbling middle-class and middle-aged man slightly out of sync with the world. 'Harry was just lovely,' recalls Stewart:

> He was a darling. He was like a cuddly toy. I never felt protective towards Patrick Cargill because he was well able to look after himself. I certainly didn't feel protective towards Sid James. But with Harry I did feel it was my job to look after him. I do think he was an insecure man. [11]

In this new sitcom Worth didn't stray very far from his tried and tested comedy persona, here playing a salesman who bumbles his way through a series of mishaps and misunderstandings when he moves into a boarding house run by the long-widowed Mrs Maybury, played by Lally Bowers. In one episode, Stewart cast ex-gangland mobster John Bindon as a policeman who has to escort Harry into the interview room: 'Right in here, sit down, don't talk,' all this kind of dialogue. Harry came over to Stewart halfway through rehearsals and said, 'Who cast that man?'

'I did, Harry,' said Stewart.

'I think he's very good, but can he soften it a bit? He frightens me.'

'He's acting, Harry.'

'But he says it like he means it. Every time we come to that scene I begin to worry.'[12]

Sadly, only one series of *My Name is Harry Worth* was made. Stewart puts the blame on Jeremy Isaacs, Thames' Head of Programmes:

> Isaacs dropped him and I was furious because the ratings were good. I think he felt it was too cosy. But Harry was adorable. He owned a beautiful big old Rolls-Royce. Can you imagine, Harry Worth sitting behind a big Rolls-Royce, it was the most incongruous thing you ever saw.[13]

***

Following on from the success of *Now Look Here*, Ronnie Corbett returned for the sequel, *The Prince of Denmark*, which saw him wave goodbye to insurance and begin a new career as a publican when he and Laura, again played by Rosemary Leach, inherit a pub.

Barry Cryer and Graham Chapman also returned as writers. Unfortunately, by this stage in his life Chapman was a borderline alcoholic. 'I think Graham lured Barry into doing more on-the-spot research than was really necessary,' Corbett later recalled. 'More time was spent at the bar than at the typewriter.'[14]

Chapman was quite the eccentric, too, and had invented this pub game called 'shitties'. This entailed placing a pint tankard in the middle of the floor, then each player was required to place a 50 pence piece or some such other coin in between his buttocks and waddle over and drop it into the tankard. Some of the cast and crew were playing this game once in the BBC bar, much to the consternation of the barman who kept removing the tankard only for Chapman to keep putting it back. 'I thought there was going to be a fist fight at one point,' recalls David Warwick.[15]

Warwick was just three years out of drama school when he was asked to play Steve, the long-haired barman. It was his first regular role on television but alas it was not a memorable experience. For a start the critics didn't like it. 'After the episode had gone out on a Wednesday night, the reviews were there on the Thursday morning and we were in the process of rehearsing and recording the following one, so it put a bit of a downer on things.'[16]

It didn't help that they lost their producer, Douglas Argent, halfway through. 'He had a bit of a nervous breakdown poor thing,' David recalls, 'and Gareth Gwenlan came in and took over.'[17] There was also a bereavement in the Corbett family and Ronnie had to leave for a funeral and so missed a few days' rehearsal. 'All this sort of put the kibosh on proceedings,' says David.[18]

The cast did get on well, though, and David saw how well Ronnie and Rosemary worked together:

Ronnie relied on her totally. She was a very no-nonsense sort of woman. You notice when comedians or comedic actors find a foil who they can rely on and are dependable, they stick with them, and Rosemary was there as a great feed and a great support to Ronnie and every comic actor needs that.[19]

Rehearsals took place at the good old Acton Hilton, then very much in its heyday when it was pretty much full all the time. 'Sometimes you had to walk through somebody else's room to get to yours,' says David, 'and I remember walking through Morecambe and Wise's rehearsal at one point.'[20] The place was a hive of activity, there would be the sitcoms, along with the light entertainment shows, and drama serials with actors being serious in togas. 'Even better,' says David, 'you'd go to the refectory and you used to get cast from lining up getting your food. Somebody would say, "Oh, you're here, are you free on such and such a day?" And you'd get a job.'[21]

Another haunt was the BBC bar at Television Centre, White City. It was here where many an actor pulled a casting trick. The BBC bar was nearly always crowded with producers, directors, fellow actors and casting directors. Outside in the corridor near the entrance was a phone, the BBC operated an internal phone system, and this phone connected to the one inside the bar. An actor would pick up the phone, dial the bar and giving his own name ask the barman if he could check to see if 'he' was in the bar. The actor would then put the phone down and rush into the bar just as the barman was calling out his name. It was a great way to get all these producers and directors to hear your name, and it was a way of raising one's profile. Who knows how many times that trick led to an actor landing a job?

★★★

ATV's two previous attempts to launch Norman Wisdom as a sitcom star had failed miserably, but *A Little Bit of Wisdom* turned out to be third time lucky and was a big hit with viewers until it came to an abrupt halt after three series, along with Wisdom's career, and all because of one tiny little screw.

Growing up, John Kane loved watching Norman Wisdom films so when the offer came to write some episodes for the show, he leapt at the opportunity. There was no doubt that Wisdom remained popular with the public. At the studio recordings Norman cooked up this little act where the floor manager came out first to explain the business of filming to the audience and slowly Norman would appear at the side of the stage. 'Of course, the audience went crazy,' John remembers. 'And the act was that the floor manager would go, "Get off, I'm busy talking to the audience, just get off," and Norman would go, "Aww," and off he'd go and there was all this warmth from the audience. They just loved him.'[22]

In this one particular episode John wrote Norman as a double-glazing installer – 'Guaranteed down to the last screw' was the firm's slogan. He and his workmates are fitting windows in a woman's flat on the fifteenth floor of a tower block and naturally the lift is out of service, cue lots of carrying material up and down stairs. When the job is finished the crew discover there's one screw missing and Norman is the one who has to go down fifteen floors to get it. Of course, as he's bringing this solitary screw up, he trips on the last step and back down it goes. They'd been rehearsing for a couple of days when Norman came in one morning very pleased with himself. 'I've got this fantastic joke.' Everyone gathered round, 'OK Norman, what is it?' He started to explain that before going back down the stairs the woman comes into the room and he says to her, 'Excuse me madam, but could you oblige my friend with a screw?' Silence followed.

'It's a funny line, Norman,' said the director. 'But we can't do that because your show goes out early in the evening, there's children watching it.'

'No, no,' said Norman. 'I've been watching television and you can get away with stuff like that nowadays. It's a great line.'

'No, Norman,' insisted the director. 'You can't say it.'[23]

Norman wouldn't let up, so the director called in the producer and Norman repeated the line. The producer laughed but agreed with the director, they couldn't use it. Norman still wouldn't take no for an answer and in the end the Head of Light Entertainment was summoned. 'We were rehearsing in a room in Wembley,' says John, 'and I remember walking away from all this to the far end of the room and looking back and there was Dick Sharples, the head writer, the producer, the director and the Head of Light Entertainment, all very tall men, and they were all standing and looking down at Norman shaking their heads and Norman was nodding. It was nothing to do with me, I thought, this was between them and Norman. And Norman was in love with this line.'[24] After much persuasion, though, he agreed to drop it.

Fast forward to the technical rehearsal in the studio. And Norman says the line. 'And because it's not in the script all the technicians, everybody in the studio fall about,' recalls John:

> There's a voice from the control room, 'Norman, you're not going to say that on the night are you?' 'No, no, no, of course I won't.' And of course, on the night with an audience he says the line and the audience laugh. And I swear they laugh for a full minute and a half, they bring the house down, and Norman looks up at the control room, spreads his arms and says, 'You see?'[25]

After everything calmed down, the director made Norman do a retake of the scene without the line and the episode carried on. After the show Norman always went to the bar for a few drinks and waited for a rough cut of the show to be made. He would take that away with him and back home would shove it into a video machine and watch it. 'He did this and, of course, the line was not in the show and he went ballistic,' says John:

He got on the line to the director, 'What have you done? Put that line back in, it's the biggest laugh I've ever had.' 'No, no, Norman.' He phones the producer, 'No, no, Norman.' He phones the Head of Light Entertainment. Now it's something like one or two o'clock in the morning, and he's getting no satisfaction. He then phones Sir Lew Grade, the head of ATV, and demands that the line go back in and if not, that Sir Lew should sack everyone involved with the show. Sir Lew, not happy with being woken up at two in the morning and being ordered to do this by Norman, says, 'No, I'm not going to do that. Furthermore, your show is cancelled,' and that's exactly what happened.[26]

This was despite the fact it was hugely popular and one of ATV's top comedy shows. 'Also,' says John, 'word got round about how difficult Norman had been and he was never on television again for years until he was cast as a cancer patient in a drama in 1981. His career hit the rocks simply because of that. So, my script was ultimately responsible for the destruction of Norman Wisdom's career.'[27]

May

1973's *Seven of One* was a BBC series of seven one-off comedy plays starring Ronnie Barker. Each individual episode hailed from a different writer and were considered as potential pilots that could be developed into a series in its own right. It turned out to be something of a golden goose, laying as it did two long-lasting series, *Porridge* and *Open All Hours*. One episode, entitled *My Old Man*, saw Barker as Sam Cobbett, a retired engine driver evicted from his terraced house slated for demolition. 'Forty years you live in a house then suddenly someone decides it's a slum,' he decries. 'So down it comes and out you goes!' The perfect solution is to move in with his daughter and his uppity son-in-law in their new high-rise flat.

When the BBC declined to develop this generation-gap comedy any further, perhaps due to its resemblance to Powell and Driver's very similarly themed *Spring and Autumn* from around the same time, writer Gerald Frow took it to Yorkshire Television. Here *My Old Man* was developed into a starring vehicle for Clive Dunn, who had made a career out of playing people much older than himself, in both theatre and television, most famously of course in *Dad's Army* and the children's series *Grandad*. Interestingly, Dunn first played an old man when he was just 19 years old in weekly rep. Still only 53 when he did *My Old Man*, Dunn was made up to appear over twenty years older. His on-screen daughter was played by Dunn's real-life wife, 38-year-old actress Priscilla Morgan. Priscilla recalls there were some problems on the show, notably the fact that the writer had never written a series before – just sketches. 'So, Clive went off and stayed with the writer and his family in the country, somewhere, and wrote it with him, and also got very fat as the wife was a wonderful cook!'[28]

Just like Corporal Jones, Sam Cobbett is a veteran of two world wars and a bit of a lively old codger with opinions and complaints about everything. It's no surprise that he proves to be more than a little disruptive to his daughter's hitherto orderly life. He also doesn't get on with his son-in-law Arthur, played by Edward Hardwicke, a snobbish, middle-class, social climber. Priscilla has fond memories of working with Hardwicke. 'He was a wonderful classical actor. I don't think he'd ever done any-thing as downmarket as sitcom TV! But when asked just said "Yes" without asking to read it or anything! I think he was just a *Grandad* fan!'[29] The cast also featured a then unknown 17-year-old by the name of Keith Chegwin.

Production-wise things ran fairly smoothly, according to Priscilla. 'The only direction I remember was, "Mind my budget, Clive" if he asked for anything! Nevertheless, we reached No. 2 in the ratings for the second series, but were not requested to do any more!'[30]

***

Up the Workers was another of those sitcoms focusing on that eternal battle between workers and management that has been a staple of British comedy since the days of *I'm Alright Jack* (1959). And in the strike-strewn 1970s it was a subject that took on added potency.

Although written by Tom Brennand and Roy Bottomley, the idea for the show came from popular comedy actor Lance Percival, who first rose to fame as a cast member of *That Was the Week that Was*, the ground-breaking BBC programme of the early '60s that brought satire to the masses. Percival was conva-lescing following a car accident and couldn't help but notice that most of the TV news was full of reports about strikes and poor industrial relations. Thinking that the British way of dealing with something serious was to make fun of it, he came up with *Up the Workers*, in which he starred as a labour relations officer at a small Midlands factory, Cockers Components Ltd, where most of the staff seem always to be on the verge of a strike. Benny Hill stooge Henry McGee plays the managing director perpetually at odds with Norman Bird's shop steward.

Up the Workers first aired as a pilot in September 1973 before ATV greenlighted a fully fledged series. Curiously, it would be another two years before the show returned for a second and final outing.

***

When *And Mother Makes Three* finished its run in June 1973 we saw Wendy Craig's scatter-brained widow Sally Harrison marry widower and antiquarian bookseller David Redway, played by Richard Coleman. Redway himself is a widower, with a young daughter, and the two families join together, hence the new title *And Mother Makes Five*.

This sequel carried on much as before, with domestic problems the centre of most storylines and the character of Sally having hardly changed at all, nor Wendy's approach to the role. 'I had got used to her rather idiosyncratic behaviour.'[31] It was a part Wendy enjoyed playing, having recognised a few similarities with her own personality. 'I'm a very vague person myself, not quite tuned into the present world and finding it difficult to keep up with the world. I'm even worse now, especially with computers and blackberries, I'm completely left behind, and I think she was a little bit like that.'[32]

Another ratings grabber, four series were made in total with Richard Waring, the show's creator, handling much of the writing, along with Brian Cooke and Johnnie Mortimer. At one point Cooke and Mortimer were unavailable, so Wendy and husband Jack Bentley, a writer himself, offered to step into the breach. 'We said to ourselves, "Look we know these characters really well, why don't we suggest that we write some." We'd previously written and suggested ideas together and I think we ended up writing about five or six episodes.'[33] They used the pseudonym Jonathan Marr.

By the end of series four in 1976 the show came to a natural end. 'Thames didn't want any more,' says Wendy. 'And you're always sad when something comes to an end. It was a bit like leaving a real family, we were all good friends. But not long afterwards Carla Lane asked me to do *Butterflies*.'[34] During that final recording a few tears were shed; after all, the cast had been together for six years. 'But that happens in showbusiness all the time,' says Wendy. 'Every play you do, it's such an intense, close relationship, and then the final curtain comes down and before you're out of your dressing room the set has disappeared, the stage is bare, and it's over.'[35]

June

When Dick Clement and Ian La Frenais first came up with the idea for *Thick as Thieves* they didn't know if it was right for a movie or a stage play. Turning it into another sitcom was by no means their first choice. 'We started to write it in my kitchen,' says Dick. 'And we wrote it very fast and had a lot of fun doing it.'[36] In the end it seemed the safer and easier option to go to television with it.

The scenario saw small-time thief George Dobbs returning to his home in Fulham after serving a three-year prison sentence, only to find his best mate Stan has moved in with his wife. Considering the circumstances, George adapts to the situation quite well and an uneasy and comedic alliance develops between the three of them as they settle down to life under the same roof.

Dick and Ian cast the show with a brilliant eye, choosing dramatic actors rather than playing it safe with sitcom regulars. Stan was played by John Thaw, already well-established in film and television, but this was his first proper comedy role. Meanwhile, hiding behind black horn-rimmed glasses as George was Bob Hoskins, appearing in his first regular TV role after several years of bit parts. Both actors share a great on-screen chemistry. 'We were big fans of Bob Hoskins,' says Ian:

> Very few people knew much about Bob but we saw him in this stage play at the Royal Court called *Veterans*, and he was hysterical. It was about the making of *The Charge of the Light Brigade* film and he played a spark with this big tool belt round his waist. As for John, he was a friend of mine and I'd seen him do comedy on stage. So, I'm sure we had those two in mind from the start.[37]

Like a lot of those early shows, *Thick as Thieves* was written in Dick's home. Ian would drive over there and they'd sit, often in the kitchen, and bounce ideas off each other and improvise before reading the script out loud over and over again until it sounded right. 'But the first and most painful part of the process is getting the plot right,' says Dick:

> Very early on we never used to work out where it was going, and sometimes you could paint yourself into a corner and suddenly found you didn't have a satisfying ending. It was kind of exciting, but that was when we were very young and inexperienced. Then we found out that it was actually better knowing where you were going, or at least have a vague idea, then you can always change it, and we often did.[38]

While *The Likely Lads* had been produced at the BBC, *Thick as Thieves* was made over at LWT and it just didn't feel the same. 'It was like going to another school,' claims Ian. 'Everything was

unfamiliar. I didn't like the atmosphere as much.'[39] Dick doesn't
think the show was handled right:

> The BBC really seemed to know how to do sitcom. It seemed
> to be something that they just did well. *Thick as Thieves* just
> didn't gel, which was a pity because we really had a wonder-
> ful time writing it, we loved the situation and we loved the
> earthiness of it. But it didn't quite work and that's why we
> only did one series.[40]

Licking their wounds, Dick and Ian went off to write *Porridge*.
As for John Thaw, he'd decided to take a chance on a new police
series written by his friend Ian Kennedy Martin called *The
Sweeney*. Hoskins, meanwhile, had to wait another five years
before winning international acclaim as East End villain Harold
Shand in the British gangster movie *The Long Good Friday*.

July

How's Your Father is your typical generation-gap comedy, a sub-
genre of the sitcom that seemed to be quite prevalent around this
time. *On the Buses*' Michael Robbins plays a hapless middle-aged
man unable to comprehend his rascally father, played by Arthur
English; he also has issues with his drop-out son.

Like Jimmy Jewel, Arthur English began his career on the
music hall circuit in the 1950s. Known as 'The Prince of the
Wide Boys', a cockney spiv character dressed outrageously on
stage with a huge kipper tie, English became one of variety's
greatest exponents. It was only in the '70s that he began to be
a recognisable face on television, as Bodkin in the popular children's drama serial *The Ghosts of Motley Hall* and most famously

in *Are You Being Served?* as Mr Harman the maintenance man frequently reprimanded by Mr Peacock for appearing on the sales floor during business hours.

Produced by Granada, *How's Your Father* was just about tolerated by the public, managing to stretch to two series.

★★★

Let's be charitable and say that *Don't Drink the Water* was at best an uninspired sequel to *On the Buses*. It was created and largely written by the team behind that series, Wolfe and Chesney, and featured Reg Varney's nemesis Blakey (again played by Stephen Lewis), who has retired from his job as a bus inspector and moved to a flat in Spain, leaving behind the Britain of power cuts and the three-day week.

Alas not everything is as sunny as the weather, since Blakey is encumbered by his spinster sister Dorothy (Pat Coombs), who quickly decides that she doesn't like Spain and makes his life a misery with her continual moaning. And there's plenty to moan about with building work still going on, dodgy food and even dodgier plumbing. And heaven forbid, Blakey discovers he's got German neighbours, along with a layabout porter called Carlos, played by Derek Griffiths, and some appallingly common expatriate Brits.

Shot entirely in the studio, with travelogue footage spliced in, the writing was just as artificial as the setting, though Lewis and Coombs made a fine comedy duo. Still, it did well enough for LWT to commission a second season, but the ghost of *On the Buses* proved hard to exorcise.

★★★

Terry Scott and June Whitfield are one of TV's great unsung comedy duos. They first worked together on Scott's 1968 BBC sketch comedy *Scott on …* Each week, a topic would be selected – Scott on Marriage, Scott on the Sex War etc, and invariably Scott and Whitfield would play a suburban husband and wife. Six years later it was their own sitcom, *Happy Ever After*, which was to firmly brand them as a husband-and-wife team in the minds of the British nation. So real was their image that many were led to believe that they were married in real life. Both actors told stories of going out socialising with their real-life partners, being recognised and getting the strangest looks. When the actors did a corporate video, the managing director of the company presented them with a top of the range camera, and had to be told they weren't a couple and he should give them a camera each.

They worked perfectly off one another. Scott's TV persona was that of an excitable, delusional, overgrown Boy Scout, while June's character had to be more mother than wife, staying keen and patient but also ready to put the brakes on her other half's madder schemes.

In real life they got on well, too, enjoying a playful relationship. Scott used to say, 'There's nothing I wouldn't do for her, and nothing she wouldn't do for me, so that's what we do for each other … nothing!'[41] Scott could be difficult to work with; June called him, fussy:

> If he didn't like the way you did something, he'd say so, and you'd say, 'Oh yes, you're absolutely right, got it,' and next time do it exactly the same way and he'd say, 'That's better.'[42]

Happy Ever After was a project close to Scott's own heart. He came up with the idea of a couple whose children have grown up and gone and are left with just each other as he contemplated his own children not being around the house anymore. Scott had four daughters, three had already left and there was now the dread of what it was going to be like when the last one left.

It began as an episode of *Comedy Playhouse*, which established the basic premise: Terry and June Fletcher are a typical middle-class couple living in a typical BBC middle-class suburban setting. With the kids gone, their new-found freedom is short-lived thanks to the arrival of Aunt Lucy (Beryl Cooke), together with a large amount of luggage and a chatty mynah bird.

After many farcical exploits covering five series writers John Chapman and Eric Merriman declared the idea exhausted and that *Happy Ever After* should end. But the BBC had other plans for Terry and June.

September

Arguably Ronnie Barker's crowning comedy achievement is his characterisation of old lag Norman Stanley Fletcher in *Porridge*, a sitcom routinely judged to be up there with the likes of *Fawlty Towers*, *Dad's Army* and *Hancock*. It started life as part of the 1973 series *Seven of One*, in which Barker played a new character in seven different stories. Dick Clement and Ian La Frenais were asked to provide two episodes and met Barker at the BBC rehearsal rooms in Acton for a coffee in the canteen. 'And all three of us were very disconcerted,' recalls Ian, 'and found it hard to focus because Pan's People were at the next table.'[43]

One of the episodes they wrote was called 'I'll Fly You for a Quid' and was set in a Welsh mining village and had Barker undertake two roles – an ex-miner on his death bed and his son Evan. As for the other story, Barker told the writers he'd always wanted to do a show about a man coming out of prison. 'And

we thought, oh f*ck, we've got to head him off at the pass here,'
recalls Ian, 'because that was the plot of *Thick as Thieves*, which
we were writing at the time. So, we said, "Oh no Ronnie, we
think it's about a bloke going into prison."'[44]

Prisoner and Escort went out as the second part of *Seven of One*
and was about a convict being taken to prison by two wardens.
The joke was that Fletcher needs a pee, pops outside the van and
does his business in the petrol tank and so they break down in
the middle of nowhere. Finding a lonely farmhouse, Fletcher
makes a break for it, wandering the countryside half the night
only to end up back at the cottage where he started. It was a brilliantly constructed piece of comedy.

It was only after the decision had been taken to turn the prison
idea into a series that Dick and Ian began to have grave doubts.
'After we'd said yes, we thought, let's look at some nicks,' says Ian.
'So, we went to Wormwood Scrubs, Wandsworth and Brixton.
Brixton was ghastly. They took us down in the basement where the
mentally disturbed prisoners were, it was awful and we thought,
we've made a big mistake, let's do the Welsh one instead.'[45]

It was when they went out drinking one night with an ex-
inmate, hoping to bend his ear on prison life, that the writers
found the hook that brought life to the project. He told them
that prisoners know they're never going to beat the system, so
they don't even try. What makes life bearable are those little
victories. 'What do you mean little victories?' asked the writers. He said, 'You know, getting a little extra bit of potato in
the dinner line, getting a couple more cigarettes than the next
bloke, getting one over a screw, tiny things.'[46] That was the key.
When asked by the press what the new show was about, Dick
answered, 'It's about survival.'

Something else the writers had was Ronnie Barker and the
enormous affection in which he was already held by the British

public. Initially Barker saw the show as a British version of *Sergeant Bilko*, a starring vehicle for US comic Phil Silvers back in the '50s, which was extremely broad in its approach and very much a comedian's show. 'We wanted it to have much more of a sense of reality to it,' says Dick. 'We wanted something a little bit grainier. And actually, the moment we wrote it Ronnie totally went along with our approach and agreed with it completely. And he said it was his favourite role, which is very gratifying.'[47]

What Barker brought to the role of Fletcher was enormous appeal, turning this unrepentant small-time villain into a likeable character, who just wanted to do his time and keep his nose clean. As he says, 'I'm only in prison because of my beliefs. I believed the night watchman was asleep.'

Cleverly, the writers decided to bring in a much younger character that Fletcher is forced to share a cell with, Lennie Godber, a first-time offender. For the role, Barker proposed the actor Paul Henry (later Benny in *Crossroads*), with whom he had worked recently. It was the show's producer, Sydney Lotterby, who had already earmarked Richard Beckinsale and he was an inspired choice. His on-screen chemistry with Barker is a joy to watch. 'Godber wasn't in all of the first series,' says Dick:

> There's a couple of episodes he's not in. But we obviously realised that we had gold dust. The idea of putting an inno-cent in the cell with an old lag meant that inevitably it became a sort of father/son relationship to some extent, although Fletcher would never have been that sentimental to admit it. There was a warmth there and an innocence about Godber, you felt his vulnerability.[48]

Everyone in the cast bonded quickly and were very close, which resulted in a wonderful atmosphere on the set. 'Richard Beckinsale was a dreadful sight reader,' recalls Dick:

The rest of the cast, if they saw that Godber had a long speech, would all groan and say, 'Oh God', which Richard took with great grace. And then you came back three days later for the run-through and he was word perfect. The camaraderie on that set was fantastic.[49]

Years later Dick and Ian were asked to do an uncredited rewrite on the war blockbuster *Pearl Harbor*. 'The first person we sat down and had lunch with was Kate Beckinsale,' recalls Ian. 'She had a role in the movie, and her mum Judy had flown out to Honolulu, too. And Kate, who was five or six when Richard died, told us that she got to know her father through *Porridge*. She watched all those series over and over, and that was very emotional.'[50]

Dick and Ian populated the fictional Slade Prison with a motley group of inmates played by familiar faces. There was Brian Glover, Christopher Biggins, Ronald Lacey (later the Nazi baddie in *Raiders of the Lost Ark*), David Jason, under a heap of make-up as dithery old man 'Blanco' and Peter Vaughan as prison kingpin Harry Grout, who maintains a luxury cell and special privileges.

Keeping order was Mr Mackay, played by Fulton Mackay, who barks out orders as if he's on an army parade ground. By comparison his subordinate, Mr Barrowclough (Brian Wilde), is far more liberal and malleable, and thus seen as an easy touch by the inmates.

As the scripts were being written, Dick and Ian scrambled around to find a suitable title. Numerous ideas were flung around, with none sticking. Finally, Barker came to the office one day saying how he'd the perfect title. The writers said they'd come up with one they liked too. After a quick argument about who was going to say theirs first, it was decided to toss a coin. Barker won. 'Porridge,' he said. 'Perfect,' said the writers, 'that was ours, too.'[51]

Porridge was an instant hit with viewers. Barker attributed much of its success to the element of realism the writers were able to conjure up. For example, there's no jaunty theme tune, just the barren sound of doors banging shut and the clanking of keys. The show certainly clicked with real inmates and became essential viewing inside Her Majesty's prisons. The prison officers liked it, too. 'A governor from one prison told us, it's a punishment in this prison for a misdemeanour: you will not be allowed to watch *Porridge* this week,' recalls Ian. 'That was the most flattering thing we'd ever heard.'[52]

The writers had managed to convey the intricate relationships between screws and convicts and the politics of prison life in a way that prisoners totally identified with and didn't think was fake. 'I think having done National Service helped when it came to writing *Porridge*,' says Dick. 'The fact that you had been in a hut with a whole lot of other blokes that you didn't know, and some of whom were scared and some of whom were frightening, that was terribly useful.'[53]

Another cast member quickly introduced was Ingrid, Fletcher's precocious daughter, played by Patricia Brake, who came to speak to her dad during visiting hours. 'Ronnie was always hugely generous to me,' says Patricia. 'I remember the first recording that I did. It was a long scene and I was very scared that I'd do something wrong and let him down. I think Ronnie picked up on it and I know that he pretended to dry, and that was so clever of him because it just relaxed me. He must have thought, she's not doing it as well as she did it in rehearsal, let's stop this now and start again, which we did. I was very young and I was in awe of him.'[54]

As Ingrid, Patricia makes quite an impression on the other inmates wearing a very tight sweater, much to Fletcher's embarrassment. 'It was quite something in those days, because I appeared braless.'[55] As a joke, some of the crew mocked up a certificate and gave it to Patricia at the end of the day's recording. 'It said: This is to certify that Patricia Brake has been seen and proved braless in the television category and hereby awarded the MBE, Magnificent Boob Exhibition in recognition of services to CND, the Campaign for Nipple Display. I'm very proud of that.'[56]

Meanwhile, American television producer John Rich, who had turned *Till Death Us Do Part* into the phenomenally successful *All in the Family*, thought *Porridge* could be another British show that might work in the States. Dick and Ian were invited to Los Angeles to work on what became known as *On the Rocks*. 'The trouble was John was unable to cast an American Ronnie Barker,' says Ian.[57] One night all three of them went to see the New York-born Kenneth McMillan on Broadway, but he either couldn't do the part or wouldn't do it. 'He would have been very good,' claims Ian.[58]

The show also had to comply with American Broadcast Standards and Practices. 'We ended up having a Jewish prisoner, a black prisoner, a hillbilly prisoner and a Puerto Rican prisoner,' says Ian. 'I mean, give me a break.'[59] There was also a lot more extensive location shooting. 'We went to a real hardcore prison called Chino,' recalls Ian, 'and spent five days filming inside maximum security. Dick and I had prison blues on, we were extras. I don't know how we weren't all taken hostage, wandering round pretending we were inmates. I can't believe we did it.'[60]

On the Rocks is something the writers do not look back fondly on. 'We didn't have fun doing it,' says Dick. 'It was a grind.'[61] Back in England, everyone met at the studio before a recording. The warm-up guy, often Ronnie Barker himself, would come out and talk to the audience, they'd record the show, do some retakes, and everyone was in the bar by ten. 'In LA we recorded it in front of two audiences,' says Ian. 'One audience goes, the next one comes in, and even then, with all that coverage, the second audience were sent home and then we would do retakes till well after midnight. And it was the same every week.'[62]

After the first series of *On the Rocks*, the executives over at ABC asked Dick and Ian to do a second series – and they said no. And nobody did that. 'I think we must be in the American TV history books as the only writers to turn down a second series,' says Ian.[63]

In the end, they just felt the show wasn't working. Essentially prison isn't funny, a hurdle the writers did manage to navigate in the UK. 'But American prison is particularly not funny because inevitably race comes into it,' says Dick,

> American prisons are divided much more along racial lines and that ain't funny. In Britain class can always be funny, and the gradations of class, you get so much humour out of it. But if you start getting into class in America you reach race before very long and suddenly everybody's prickly and sensitive and nervous because it's a difficult subject.[64]

Back in Blighty, Dick and Ian started working on series three of *Porridge* and more memorable episodes, including a two-parter that saw a new inmate arriving at Slade Prison that just happens to be the judge that sent Fletcher down. 'We had *On the Rocks* to thank for that one,' says Dick. 'Because in America they needed twenty-two episodes for a season, we ran out of original *Porridge* episodes, and we came up with that idea, and then when we went back to do series three of *Porridge,* we ended up re-translating the US shows back into the English show.'[65]

Following series three in 1977, Ronnie Barker decided to call it a day. The comedy actor always feared being typecast or getting stuck in a rut, and even the personal intervention of Bill Cotton, then BBC Head of Comedy, couldn't change his mind. 'I think we should have pressed Ronnie and we should have pressed ourselves to do more,' admits Ian. 'I think *Porridge* is definitely a series short. It was ridiculous for something that popular to only do the three series.'[66]

Then in 1979 Barker and Beckinsale were back in stir when TV and film tycoon Lord Lew Grade financed a cinema version of *Porridge*. Filmed on location at Chelmsford prison, then empty and undergoing refurbishment, the plot involved Fletcher and Godber being coerced into aiding an escape attempt during a celebrities-against-prisoners football match.

Thanks to numerous repeats *Porridge* has never really left us, it remains firmly rooted in the consciousness of the nation. And it's as good an example as any of the artistry of sitcom writing at its finest.

***

Performing in a play at the end of Eastbourne pier is an odd place to get 'discovered', but that's exactly what happened to David Jason when producer Humphrey Barclay was looking to add another comedy face to the cast of 1968's *Do Not Adjust Your Set*. Barclay saw Jason's potential immediately. 'When he came on the stage, he just had the whole house in the palm of his hand from the word go.'[67]

Barclay liked Jason enormously and was keen to find a comedy vehicle that could launch his career, 'and make him a star'.[68] Another admirer was the writer Bernard McKenna, who'd worked on several *Doctor* episodes for Barclay, 'along with keeping fellow writer Graham Chapman on the rails'.[69] Barclay and McKenna looked at a few possibilities, including the idea of bringing the character of Inspector Clouseau to television and casting Jason in the role. 'In the end we thought we'd never get the rights, and also that it would be silly to try and follow Sellers.'[70] But the concept of having Jason play a bumbling character remained, which would play to his strengths as a physical comedian. Inspired by the '60s US TV comedy spy spoof *Get Smart*, McKenna and his writing partner Richard Laing came up with *The Top Secret Life of Edgar Briggs*. 'And we just had a wonderful time making it,' says Barclay.[71]

The concept was amusing: Edgar Briggs, a humble pen-pusher, is transferred by mistake to counter-espionage duties at the Ministry of Defence. Obviously, he's completely hopeless but somehow manages to get the job done and solve his cases. These escapades usually involved a lot of pratfalls and other physical comedy, with Jason keen to do his own stunts such as dodging cars and jumping into canals.

After years of hard slog, Jason hoped that *Edgar Briggs* might be his breakthrough, but despite being well received critically the ratings were not up to much. It didn't help that LWT put the show up against the BBC's top drama series at the time, *The Brothers*. Barclay thinks that given another chance it might have caught on, 'so it was a huge disappointment that it wasn't taken on as a second series'.[72]

October

Carla Lane's first sitcom since her success with *The Liver Birds* was something of a disappointment. *No Strings* starred Rita Tushingham and Keith Barron. Its amiable premise was about a single man and a single woman trying to share a flat and the inevitable clashes and romantic murmurings. The show only lasted six episodes, no time really to develop any meaningful relationship between the two characters, and Carla always viewed it as a personal disappointment.

★★★

It's strange how some actors get cast in a show, sometimes even when they're not right for a part in the writer's mind's eye. Take Patricia Brake in *Second Time Around*, a romantically themed sitcom from Richard Waring that starred ex-matinee idol Michael Craig as 50-year-old divorcee Harry, who falls in love with a much younger woman. Patricia was at home one evening when a girlfriend of hers called. 'I've been up for something today, Pattie, at the beeb and you are so right for it.' It was for *Second Time Around*.

As it happened, Patricia's husband knew Richard Waring quite well and had his phone number. 'Why don't you call him up?' he urged. 'I wasn't very good at that sort of thing,' confesses Patricia. 'I didn't have the confidence.'[73] Patricia had done quite a bit of television before and also been with the Royal Shakespeare Company, but at this point no comedy. This was before she had been cast in *Porridge*.

Anyway, her husband filled her with enough wine to summon up the courage to call Waring. 'Hello Pattie darling,' he said, 'it's lovely to talk to you, but no, no, no, no, I really envisaged an Audrey Hepburn type of girl, not you at all.'[74] It must have occurred to Waring to do the decent thing and at least call her in for an interview. And as it happened, Patricia ended up in competition with one other actress and after two weeks of testing won the role. 'It just goes to show,' says Patricia, 'even though I wasn't the writer's idea at all. And if I hadn't been brave that night, probably I would not have got *Porridge*.'[75]

Second Time Around was a moderate success, lasting for two series. Patricia plays Vicki, a young girl who falls in love with an older man. The first series dealt with the perils of dating, the inevitable clashes with her parents and an eventual wedding. Series two focused on their early days as a married couple. What surprised Patricia the most about the show was the reaction she sometimes got in the street. 'Older women would see me and approach me and say things like, "Oh, I suppose you think it's clever getting an older man."'[76]

★★★

No, Honestly also traded on romance but was a little bit different. Humphrey Barclay had known Charlotte Bingham for years, been to some of the same high society parties and saw her come out as a debutante. When she married the Irish actor Terence Brady, many thought it an unlikely match, but when she wrote of their experiences in a memoir it became a minor bestseller.

When the couple approached Barclay at LWT with the idea of adapting the book for television the producer knew exactly how to approach it. He was going to replicate Charlotte's anarchic way of writing straight on to the screen:

> I was going to throw captions on the screen, like a comic book, do abrupt changes, play stuff upside down. I had an image of making the visual presentation jokey and imaginative in a way that had never been done – and thank God I was talked out of it by the wise director of programmes Cyril Bennett who said, 'It's a love story.' Which was very perceptive because it didn't seem like that to me, it seemed like social satire. So, we put together a much more straightforward script.[77]

Real-life husband-and-wife team John Alderton and Pauline Collins, coming off the highly successful *Upstairs, Downstairs* and their own spin-off series *Thomas and Sarah*, voiced an interest in playing the couple, which automatically got the project green-lit. 'They really were an enchanting couple on screen,' says Barclay.[78]

The actual premise of the series was that the couple are look-ing back at events ten years previously, when they first met and began their relationship. Consequently, each programme opened and closed with both of the characters talking directly to the viewer about that week's story. There was a lot of discussion about how best to do this. 'Terence and Charlotte were sure that we needed to do it with a visible studio audience to show them sharing the joke before we went into the sitcom situation,' says Barclay.[79] In the end the director David Askey said, 'Just for the time being, let's put them on stools against black and they can talk to camera.' It worked so well they kept it. 'But it was very inter-esting because John couldn't find a way of doing it at all,' Barclay recalls. 'He said, "I don't know who I am. Am I the character?" I said, "Yes, you're in the character." And he said, "Then why I am talking to the audience?" He couldn't get it intellectually. I gave him a helpful clue, which was simply to treat the camera as his favourite member of the audience. And that was a great help.'[80]

No, Honestly was an instant hit, helped no doubt by the enor-mously catchy theme tune by Lynsey de Paul that was a top ten hit. 'The public loved it,' says Barclay, 'which was surprising because it was about this posh girl. There was a joke in episode one that included a reference to the Brecht play *Mother Courage*; now that wasn't very ITV, but it got a laugh.'[81]

LWT were obviously keen for another series but Alderton and Collins said they would not do another thirteen episodes; at best they'd commit to half a series. 'Cyril Bennett got cross and said, "They either do it or they don't,"' Barclay recalls. 'So, they said, "Well, we won't." And before we let them go, Cyril said to me, "Could you make the formula work with another couple." And I said yes.'[82] The result was *Yes, Honestly*. But more of that later.

December

The final sitcom of 1974 turned out to be arguably the finest that ITV ever produced, certainly one of its most enduring – *Rising Damp*. Much of its popularity rests on the magnificent central performance of Leonard Rossiter as Rigsby, Britain's most obnoxious landlord, who owns a rundown boarding house in a northern university town. In Rossiter's hands this lecherous bigot became almost loveable, while his cack-handed pursuit of lovelorn spinster Ruth Jones, played by the RSC's Frances de la Tour, generates sympathy rather than loathing. It's one of the great unrequited romances in British television history.

The bulk of the comedy derives from Rigsby's interaction with what appears to be the only other tenants living in the building, long-haired medical student Alan, played by Richard Beckinsale, who writer Eric Chappell remembered from *The Lovers*, and Don Warrington, just out of drama school, as fellow student Philip, who claims to be the son of an African chief.

The origin of the show went all the way back to a stage play written by former Electricity Board accountant Eric Chappell. *The Banana Box* starred Wilfrid Brambell as a seedy bedsit landlord ruling the roost over a motley collection of tenants. Chappell based the character on several people he knew and their cynical attitude to the increase in Afro-Caribbean immigration into the UK. Indeed, the idea for the play first came about when Chappell read a newspaper article about a black man who had stayed as a hotel guest for twelve months pretending to be an African prince, where he received the royal treatment. The role of Philip was clearly based on this.

The Banana Box was first performed at the Phoenix Theatre, Leicester, in 1971 before going on a short tour in 1973, with Leonard Rossiter replacing Brambell. Chappell recalled

Rossiter's appearance in a *Steptoe and Son* episode playing an escaped convict and thought he would be perfect casting, having come on to that show and almost overpowered the two established leads. Playing the hapless tenants were Don Warrington, Frances de la Tour and ex-singer turned actor Paul Jones. Arriving in the West End later that year, John Duncan, then Head of Light Entertainment at Yorkshire Television, spotted its potential as a sitcom and commissioned a one-off pilot episode in September 1974, starring most of the stage cast but with Richard Beckinsale replacing Paul Jones. The title was also changed, becoming *Rising Damp* after a line in the script that highlighted the squalid conditions the tenants had to live under.

When the pilot garnered a respectable audience of 6 million and critical praise, a series was commissioned immediately and went on air that December. It was a personal triumph for Leonard Rossiter, in his first sitcom role, turning Rigsby into one of British TV's great comedy characters, the equal of a Basil Fawlty or Captain Mainwaring. He took it over, to the extent that he began saying to Chappell, 'Rigsby wouldn't say that.' To which Chappell argued, 'Wait a minute, I created this character, now you're telling me what he'd say.' That was Rossiter, though, in rehearsals he was a perfectionist, some would say difficult and demanding. 'He was a hard taskmaster,' says Eric Chappell. 'He gave 100% and expected everyone else to do the same.' Writer Brian Cooke worked with him on the '80s sitcom *Tripper's Day*:

> Len had this line and he came to me and said, 'That won't work.' I said, 'I think it will work.' 'No, no it won't,' he said. And I said, 'Well, let's just try it.' He said, 'Yeah, I'll try it but it won't work.' So comes the show, he does the line and it gets a roar from the audience and afterwards I said, 'That line, it

worked, didn't it?' He said, 'The audience was wrong,' and walked off.[83]

Rigsby stalks the corridors and rooms of his boarding house almost like a restless spirit, barging into the boys' room without knocking, mocking Philip's race and his culture, while trying to be a father figure to Alan. Rigsby's prejudice towards Philip makes for uncomfortable viewing today, but like Alf Garnett's bigotry the joke is on him, and Chappell must be congratulated for creating in Philip arguably the first fully rounded, non-caricature black leading character on a British television comedy show.

The cast mostly got on well together. Rossiter had a particular fondness for Beckinsale, and the young actor generally acted as a calming influence over everyone when things got too heated. For several of the episodes Beckinsale had to wear a wig because he was playing Godber (with obligatory short-cropped hair) in *Porridge* at the same time as recording *Rising Damp*. Rossiter's relationship with Frances de la Tour was less happy; they didn't click at all, being not remotely similar personally and certainly politically, with Rossiter a Tory and de la Tour very left-leaning.

During its four series, there was the occasional new tenant, notably a smarmy con man played by Henry McGee, Peter Bowles' hysterically camp theatrical and Brenda, who posed nude for art life classes, otherwise the cast remained constant until the final series, when Beckinsale dropped out due to other work commitments.

During its time *Rising Damp* only gained in popularity, at times commanding massive audience figures of over 18 million, won a BAFTA for Best Comedy and rocketed Rossiter to stardom. Tragically, the death of Beckinsale meant there was no chance of any further series, although by then both Chappell and Rossiter had agreed to end it, feeling twenty-eight episodes was enough. 'I thought the subject was exhausted,' says Chappell, 'and so was I.'

However, in 1980 a feature film was made, directed by Joe McGrath, with Christopher Strauli taking the place of Beckinsale. By no means the worst sitcom movie – after all it did win Best Comedy at the Evening Standard Film Awards and Frances de la Tour won Best Actress – it did regurgitate several storylines from the television series, notably the con man episode, with Henry McGee replaced by Denholm Elliott. The big revelation of the film is Philip's confession that he isn't the son of an African chief after all but comes from Croydon, much to the disappointment of Rigsby. This revelation was part of the original play *The Banana Box* but dropped from the TV series.

Chapter Six

1975

March

Since the death of writing partner Harry Driver, Vince Powell had been employed as a comedy consultant for Thames Television, during which time he developed an idea for a sitcom about a working-class Liverpool family. Powell hailed from Manchester himself but had lived in the city of Liverpool for several years. Valuing Powell's expertise and liking the idea, his boss Philip Jones discarded the idea of doing a pilot first and commissioned a full series straight away.

The Wackers focused on the Clarksons, a family divided by loyalties, both on religious grounds and, more importantly, football. They live in the deprived Dingle area of the city, with its streets of back-to-back houses. Liverpudlian Ken Jones was cast as the head of the household, alongside his real-life wife Sheila Faye. Their teenage kids were future children's television presenter Keith Chegwin and Alison Steadman – just two years away from her breakthrough role in *Abigail's Party*.

Powell was positive he was on to a winner, and so it came as something of a shock when the press turned on the show, calling it out for its vulgar humour and hackneyed stereotypes of Liverpool people. Forced to act, Philip Jones asked director Anthony Parker to edit out all the crude references from each episode. Parker and Powell resisted such a move and complained to Jeremy Isaacs, then Controller of Programming at Thames. Isaacs' bizarre compromise was to request both men to nominate the worst offending episode, which would not be broadcast, but the rest could go out uncut. At the same time a newspaper carried out a survey of Liverpool people and the result saw a 50–50 split over those who hated the show and those who loved it. Nevertheless, only one series was ever made, though Powell remained unrepentant and proud of the work, classing it as a probable forerunner of the much more popular *Bread*.

Things did not improve for *The Wackers* when it was shown out in Australia, as a lot of British comedy was in the 1970s. Melbourne-based television critic John Pinkney, writing in *The Age* newspaper, described the show as, 'a half-hour lavatory joke that's hardly worth the toilet paper on which it seems to have been written'. Indeed, after its first broadcast 116 people rang up the TV station demanding the show be cancelled.[1]

April

The inspiration behind one of the BBC's most cherished sitcoms was the fact that writer Bob Larbey was approaching his 40s. This is indeed one of those landmark dates, prompting one to think, 'What have I done with my life so far?' Larbey and his writing partner John Esmonde began to think about this and came up with a character nearing his 40s who wasn't happy with the way things had gone, especially where his career was concerned. 'So, what should he do about it,' recalls Bob. 'Then we came up with the idea of self-sufficiency in Surbiton, and *The Good Life* was born.'[2]

Tom and Barbara Good are a middle-class suburban couple. Tom is fed up with his life in his office and the hurly burly of modern existence, commuting and all the rest of it, and decides to pack up his job and go self-sufficient, turning his garden into an allotment. Inevitably, their neighbours, Margo and Jerry Leadbetter, are shocked by the idea of their genteel neighbourhood being overrun by pigs and sundry muck.

Seen very much as a star vehicle for Briers, the actor at first paused about whether or not to accept the job after reading an initial script. Following his hit 1960s sitcom *Marriage Lines*, Richard had done plenty of TV work but nothing quite as successful and pondered whether he wanted all that fame and recognition again:

> There's always a conflict between wanting to be a legitimate actor and being a well-loved personality. I realised, in all honesty, because I was then getting on a bit, that I wanted to be loved and well known.[3]

Something else made him cautious. It all felt, well, a bit too safe. 'A bit middle-class southern. Will it have a wider appeal? But then what I didn't know was that as soon as Tom left his job and got his spade out and dug it in the ground the whole thing became class-less.'[4]

Originally Peter Bowles was going to play Jerry, 'but he was under contract to do a play at the Royal Court, poor devil,' recalls Richard, 'and he missed out. But on the other hand, Paul Eddington was definitive.'[5] At the time Eddington was a jobbing actor with a big family to support so wasn't particularly well off. Richard recalls that during filming of the second episode Eddington came up to him at the studio and asked, 'Have you had your cheque yet?' Richard had. 'Well, I'm still waiting for mine and I need it.' Richard put in a word with the right people and Eddington got his cheque the next day.[6]

For the two wives, Richard urged the writers to go and see Felicity Kendal and Penelope Keith, then appearing together in a West End production of Alan Ayckbourn's *The Norman Conquests*. The team was complete and very quickly everyone bonded. 'We were a family,' says Richard. 'We'd all done repertory, we were all stage people, and we all admired each other's work. And the fondness we genuinely had for each other comes across on the screen and that gave the show a nice feel.'[7] John Howard Davies was the producer and saw first-hand what a special atmosphere there was. 'Throughout the whole of that show we did not have one single cross word or irritation about anything. It was just magical. I'd never known that happen before.'[8]

Something else, too, it soon became apparent that it was the interplay between the two couples that really gave the show its appeal. 'After a few episodes,' relates Richard:

the writers took me aside and said, 'Penelope's a bit of a gold mine, isn't she?' I said, 'Yes, she is.' They said, 'Would you mind if we wrote her up?' So instead of two starring parts and two supporting parts, it became a quartet and when we became a quartet — bang! And John Howard Davies, I'll never forget it, he came into the rehearsal room one day and said, 'You'd better all sit down.' I thought, oh God, we're all going to be sacked. He says, 'The trouble is the audience don't like you, they love you.' And I said, 'What an awful responsibility.'[9]

After a slow start, *The Good Life* did endear itself to the public, who seemed to gain a real affection for the characters and wanted Tom and Barbara to succeed. 'Theirs was a revolution,' says Bob Larbey, 'but one that harmed nobody else and perhaps the idea of living outside the system reaches a lot of us – even if we don't try it!'[10]

The production routine followed the same pattern as other shows: read throughs and rehearsals during the week, then a couple of run-throughs on Saturday at the BBC studios, in at ten on Sunday morning for camera rehearsals, a break for dinner before the recording that evening. By then the nerves were starting. 'Just outside the dressing room is where the audience queued,' recalls Richard. 'You could hear them and that terrified the life out of you.'[11] Richard always made a point of introducing himself and the cast to the audience prior to the recording, 'then when it was all finished, it was straight to the bar.'[12] Exterior filming took place at a house in Northwood, Middlesex, which was deemed to be the perfect suburban setting.

One memorable recording took place in front of the Queen and the Duke of Edinburgh. The Royal couple had been offered the opportunity of watching a BBC show being recorded and it was between *The Two Ronnies* and *The Good Life*. Since it was reported to be their favourite television programme, it was no surprise they chose *The Good Life*.

The first Richard heard about it was when he was collared one afternoon at BBC Television Centre by Bill Cotton. 'You do realise, don't you, that it will have to go out live.'

'Sorry, Bill,' answered Richard. 'Did you say live?'

'They can't hang about for retakes.' Cotton didn't think the Royals would put up with reshoots if things went wrong.

'I'm terribly sorry Bill, but if you do that, you'll have to recast Tom Good. I don't have the nerves to do it. I forget lines sometimes.'[13]

In the end the episode went ahead as usual and was recorded. 'And I think we made five errors and, of course, she loved it,' recalls Richard. 'Like anybody, they love the mistakes.'[14] No members of the public were in the audience that night, instead the seats were filled by senior BBC management and staff. The cast were in make-up when the Rolls-Royce carrying the Royal couple turned into the gates of BBC Television Centre. 'Oh my God,' cried Penelope Keith, as they all looked out of the window. 'It's her and she's coming to see us!'[15] After the recording the cast were introduced to Her Majesty. For Richard it was a terrifying evening, so far as nerves went, but one of which to be immensely proud, too.

As for the scripts, the actors hardly ever found themselves challenging anything or even altering lines. 'Those scripts were gold,' says Richard.[16] The actor did have a few ideas, notably concerning Tom's relationship with Barbara:

> I began to realise it was getting a bit lovey-dovey, a bit nice, and I said to Bob, 'Any chance of us having a couple of rows? Because she's under an awful lot of stress; no clothes, no child, no social life, no fun. And Tom is such a selfish bugger. I think to make it more real we should have an up and a downer every few episodes.' And that gave it another dimension.[17]

After four series and two specials (a 1977 Christmas offering and the Royal performance in 1978), Larbey and Esmonde decided to call it quits. The BBC were anxious to continue, but the writers just felt the situation had run its course and they'd only be repeating themselves. The cast agreed, they didn't want to be typecast anyway. 'It was sad because we'd become such good friends,' says Richard. 'But we felt that we'd kind of done it, and it was a good time to get out. We went out on top. For God's sake don't drop that standard, don't let people say, "Oh it's that bloody *Good Life* again," it would have broken all our hearts.'[18]

There were always whispers about a return, and even a few rumours concerning a possible film version, but nothing came of any of them. 'I can't say I'm sorry we didn't end up making a film,' says Bob Larbey, 'because nearly all of those films made from sitcoms were fairly awful.'[19]

Thanks to numerous repeats over the years *The Good Life* is now something resembling a national institution. Watching an episode is like sliding underneath a warm duvet into a comfortable bed. Richard was in no doubt, regardless of what any of the four of them might later achieve, that they would always be remembered for it:

> I said to dear old Penny Keith, 'I suppose we're stuck with it now darling. Whatever you've done, bloody Ophelia, I've done King Lear, it doesn't matter. When the obituary comes out it'll be Margo and Tom. That's what it will be.'[20]

***

Sadie, It's Cold Outside was noted writer Jack Rosenthal's third comedy series, after *The Dustbinmen* and *The Lovers*, and was a sympathetic domestic sitcom full of the writer's trademark closely observed characterisation. Rosemary Leach and Bernard Hepton, two actors equally at home in comedy and straight drama (Hepton had only recently played the stern kommandant in the BBC serial *Colditz*), star as Sadie and Norman Potter, a middle-aged married couple stuck in a humdrum, middle-class, semi-detached suburban rut with nothing much to live for now that the children have flown the nest. Norman spends most of his spare time watching television, while Sadie is thoroughly fed up of her domestic chores and wonders how life has managed to pass her by. Both once had dreams, but these have long since disappeared, slowly eroded by the grey dreary reality of everyday life in '70s Britain, with its oil crises, inflation, wage stagnation and strikes.

Rosenthal claimed that he got the idea while sat in a cafe and saw a middle-aged couple stop outside, peek through the window at the customers, glance at the prices on the menu and then shuffle off.

Only one series of six episodes was ever made by Thames. The dull entrapment that can be married life was perhaps a subject better suited to a drama than belly laughs. And perhaps too many couples recognised their own situation mirrored on the screen and never switched back on.

June

Back in 1969 Johnny Speight and Spike Milligan collaborated on the controversial sitcom *Curry and Chips*, which saw Spike brown up as an Irish-Pakistani. As with Speight's *Till Death Us Do Part*, the aim was to satirise bigotry, but too much of its humour relied on the use of crude racial abuse and stereotypes. ITV dropped the show after one series.

When in 1975 the BBC approached Milligan to create a new series, the comedian intended to have another go at the issue of race and brought in television comedy writer Neil Shand, who'd worked with Spike before, along with the likes of David Frost and Mike Yarwood. The result was *The Melting Pot*, which not only saw Milligan don brown face once again, but play an illegal immigrant. He and satirist John Bird are cast together as a Pakistani father and son who make their way across the channel in a rowing boat. Arriving in London, they take up residence in a boarding house run by an Irish Republican coal miner, played by stand-up comic Frank Carson (no, I'm not making this up). The place is a mad house, filled with a disperate collection of lodgers including a Chinese cockney, a Scottish Arab, a crude Australian, a racist ex-Indian army officer and an orthodox Jew.

One wonders if anyone at the BBC actually read the scripts before they went in front of the camera because after the first episode was screened the remaining five episodes were pulled and have never been broadcast. Milligan later speculated that maybe the scripts weren't funny enough, others felt the material too ill-judged to put it mildly.

Despite the disastrous reaction to the show, Shand enjoyed working with Milligan. 'When his manic depression was at its peak of mania, he was impossible to work with, and when he was in the bottom of a depression you couldn't talk to him, but at all other times he was incredible. He was the master of brilliant nonsense.'[21]

July

Reg Varney was always going to find it difficult to escape his image as the cheeky chappie bus driver from *On the Buses*. And after fronting a couple of television variety shows he returned to the world of sitcom. Inspired by the characters he met while buying fish at Billingsgate Market, Varney came up with the idea for *Down the 'Gate*, written by Roy Tuvey and Maurice Sellar, in which he played porter Reg Furnell. At the time Billingsgate was Europe's premier fish market and its bustle and banter provided an interesting backdrop. Varney and the writers made several visits there, at 4.30 in the morning, to absorb the atmosphere and research story ideas. Location work also meant that the cast and crew were required to show up at the crack of dawn. Most of the episodes, though, were shot at the ATV studios in Birmingham, where the crates of fresh fish and shellfish usually stunk the place out.

The working-class setting of *Down the 'Gate* had definite echoes back to *On the Buses*, along with the script's reliance on saucy double entendres and the Blakey-esque foreman, played by Percy Herbert. One difference is that Reg is married here to Irene, played by Carry On actress Dilys Laye, although that doesn't stop him ogling the ladies, especially the canteen's well-proportioned cook.

Confident they were on to a winner with Varney on board, the show was given a prime-time midweek slot, usually reserved for big hitters like Tommy Cooper and Benny Hill. Indeed, the first series was a regular in the Top 10, but the popularity of the second series fell away and it was dropped. Varney did not star in another television series and spent his later years working as an entertainer on cruise ships and touring Australia with his one-man show.

***

Executives can sometimes take a while before reaching a decision to commission a series, but the BBC's *The Rough with the Smooth* must hold the record; first appearing as a *Comedy Playhouse* pilot back in 1971, it took another four years before it was made into a series. Was it worth the wait – not really, despite the enjoyable presence of Tim Brooke-Taylor and John Junkin, who also devised the series, playing a pair of comedy writers sharing a flat and rivals in pursuing women; a sort of prototype *Men Behaving Badly*.

Harold Snoad was asked to come in and direct:

> Directing a sitcom series is extremely hard work. I used to work six and a half days a week and sometimes very long hours. The great thing was that, in those days, the BBC had its own camera crews, lighting and sound supervisors, vision mixers, costume and make-up departments etc. We all knew each other very well and worked together happily for many years. Nowadays people doing these jobs are just hired in from the outside world.[22]

The *Rough with the Smooth* lasted just the one series.

***

Fairing much better was ATV's *The Squirrels*, which was set in the accounts department of a television rental company, 'and was written entirely from my experience of office life,' says Eric Chappell,[23] who before he became a writer was for many years a travelling auditor with the East Midlands Electricity Board.

Most of the comedy springs from the frictions and relationships between the staff. Bernard Hepton plays Mr Fletcher, the firm's neurotic boss, contrasting effectively with the downtrodden working man personified by Ken Jones, an actor who learned his trade in the late 1950s at Joan Littlewood's Theatre Workshop. At the time Jones was also appearing in *Porridge* as 'Horrible' Ives, who earned his nickname – from both inmates and warders – through displaying the loathsome qualities of being a creep and a snitch. Jones managed to juggle both recording schedules for a while, working on *Porridge* in the mornings and *The Squirrels* in the afternoons, but this eventually became unfeasible and he left *Porridge*; the reason why he's only in some of the early episodes.

The Squirrels was an immediate ratings hit, but during the second series Chappell was unable to write all of the scripts, no doubt busy with the demands of *Rising Damp*, and so other writers were brought in, something he came to regret, and the quality noticeably slipped as a result. Very few series with a mix of writers work as effectively as a writer working alone or part of an established team such as Galton and Simpson or Larbey and Esmonde. Even so, *The Squirrels* was popular enough to go into a third series.

***

In *My Honourable Mrs*, Derek Nimmo was delighted to take a breather from 'holy orders' to play an amiable publisher who encourages his wife to take up a hobby, only to discover not only has she got into politics but she has been selected to fight a by-election. The inevitable happens, of course, when she wins a seat in the House of Commons.

Written by Richard Waring, *My Honourable Mrs* was quite an innovation at the time, having a woman play an MP, especially in something like a sitcom. Back in the 1970s politics was seen very much as a man's world. It's interesting too that Waring chose his protagonist Jane Prendergast to be a Conservative MP and Pauline Yates' performance may very well have been modelled on Margaret Thatcher, who earlier that year had become, against all odds, Conservative Party leader and Leader of the

Opposition. One can speculate that had the series lasted more than just seven episodes, Waring might have been tempted to follow Jane's career to, who knows, Number 10 itself. As it was, the comedy revolves more around Nimmo's silly ass antics and the domestic disruptions Jane's move to Parliament brought to her husband's life.

August

I Didn't Know You Cared is one of those sitcoms that deserves to have a far better reputation than the one it has. A hit back in the day, running over four series, it's been largely forgotten, perhaps because it had the misfortune to be rolled out by the BBC at roughly the same time as those twin juggernauts *The Good Life* and *Fawlty Towers*.

Peter Tinniswood's wonderful comic creation, the Brandons, a dour, extended northern family that take a phlegmatic view of life, first appeared in a series of books and were brought wonderfully to life on screen thanks to adroit casting. There's relentless pessimist Uncle Mort, a newly widowed pensioner. At his wife's funeral he moans the service is taking so long that he's going to miss the football results. Robin Bailey, an actor known for his upper-crust Whitehall-type figures, relishes playing against type here. There is his sharp-tongued sister, Annie, played by Liz Smith, constantly arguing with husband Les (John Comer of *Last of The Summer Wine* fame), their laid-back son Carter, a young Stephen Rea, and his headstrong fiancée Pat, played by Anita Carey. The clan is completed by Uncle Stavely, who wears a small cardboard box around his neck containing the ashes of his friend from the trenches in the First World War.

Well acted it may be but it's Tinniswood's acute observations of working-class life and pithy dialogue that raises this sitcom above the norm. It depicts the world of married life as a battle-ground, where the women give as much as they get, but still do all the housework and while the men go to the pub stay waiting at home, the dinner getting ruined in the oven. 'If the men don't exactly detest the women,' said Tinniswood, 'they at least rec-ognise their worth as reslaters of wash house roofs and reluctant companions to while away the dog hours between darts matches and crown green bowls tournaments.'[24]

By series two Carter and Pat tie the knot, although Carter finds it difficult adjusting to married life. Both Rea and Carey then left the series and their roles were taken by Keith Drinkel and Liz Goulding for the rest of the run.

Coming to an end in 1979, Tinniswood penned a further six series of adventures revolving around the Brandon family for Radio 4 between 1987 and 1996.

September

What is generally considered to be the best sitcom of all time, *Fawlty Towers*, may never have seen daylight had the BBC taken the advice of one of their commissioning editors, who said of the first script:

> I'm afraid I find this one as dire as the title, it's a sort of *Prince of Denmark* of the hotel world, a collection of clichés and stock characters that I can't see being anything but a disaster.[25]

Admittedly, things didn't look too promising at the beginning. 'It was transparently obvious at the read through that everything was not all right,' recalls producer John Howard Davies. 'We worked quite a lot on the script.'[26] Davies was given the job of producing *Fawlty Towers* by Jimmy Gilbert, the BBC's comedy chief, thanks in part to his relationship with John Cleese after working on the early *Monty Python* shows.

The early stirrings of *Fawlty Towers* began during the second series of *Monty Python* when the cast and crew travelled to Torquay in Devon for some location shooting. They stayed at the Gleneagles Hotel, a four-star establishment run by what turned out to be the prototype for Basil Fawlty. That first day the *Python* boys arrived late back at the hotel after an evening out only to see the owner in his pyjamas and slippers looking at his watch. He then proceeded to eye them accusingly as they ascended the stairs to their rooms like some headmaster at a boarding school. The odd behaviour continued. At dinner he demonstrated to the American Terry Gilliam how British people use their knife and fork at the table, and when Eric Idle left his briefcase at reception the thing was thrown outside by the owner, who feared it was a bomb left by a disgruntled ex-member of staff.

The Pythons deplored their stay, but for Cleese it planted a comedy seed that first sprouted in an episode he contributed to ITV's Doctor series when Barry Evans stays at a small hotel run by a crabby Timothy Bateson, with his huge wife lurking in the background. Bateson had lines including, 'How quick can you cook a kipper?' After the episode was recorded, producer Humphrey Barclay took Cleese to one side, 'There's a series in that hotel,' he said. 'About two years later,' recalls Barclay, 'John took me out to lunch and said, "You were right, there was and I'm doing it for the BBC".'[27]

Like many a classic sitcom character, think Rigsby, Captain Mainwaring or Harold Steptoe, Basil Fawlty is a man approaching middle age staring at a life that is empty and going nowhere.

'It's what a lot of sitcoms are about, when you analyse them,' says John Howard Davies. '*Steptoe and Son*, that's the same thing, Harold is never going to go anywhere, is he? It was the same with Hancock.'[28]

Cleese sat down and wrote the series in collaboration with his then wife Connie Booth, who also played Polly, the down-to-earth maid/waitress always embroiled in Basil's schemes and their inevitably disastrous consequences. The remainder of the main characters were filled out memorably: Andrew Sachs earned a place in British comedy immortality as Manuel, a Spanish waiter and general dogsbody that Basil has improbably hired, and Prunella Scales is devastating as Basil's wife Sybil. It was John Howard Davies who suggested Prunella for the role, and early in rehearsals gave her a little hint as to the character. 'I remember saying to her, this is a woman who can paint her nails and make love at the same time.'[29]

Davies liked Cleese enormously:

It was like working with a huge laughing praying mantis. He was highly intelligent. The only thing he was occasionally missing was a kind of instinct, he didn't know when he'd gone too far or when he hadn't gone far enough.[30]

Besides that, he was easy to work with. 'John came up with suggestions and he didn't mind if they were thrown out, and they quite often were,' recalls Davies. 'He was very rigorous in his work ethic, too, as indeed we all were. And we laughed, and laughed and laughed and laughed. There was such huge joy because we knew for four or five hours that morning we were going to roar with laughter.'[31]

All twelve episodes were intricately plotted, with the comedy often straying into Whitehall farce, with people falling off ladders, hiding in cupboards and moose heads plummeting off walls and cracking skulls. There is a fair level of violence, too, usually directed at poor Manuel, but the real victim is Basil as he appears by the end of most episodes to be hurtling towards a complete mental breakdown.

One of the earliest episodes was 'The Builders', in which Basil decides to have some alterations made to the hotel and, going against Sybil's wishes, hires a dodgy builder called Mr O'Reilly. 'When I read that script, I knew it was pure gold,' recalls David Kelly, who memorably played the incompetent builder. 'And I was a great fan of John Cleese anyway and we got on like a dream. It's extraordinary, I think I've had something like seventy-eight repeats of that episode. It made me very big in Malawi.'[32] Amusingly a builder in Wales by the name of O'Reilly tried to sue the BBC. 'He believed they were having a go at him,' says Kelly. 'It didn't work.'[33]

Kelly seems to recall that Cleese didn't want a studio audience. 'But the BBC liked the idea of an audience and we the actors did too because it was like being on stage.'[34] Virtually every sitcom recorded at BBC TV centre was in front of a studio audience. 'There were two main reasons for this,' says producer Harold Snoad:

> For a start their reaction is something that the cast appreciate and can build on. Also, the reaction of one character to what another has just said or done builds the laughter. Another important factor is that laughter is infectious. When you go to the theatre or a cinema to see something comedic you are part of a large audience, but when you're sitting at home, on your own or with someone else, it's not the same. However, if you are hearing the studio audience laugh at what is happening or has just been said you become part of it.[35]

Something else, too; in those days, according to Harold, it was never the practice to add a pre-recorded laugh track, which was not the case later on. 'What you heard was the genuine studio audience reaction. They were also shown any scenes shot on location and, again, it was their reaction to this material that the viewers heard at home.[36]

However, the BBC were not always very good at getting a cross section of the British public, as David Kelly recalls:

For my episode we had, I think they were the society of young Conservative farmers from Wiltshire, and they're not a barrel of fun I can tell you. At one point, John came over to me with his head in his hands, 'I think we're dead, we're dead.' The BBC also went to Thomas Cook, apparently, and brought in a group of visitors from Iceland. 'They're all out there,' said John. 'They won't laugh, they're smelling of fish and they don't want to be here.' And it was a fairly dead reaction to begin with, but somehow it warmed up and, in the end, it worked out beautifully.[37]

After the success of the first series, it was inevitable that the BBC wanted more. Cleese and Booth were less inclined to give it to them, and it was another four years before they sat and wrote a further six episodes. By this time their marriage was in steep decline and the writing process became almost a form of therapy as the union dissolved into eventual separation and divorce. Despite the long gap, the standards remained fantastically high and the BBC craved a third series. But that was it. There was brief talk of a film. Cleese even came up with a premise: Basil and Sybil fly to Spain to visit Manuel when the plane is hijacked. Basil gets so annoyed he overcomes the hijackers, but when the plane is diverted back to Heathrow, he hijacks the plane himself to return to Spain, where he spends his entire holiday in prison. What a shame it was never made.

***

After writing and appearing together in the popular Doctor series, along with providing scripts for *On the Buses* and *Romany Jones*, George Layton and Jonathan Lynn decided the time was right to devise and star in their very own sitcom – the result was Granada's *My Brother's Keeper*. They play twins with completely opposing views on life, except a shared passion for chasing women. Layton is a naïve and ambitious young policeman, Lynn is a militant firebrand student, happy to sponge off his sibling. Hilary Mason was cast as the lads' exasperated mother.

My Brother's Keeper lasted for two series, after which Layton and Lynn went their separate ways and into successful solo careers. Layton created and wrote the comedy series, *Don't Wait Up* starring Nigel Havers and Tony Britton, and *Executive Stress* with Penelope Keith, while Lynn co-created and co-wrote *Yes Minister* and *Yes, Prime Minister*.

***

When Vince Powell's *The Wackers* was cancelled at Thames, the executives suddenly found they had a huge hole in their schedules. And it was Vince Powell who took it upon himself to be the one charged with filling it. His idea was a comedy about a middle-aged Jewish bachelor called Reuben Greenberg, played by Bernard Spear, carrying on his late father's dry-cleaning business, but still tied to his mother's apron strings. As essayed by Lila Kaye, Fay Greenberg is the stereotypical smothering mother.

When Reuben finally musters enough courage to leave home, Fay takes a leaf out of Albert Steptoe's play book and feigns a heart attack to bring him back again.

For a title, Powell originally suggested 'My Yiddisher Mother', but the Thames executives objected saying it was anti-Semitic. *My Son Reuben* was the less controversial alternative. Unfortunately, like *The Wackers*, it lasted just one series.

***

LWT had much better luck with *Two's Company*, starring the renowned Broadway star Elaine Stritch as an abrasive American author of thriller books who employs an English butler, played by Donald Sinden, to run her Chelsea townhouse. Elaine was living in London at the time and seemed ideal casting, but she and her producer, Stuart Allen from *On the Buses*, clashed and Humphrey Barclay was brought in to oversee things following the first series.

Barclay knew from his first read through that things were going to be difficult when Elaine arrived with a script entirely covered in crossings out and rewritten dialogue in blue felt-tip. Nobody else had this version. And there she sat reading this script while everybody else was scrabbling through the pages trying to find out where they were. At one point, Elaine came to the end of this long speech, paused, then said, 'Come on Donald, it's your line.'

'Elaine, I haven't got the faintest idea where we are.'

'Oh, for God's sake. I've stopped talking so it must be your turn.'[38]

Sinden was very much from the old school of acting, while Elaine had gone to drama school with Marlon Brando. 'If you had to do a retake, Donald knew exactly how far down the cigarette had been smoked,' says Barclay. 'Elaine wouldn't have a clue whether she was smoking in that scene or not.'[39]

It was, in the words of Barclay, a nightmare:

> And it was a nightmare because she was drinking. It was a nightmare because she had a credo that an improvised line was by definition going to be better than the one that had been rehearsed. And this also applied to moves, looks, use of camera, whatever. She was just very difficult to handle on the floor of the studio.[40]

For one episode, the director John Reardon had built a beautiful shot that would follow Elaine as she left the front door, walked through the living room and called the butler. However, on the take Elaine decided to make a different journey through the set, so none of the shots worked. 'Stop, stop,' cried Reardon, then to his assistant, 'Can you please ask Elaine to do it the way we have rehearsed.'

'For God's sake!' shrieked Elaine, talking directly to the studio audience. 'He's got five f*cking cameras and he can't get me on one of them!'[41]

Barclay reached the point where he was convinced Elaine changed things just for the sake of changing them. 'And it drove us all mad. And yet there was something exciting going on.'[42] And it was Barclay's job to make it all work. Sometimes Elaine's instincts about things were right, sometimes they weren't, sometimes there were other motivations. Going through one script, Elaine said to Barclay, 'I think this scene is next day.'

'No, I don't think so, Elaine, because this event happens here and that comes in …'

'It's next day!'

'Why is it next day Elaine?

'I just feel it's next day.'[43]

Well, next day meant a new frock from Mayfair boutique Nicole Farhi, which she got to keep.

Despite all the problems and stress, Barclay remained 'admiring friends' with Elaine for the rest of her life and *Two's Company* continued its successful run across four series.

★★★

Over at the BBC, Roy Clarke was crafting another homely piece of comedy drama, typically full of fascinating northern folk. *Rosie* was about a young, idealistic police constable, played by Paul Greenwood, and drew heavily upon Clarke's own experiences. 'I spent a couple of years as a fresh-faced young copper, so that character was pure me.'[44] His beat was a little mining town in South Yorkshire and he found the job a wonderful background for becoming a writer, 'because apart from the shocking things that happen there's a huge number of silly things that happen and quite a lot of laughter.'[45]

By the mid-'70s, Roy had enough of a track record that his ideas were always welcome at the BBC, even if not everything he submitted was accepted:

But what was a huge advantage in my day was that they would tell you straight away, and a no, while not pleasant, was as useful as a yes because you don't waste any more time on it. These days they can drag you out with a potential programme for literally years, going through various processes. And that's a bit soul destroying, actually. But in those days, they were very laid back. We'd record the pilot, after that we'd go into the bar at the BBC and the producer would say, 'Well that's never going to go, is it?' or he'd say, 'How many do you want to do next year? It was wonderful.'[46]

The reason for this was very simple. Back then the Light Entertainment department was being run by people who had a show business background and knew what they were doing. Take John Howard Davies, for example. He'd been a child actor, notably playing the title role at the age of 9 in David Lean's production *Oliver Twist* (1948). He arrived at the BBC in 1966 and became a producer in 1968, working on early episodes of *Monty Python* and then *Steptoe and Son*. 'That was a learning process of how to do it.'[47] For John, the creativity and decision-making were more free at the BBC during those days. 'There were no focus groups or committees deciding which direction a show should go in. If a good comedy came along, we just knew it and if it didn't work, we just shrugged our shoulders and went on to something else.'[48]

The general consensus was that *Rosie* had the potential to be a good comedy. It started life as *The Growing Pains of PC Penrose*. Set in the fictitious Yorkshire town of Slagcaster, it saw the young and naïve PC Penrose taken under the wing of a seasoned officer and shown the ropes. Following the opening series, the programme underwent a revamp with a new title, *Rosie*, after Penrose's nickname, in which the young constable leaves Slagcaster and returns to live with his domineering mother in his hometown of Ravensby. There was even a new theme tune, co-written and sung by Paul Greenwood.

Rosie was a reassuringly safe slice of comedy and found a large and loyal audience that stayed with it over five series until it came to an end in 1981. And it was another winner for Clarke, who always approached his work in exactly the same way:

> The first person you've got to entertain when you're looking at a blank page is yourself. I've got to find something that I think is funny to get through the inertia of that blank page,

until I've got something that is, in a way, turning me on. And when I've had a good writing session, when it's working fine, when I'm finished, I find I've been sweating. You feel the emotion. It's physical for me.[49]

October

Vince Powell's latest attempt at cultural cohesion, *Rule Britannia*, lasted just seven episodes and was a twist on that old joke – there was this Englishman, Irishman, Scotsman and Welshman.

A group of former shipmates arrange a reunion twenty-five years after going their separate ways. Prolific character actor Tony Melody played the hapless George, who finds himself led astray into drunken binges and punch-ups with Jock, played by Russell Hunter, famous for his role as Lonely from crime series *Callan*. Then there is the imaginatively named Paddy, played by Joe Lynch, still best remembered as the Irish tailor in *Never Mind the Quality, Feel the Width*, and Taffy, played by Richard Davies, probably best known for his performance as an exasperated schoolmaster in *Please Sir!* A solid cast, but it just didn't gel. According to Powell, Lynch insisted on not only rewriting his own dialogue but the rest of the cast's too, leading to friction with the director during recordings. Combined with low audience figures, no second series was commissioned by Thames, who had much better luck with another sitcom launched just a week later.

***

Military sitcoms had always been a bit of a mainstay where British comedy was concerned, going all the way back to the 1950s and *The Army Game*. The first ever Carry On film had a military setting and *Dad's Army* and *It Ain't Half Hot Mum* were more recent examples. For the winning team of Bob Larbey and John Esmonde it made sense to turn the sitcom spotlight on to National Service. 'John and I had both done our two years,' recalls Bob, 'so could write from experience, which is always a help, and felt it might work. Luckily, so did Thames.'[50]

Get Some In! harked back to the mid-'50s and the era of compulsory National Service, and followed the misadventures of a group of young conscripts and their permanent adversary, drill instructor Corporal Marsh, a nasty piece of work who loathed and despised the lot of them. It was a great part and one written especially with Tony Selby in mind, who had previously appeared in a similar kind of role in an episode of Esmonde and Larbey's *The Fenn Street Gang*. Tony was an actor hitherto known for straight drama, stuff like Pinter and *The Wednesday Play*, and approached the part of Corporal Marsh like any other:

> As an actor I always find the character through the writing, and the writing here was so good. Marsh was a prat, so I played a prat in uniform. I didn't really think about it that much, because as soon as I put the uniform on and the boots, that was it, I was him.[51]

The lads in his charge came from contrasting backgrounds, and some were based on people the writers had served with. There was a reformed teddy boy, played by Robert Lindsay, in his first major TV role, a cynical Scot, a former grammar school pupil and a vicar's son, 'Little namby-pamby darlings just off their potties,' as Marsh affectionately described them.

Its sharp humour made *Get Some In!* an instant success, especially among young audiences, who related to these 18-year-old conscripts battling against the system, as represented by the monstrous Corporal Marsh. 'And the servicemen loved it,' recalls Tony Selby. 'I used to get letters galore from ex-servicemen saying, we had a bastard just like you.'[52]

Such was its popularity that Larbey and Esmonde wrote a stage version that played two summer seasons in Torquay and Blackpool. 'That was a killer,' recalls Tony, 'because we did two performances a day, twelve shows a week. It was hard graft because everybody knows you as that character from the telly so you can't let an understudy go on, even if you're not well.'[53]

After five series Tony recalls having a drink with the writers in a pub and the general feeling was, where are we going to take this show next? The lads had by now finished basic training, moved bases and been posted abroad. Tony thinks it was the right decision to stop when they did and says that working on the show was a career highlight. 'I loved doing it. I couldn't wait for it to come round, and we did have a laugh. We used to sit at the read through and fall about laughing.'[54] He recalls that Philip Jones, Head of Light Entertainment at Thames, was there for every recording. 'He was always backstage saying, "good luck Tony. Good show. Love it." He was always around and very supportive.'[55]

That seems to be what a lot of people say about Philip Jones, that he was always there, a great source of encouragement, and like a lot of the people overseeing comedy in the 1970s, he had an incredible ability for spotting talent and hit shows from *Father Dear Father* to *Bless this House*, *Love Thy Neighbour* and *Man About the House*. 'People always used to say to me,' recalls William G. Stewart, 'what is it about Philip? And I used to say, I don't know, but it's success. And he was such a mild sort of chap, always jingling his keys in his pocket nervously, but he was wonderful.'[56]

★★★

Monday night on ITV at 8 p.m. was always considered to be one of the prime slots for any new show, following as it did the nation's most watched programme *Coronation Street*. Granada were hedging their bets on something called *The Cuckoo Waltz*, starring a trio of little-known actors: David Roper, Diane Keen and Lewis Collins. Granada needn't have worried, by the end of the first series the show had become a regular feature in the nation's top ten and the three fresh-faced cast members were stars. 'It was weird to walk along the streets of Manchester and be recognised by virtually everybody,' recalls Roper:

'Great show. Loved it,' many called out. Fame can bring its bizarre moments, too. I was once fast asleep on a train to London, when a young woman woke me up to tell me who I was! She shook me awake, 'You're David Roper,' she shouted – she was right, I'll give her that, but funnily enough I did in fact already know that.[57]

One of the show's biggest fans was Betty Driver, who played Betty Turpin in *Corrie*. 'She was really supportive,' David remembers, 'and would tell us how much she had enjoyed each episode.'[58]

The Cuckoo Waltz was inspired by true events from writer Geoffrey Lancashire's days as a struggling journalist. Lancashire was recently married and starting a family when his friend and fellow writer Jack Rosenthal showed up on his doorstep, his first marriage on the rocks. Moving in as a temporary lodger, Rosenthal ended up staying three years! Instead of Lancashire we have Chris Hawthorne, played by David Roper, a junior reporter who along with his wife Fliss and twin babies are struggling to make ends meet in their sparsely furnished first home.

The couple's problems aren't really solved when their friend Gavin, recently broken up with his wife, moves in as a lodger and is soon filling the place with expensive furniture, flashy gadgets and a succession of decorative young ladies.

Playing Fliss was Diane Keen in her first sitcom role after years playing in mostly drama. Diane wasn't the first choice; she thinks she was perhaps the fourth:

> And Geoff and I used to laugh about it and at the end of the series he very sweetly said to me, 'I could not have had a more perfect Fliss if I had the choice of any actress in the world.' And what a great compliment to come from a writer.[59]

Lancashire later wrote the hit '80s sitcom *Foxy Lady* for Diane.

Diane had always loved playing comedy and saw this as a wonderful opportunity:

> But once I'd read the scripts and realised how good they were I thought, crikey, I've got to get this right. I said to my agent, 'I just feel a great sense of responsibility.' And he said, 'These lines are a gift for anyone. If you do what you do best, you can't go wrong. So, don't worry about it, just do it.'[60]

Diane relaxed and eased into the role, 'and I loved every minute of it'.[61]

Playing Gavin marked a breakthrough in Lewis Collins' career, not only turning him into a TV star but a sex symbol. 'Lewis and I also got on well,' says David, 'and would play squash at Salford Rugby League Club's courts most mornings, challenge each other to rounds of pitch and putt and even spend holidays together. In my opinion, Lewis was a much better comedian than he realised. He often thought that he had to push himself to get laughs, but when he relaxed and let his natural humour show through, he really came into his own as a comic actor.'[62]

Diane also liked Lewis enormously and they became good friends. 'While we were making *Cuckoo Waltz*, he used to live in a converted ambulance that was parked in the car park at Granada.'[63] Collins had used this ambulance since his days on the road as a young stage actor in repertory theatre, although it was by no means his only residency and did lead to false rumours that he was homeless.

After three series Collins left *The Cucko Waltz* to go on to even greater fame in the action series *The Professionals*. 'Successful as he undoubtedly was in *The Professionals* and *Who Dares Wins*,' says David. 'I would love to have seen him succeed in what I believe was his true area of talent: Comedy.'[64]

Without Collins, *The Cuckoo Waltz* seemed to be at an end, but three years later in 1980 a final series was made in which Chris and Fliss had to contend with another lodger, who like his predecessor turned out to be something of a scoundrel. But the old magic just wasn't there, it missed the presence of Collins. 'My lasting image of Lew,' says David, 'is not of the gun-toting hard man who wanted to be feared, but of the little boy with a twinkle in his eye who just wanted to be loved.'[65]

Chapter Seven

1976

January

Bill Maynard, a familiar face to audiences for years, conceived a show based around the characters he used to know at the working men's club in his home village of Sapcote, Leicestershire; one patron in particular for whom everything he touched turned to disaster. He'd given the idea to an old pal of his Duncan Wood, a producer at the BBC. Things went very quiet for a while. A little exasperated, Maynard phoned Wood to see if he was ever going to do anything with it. Wood's reply was encouraging, he was leaving the BBC after twenty-five years to accept a position at Yorkshire Television as Controller of Light Entertainment, and Maynard's show was going to be his first commission.

True to his word, Wood brought in Roy Clarke to write a pilot. Clarke also came up with a title – *Oh No, It's Selwyn Froggitt*. The pilot went out in September 1974, after which Clarke walked away due to other work commitments. Things went quiet again. In 1975 Maynard was offered another sitcom,

The Life of Riley, playing a man whose carefree lifestyle comes under threat when his puritanical son walks back into his life, but that faltered after just one series. It was *Selwyn Froggitt* that came to his rescue when it became one of ITV's biggest comedy hits and established Maynard as a household name.

Set in the fictional Yorkshire town of Scarsdale, hapless council labourer and all-round public nuisance Selwyn Froggitt was basically ITV's version of Frank Spencer, spectacularly incompetent at everything he turned his hand to and something of a man child; Maynard referred to him as 'a naïve boy who never grew up'. Like Frank Spencer, Froggitt had his own catchphrase – 'Magic!' uttered while sticking up both thumbs – and it became the popular vernacular of the day.

With Roy Clarke unavailable, the writing duties were handed over to northern dramatist Alan Plater, marking his only foray into sitcom writing. As a result, the show is an interesting hybrid of slapstick comedy alongside Plater's typical northern humour and humanity; Froggitt keeps a copy of *The Times* tucked up the sleeve of his donkey jacket in a bid to make him look an intellectual.

Bizarrely, Froggitt is secretary of the local Working Men's Club, where his fellow committee members view him with disdain, while taking advantage of his honest and hard-working nature. At home, he lives with his ever-exasperated mother, played by Megs Jenkins, and his brother – 'our Maurice'.

In 1978, after three successful series, Yorkshire Television changed the format of the show radically. Now just called *Selwyn*, Maynard is the only surviving member of the cast as Froggitt departs Scarsdale to become entertainments officer at a seedy holiday camp. The holiday camp setting was arguably Maynard's suggestion, having made his professional stage debut at Butlin's Skegness in the early '50s. Plater was also missing and that's perhaps why *Selwyn* fell flat with audiences and a planned follow-up was cancelled.

After a long period out of the public eye, Maynard returned to television in the 1990s playing Claude Jeremiah Greengrass in ITV's nostalgic police drama *Heartbeat*.

***

When John Alderton and Pauline Collins decided not to make another series of *No, Honestly* LWT remained keen for the show to continue and that the formula be reworked with another couple. The result was *Yes, Honestly*.

The format did indeed remain very much the same: two young people meet and fall in love, and it was once again written by husband-and-wife team Terence Brady and bestselling author Charlotte Bingham. The new stars were Irish actor Donal Donnelly as struggling music composer Matthew Browne, who hires a secretary, played by Liza Goddard, and over the course of two series we watch their romance blossom into eventual marriage.

Goddard had only recently come off a regular role in the BBC's hit drama serial *The Brothers*, and had also worked with Terence and Charlotte on *Take Three Girls*, their television drama that ran on the BBC between 1969 and 1971 and which followed three young women sharing a flat in 'Swinging London'. Liza knew the writers very well and liked them enormously:

> They had an extraordinary partnership. She was the comedy genius and Terry was very good at English. He'd been to Trinity College in Dublin, and he was marvellous with grammar and syntax and structure, so they really were a marvellous team. And they were very funny together in real life. Their parties were legendary.[1]

Donal Donnelly also knew the writers well, a friendship that no doubt helped him land the role, although he was already an established film and theatre actor, if unheralded. 'Donal was lovely,' recalls Liza. 'Absolutely stark staring bonkers, though. He was such a funny man, with wonderful anecdotes. After our coffee breaks, we'd have to say, "OK Donal, you can't do any more anecdotes, we've got to go and rehearse." And he was a marvellous actor. I adored him, bonkers as he was.'[2]

Another aspect of the show that didn't change from *No, Honestly* was the two leads sitting on stools addressing the audience both at the beginning and the end of each episode. Liza never quite understood why these monologues were always the last things to be recorded, which often led to a bit of a rush. 'Back then you had to finish in the studio at ten o'clock, otherwise they just pulled the plugs, so we sometimes had just fifteen minutes to record those two monologues. It was quite nerve wracking but very exciting at the same time.'[3]

With the theme song again provided by Lynsey de Paul, *Yes, Honestly* met with popular success but only two series were made. 'I absolutely loved doing it,' says Liza. 'We were so lucky to do something that we absolutely adored.'[4]

★★★

At the same time as *Yes, Honestly*, LWT presented us with a very different kind of couple in Arthur Mullard and Queenie Watts in *Yus My Dear*, a sequel to *Romany Jones*. Leaving behind their gypsy caravan, Wally and Lily Briggs are starting a new life in a council house, where they are joined by Wally's layabout brother Benny, played by stand-up comic Mike Reid in his first acting role. Reid had been a stunt man back in the '60s and was currently the popular host of kids' quiz show *Runaround*, but *Yus My Dear* represented a new challenge. While he was by no means camera shy, 'on reflection, I was bloody awful,' he later admitted.[5] Reid continued his career as a comedian, occasionally dipping his toe into the acting world, until his celebrated turn as Frank Butcher in *EastEnders*.

Although it garnered modest ratings, and ran for nineteen episodes over two series, *Yus My Dear* ranks as one of the worst sitcoms of the decade; it makes *Queenie's Castle* look like *The Forsythe Saga*.

February

From one of the worst sitcoms in *Yus My Dear* to a perennial favourite in *Open All Hours*. This derived from 1973's *Seven of One* series, which also spawned *Porridge*. Numerous writers were brought in to come up with different characters for Ronnie Barker to play and see which ones worked the best. One of those writers was Roy Clarke. 'I met with Ronnie and we talked and for openers he said that he'd always wanted to do something about one of those little shops that sold everything. And that suited me because when I was teaching my wife owned a little corner shop, so I had a bit of an idea what went on.'[6]

What came out of that discussion was the curmudgeonly, penny-pinching shopkeeper Arkwright. Much of his character and personality was laid out on the page by Roy. 'But Ronnie gave him that stutter, and played it brilliantly. The trick with Arkwright was not making him too unpleasant because if you just read the lines, he was such a money-grabbing old bag no one would like him. But with the magic of somebody like Ronnie audiences were able to warm to him.'[7]

Arkwright shared his corner shop with his nephew Granville, played by David Jason, for whom he's a rather reluctant father figure. Lamenting his lowly existence as an assistant-cum-delivery boy, Granville spends most of his time wistfully dreaming of a better life and fantasising about any kind of physical experience with the opposite sex. It was a role and performance that marked a career breakthrough for Jason, and Roy saw the important role Barker played in it:

> David at that time was a young man starting out that Ronnie had spotted for the huge talent that he was going to be. And there is many a man in Ronnie's position who wouldn't have wanted someone as good as David at his elbow, but Ronnie did and he encouraged him and was helpful in every way. Ronnie was very generous with his talent. He didn't throw his power about to be unpleasant. [8]

It took a while for the BBC to be persuaded to give *Open All Hours* its own series, and when it finally made its appearance everyone crossed their fingers and hoped for the best. 'When you think of the talent involved with Ronnie and David, I thought, if this isn't going to work, nothing is,' Roy recalls. 'So, I had good expectations, although you really can't foresee what's going to be a hit because nobody knows. But when it is a hit, and touches something in people's bloodstream, it really does work. But there's no way of calculating that.' [9]

Barker did raise objections with the decision to put *Open All Hours* on BBC 2 rather than the main channel and as a result the viewing audience was small. It was another five years before it returned, this time on BBC 1, to finally achieve the huge ratings it deserved.

Equal to Arkwright's desire to make money is his unrequited love for local District Nurse Gladys Emmanuel, played
by Lynda Baron, who must constantly fend off his lustful
advances and endure lewd remarks about her generous bosom
and backside; while at the same time leaving the faintest hint
that romance might one day be in the air. Clarke's script does
occasionally stray into the arena of laboured innuendo, albeit
of a rather gentle kind that fits into the series' wistful evocation
of bygone days.

The cast formed a close-knit bond with each other during
production, but Clarke rarely if ever turned up for the recording, leading to his nickname of the 'Yorkshire hermit'. For
him, having to hang around the studio is deadly dull, and it's
always been the case. 'I keep well away.'[10] The first time Clarke
sees an episode is when it's broadcast to the public. 'I love what
I do. I love the writing side, but I do feel that when it's done,
providing anything that comes up that needs changing I'm the
one who changes it, I've got no qualms about leaving it to producers; provided I have a good relationship with them and I
trust them.'[11]

For exterior shooting, a corner shop was located in a suburb
of Doncaster. Although it was a hairdressing salon a quick
makeover by the BBC design team rendered it perfect for the
job. Inevitably it became a local tourist attraction. Arkwright
doesn't appear to be overly burdened with customers during
each episode. It's fun, though, to spot the odd familiar face:
Kathy Staff as a cheerless woman not a million miles away from
Summer Wine's Nora Batty, a matronly Stephanie Cole, there's
Liz Dawn before she became *Coronation Street*'s Vera Duckworth
and before his immortalisation as Boycie in *Only Fools and Horses*
John Challis appeared occasionally as a randy breadman.

Open All Hours ran until 1985, twenty-seven episodes in total. Much of its popularity and enduring appeal stems from a steady flow of repeats and the fact that its situation strikes such a familiar note with viewers. Most sitcoms take place in banal surroundings, like shops, offices and the home. Once a sitcom moves into the realm of the fantastic and the unreal, outer space for example, it usually misfires. 'That's why *Open All Hours* worked,' says John Howard Davies, 'because it looks so much a part of our lives and everyone's familiar with it.'[12]

The show's ongoing popularity led to a revival in 2013 as *Still Open All Hours*. Written by Roy Clarke, David Jason returned as Granville, who now runs Arkwright's grocery shop with the assistance of his son.

April

It was never that unusual for a British sitcom to be bought and remade by an American network, but it rarely happened the other way round. One of those exceptions was *The Fosters*, which was based on the popular US series *Good Times*, aired on CBS from 1974 to 1979, and set in a housing project in a black inner-city neighbourhood in Chicago. Michael Grade, Deputy Controller of Programmes at LWT, saw potential in the idea and made a deal to bring it over to the UK, with the condition that the original scripts be used, give or take some adaptation for the domestic audience. Whether he intended it to be or not, Grade's decision broke new ground when *The Fosters* became the first British sitcom to feature an all-black cast.

With the setting changed to a tower block in south London, Guyana-born actor Norman Beaton was to make his television breakthrough playing Samuel Foster, an honest, hard-working man who, along with his wife Pearl, played by Isabelle Lucas, tries his best to raise a family while struggling to make ends meet. *The Fosters* was also a turning point for 17-year-old Lenny Henry, who had recently come to public prominence with his appearances on the TV talent show *New Faces*. Henry has spoken about how he felt a little out of his depth during the making of the series, but that he tried to learn as much as he could from Beaton and was amused by some of his activities. Beaton certainly lived life to the full and Henry recalled him sometimes arriving for rehearsals with a hangover or still plastered from the revelries of the previous night.

Beaton was to later reveal how much pressure he and the rest of the cast felt under to make a success out of the show: 'If we blew it,' he suggested, 'the possibility existed that there would be little justification for giving other blacks a break for God knows how much longer. We all knew this was a searching test. As the studio countdown began [on that first episode] I thought to myself, we're picking up the tab here for a whole community, a whole generation, please God, don't let us fail.'[13]

Unfortunately, given the restrictions of having to use the American scripts, *The Fosters* was never really able to make its own mark, although it got good ratings, and lasted just the two series. It did, however, help launch the careers of Lenny Henry, who went on to become one of Britain's biggest comic entertainers, and Norman Beaton, who played another patriarch in Channel 4's award-winning sitcom *Desmond's* (1989–94).

September

Lucky Feller was Humphrey Barclay's latest vehicle to make David Jason a star. It was the brainchild of playwright Terence Frisby, most famous as the author behind the stage hit *There's a Girl in My Soup*, which was turned into a film starring Peter Sellers and Goldie Hawn. The premise was two brothers, 'Shorty' and Randolph Mepstead, who run a small plumbing business in south London and live together with their mum. 'Shorty' is the more sensitive brother, while Randolph is a bit of a Jack the Lad, a consummate chat-up artist with dishonourable intentions towards 'Shorty's' girlfriend.

Frisby intended to cast his friend Sylvester McCoy as 'Shorty', but Barclay wanted the show for Jason:

> I managed to talk Terence round, although at first he wasn't too keen. And David wasn't too keen either. Finally, David said, 'Well, OK, if you think I should do this.' What I liked about *Lucky Feller* was that it took David on the first path towards acting. He was playing a character, not a comic character, and I thought it was a smashing series.[14]

By and large audiences agreed and press reviews were so good that LWT offered Frisby the chance to do a second series, only he felt he didn't have enough ideas for the show to continue. And so, another opportunity for Jason to carry his own sitcom hadn't taken off, and the actor must have wondered whether he was ever going to get another chance. Around this time a letter appeared in *The Stage* newspaper. It rather prophetically read: 'Somewhere there is a writer whose ideas Mr Jason can execute to great effect, but they have not yet met.' They would soon – the writer would be John Sullivan and the show was the most successful comedy series of the '80s, *Only Fools and Horses*.

★★★

The Many Wives of Patrick starred Patrick Cargill and while it wasn't technically a spin-off from the hugely successful *Father,*

Dear Father, it did suit his style very well, playing as he did a Bond Street antique dealer who had been married no fewer than six times! And he's well on his way to divorcing his latest wife, while his exes keep popping in and out of his life with alarming regularity.

Father, Dear Father's original producer, William G. Stewart, first took the idea to his agent, Michael Grade, who told him he'd try and place it somewhere. 'Then I got Richard Waring to write it,' recalls Stewart:

> Things went quiet for a little while, and then Michael went to LWT and rang me up, 'Do you want to bring your idea in?' And he was really good because he said, 'I meant it as an agent when I said I liked it and I'll try and sell it, and now I'm in a position to buy it, I will.' And he did, he bought it.[15]

The Many Wives of Patrick in no way matched the success of *Father, Dear Father* but did well enough, running for three series. All of which says much about the durability and popularity of Patrick Cargill. Stewart knew Cargill could still headline a sitcom; he didn't need focus groups to tell him that. Back then producers made all the decisions. He cast the show and put everything together. Today everything is done by committee with decisions taking forever because so many people have to be consulted. As a rule, Stewart never did any market research, either, or even considered the audience, thinking, this is a show for a certain type of audience. 'My philosophy about television has always been, if it's good of its kind there will be an audience for it.'[16] That's how they used to make television.

***

When *Man About the House* was in its fourth series, Philip Jones said to Brian Murphy and Yootha Joyce, who played landlords George and Mildred, 'You do realise there's a lot of mileage to be got out of these characters.' The actors nodded sagely and said, 'Oh, that would be nice,' before looking at each other rather cynically and thinking, we'll believe that when it happens. 'And we didn't really give any serious thought about it,' recalls Brian. 'But we were hopeful, of course.'[17]

It wasn't until one of the stage carpenters said to them one day on set, 'It's good news about your show, ain't it?'

'What do you mean?'

'*George and Mildred*,' he said.

'Well, it will be if we do it,' Murphy replied.

'What do you mean if we do it?' said the carpenter. 'We're building the sets now.'[18]

The writers themselves knew pretty early on in the run that they were on to a winner with the Ropers and for the spin-off decided to move them upmarket into a new home in a posh suburb of London. The actual house used for exterior filming was in Teddington, not far from the Thames studios. For Mildred it was her long-awaited climb up the social ladder, while George remained resolutely working class, and for the most part unemployed. 'George only ever had two jobs,' recalls Brian Cooke:

> One of them was a traffic warden. He had this interview with the head traffic warden who said, 'You see this yellow band on your hat, you know what that means?' and George said, 'You can't park on it.' George loved the authority of being a traffic warden, and of course the first person he booked was his new next-door neighbour.[19]

Much of the conflict in the show comes from the posh family next door, the Fourmiles – wife, husband and young child – who are befriended by Mildred but loathed by George. Jeffrey Fourmile was played by Norman Eshley, who only recently had played Robin Tripp's brother in a couple of *Man About the House* episodes. Before starting work on *George and Mildred*, Norman went on holiday to Spain with Yootha and their partners:

> We were staying up in the mountains and I said to Yootha one day, 'Shall we go down to the beach?' And she said, 'I don't think you really want to do that, Norman.' Yootha finally agreed and we all went down there and within two minutes we were surrounded by a crowd of over a hundred people. It was just bizarre. I didn't realise the effect that a programme like that had. So, we packed up and went back to our villa.[20]

Jeffrey rapidly realises that George is not his type of person. In fact, George gets on better with the Fourmile's young son Tristram, played by Nicholas Bond-Owen. Due to rules governing child actors, Bond-Owen was not allowed to work at the studio for the whole day of recording, instead all his scenes were pre-recorded. He was, though, allowed to come and watch the episode being filmed along with the studio audience. 'Those scenes with Nicholas were lovely to do,' recalls Brian Murphy. 'And they worked so well because in a way George was a child.'[21]

The only other regular character was Jerry, played by Roy Kinnear. 'We'd always have Roy in one or two episodes of each series,' says Cooke:

He was George's only friend. He was a wheeler dealer, always coming up with hair-brained schemes. There was this one, he said, 'I've got three words for you George, Kentucky Fried Pigeon. There's no money involved, just go down to Trafalgar Square, they go along the arm, wham you've got them.'[22]

Like its predecessor, *George and Mildred* was another ratings smash, even the repeats got huge numbers. Maybe audiences could identify with the characters. 'People used to say to us, "You're just like the people that live next door,"' recalls Murphy.[23] And although the humour could be saucy, families were able to safely watch it together. 'We got fan letters from children,' says Murphy. 'I remember in one episode the ceiling fell in on George and there was a card from a 5-year-old saying, I do hope George is alright and his head wasn't really hurt.'[24]

Relatively new to sitcom, Norman Eshley paid careful attention to every single rehearsal during that first series and every scene with Brian and Yootha to see how they played it and developed it. 'They had such a rapport.'[25] He liked them both enormously and found it amusing that despite being firm friends they were diametrically opposed politically; Murphy was left wing and Yootha right wing, 'and there would be huge political arguments between the two of them'.[26]

Brian Cooke found the whole cast easy to get on with, too, though Yootha had a habit of inserting more cries of 'George!' than had been written, using the word as a comedy crutch because she knew it would get a laugh. 'One episode we counted them and there were thirty-four more "Georges" than we'd put in the script. So, we stopped using George at all, and still she managed to get ten or twelve in.'[27]

Each episode was usually shot as live and in sequence. 'They might take a break if you had a big change of costume,' recalls

Murphy, 'but sometimes they would build in a scene that could be done in between your changes. But they ran through from the top without too many breaks because that carried an audience with you. If there are lots of breaks you have to pick the audience up and start again, and that's not very conducive to a good audience reaction.'[28]

The show's success led inevitably to a film version, released in 1980, which no one working on it particularly liked, and a stage adaptation that played in Bournemouth during the 1977 summer season. Brian Murphy recalls they did two shows nightly, which was a tough chore, but every performance was packed out:

> The reaction of the audience was amazing. They laughed from the moment the curtain went up because they were familiar with us and we couldn't put a foot wrong. And when that washes over you, all that laughter and warmth, you just bask in it and you don't want it to stop.[29]

Brian and Yootha also appeared as the ugly sisters (Mildred and Georgina) in the London Palladium's 1977 Christmas panto *Cinderella*, with Richard O'Sullivan as Buttons. The following summer they were back doing the stage play, then it was off on tour to New Zealand and Australia.

For Brian and Yootha the only regret with the success of *George and Mildred* was the fact that those characters took them over so completely. 'We were being George and Mildred for the best part of each year,' says Brian, 'and probably getting itchy feet to do other things.'[30] By the end of the fifth series, which closed with a 1979 Christmas special, everyone agreed to do another eight episodes and then bow out, while the show was still on top. Sadly, as Cooke and Mortimer were putting the finishing touches to the scripts in the summer, Yootha Joyce died from liver failure.

Her death was a huge shock to everyone. Brian Murphy knew she hadn't been well but when they were doing promotion duties for the movie, he was disturbed to see how much weight she had lost. A decision was made to put her into a clinic before the new series started. Brian visited and things didn't look too good:

> Then she seemed to rally, come her birthday, she was sitting up in bed, her glasses perched on the end of her nose giving me orders, as she did, and doing replies to all the cards she'd got. Her room was filled with flowers.[31]

Convinced Yootha seemed to have turned a corner, Brian went out for a little celebration:

> That night a friend rang me up and said, 'It's not good news.' I said, 'What do you mean? I've just been in to see her.' He said, 'That happens. Things are beginning to pack up.' And I couldn't believe it. I went back and she died while I was there.[32]

Yootha Joyce was only 53.

What few people knew was how much Yootha was drinking. Norman Eshley believes she wasn't happy with her life. Having enjoyed a career in straight drama, done kitchen sink stuff and won awards in the theatre, whenever she was recognised now it was as Mildred, and maybe that had begun to grate with her. She had also recently split from her boyfriend, had no children and was living alone in a flat in Paddington. 'I think she died of a combination of loneliness and alcohol.'[33]

★★★

Just two days after *George and Mildred* made its debut, the BBC launched what turned out to be one of its most highly regarded comedy series. David Nobbs experienced something of an up and down career in the '70s. Writing successfully for the likes of Frankie Howerd and the Two Ronnies, his attempts at sitcom were less rewarding. That all changed when he was asked to contribute a script for a BBC series of half-hour plays on the issues of the day:

> I put forward the idea of a businessman that goes berserk and they turned it down. I was very disappointed but it turned out to be a fantastic stroke of luck because I made it into a book and that was the forerunner of Reggie Perrin.[34]

If anything, the kernel of that idea went even further back, to David's childhood when he used to go to school on the same train every day and saw the same businessmen in the same carriages with their rolled-up newspapers, umbrellas and dark suits. That image came back into his mind when he read an article in the Sunday papers about a firm of jam makers and how they researched various flavours, tested them out, discussed them sitting round a boardroom table and then went out knocking on people's doors with samples to ask if they liked their jam. 'I thought, this would drive me absolutely and totally up the wall.'[35] Thus, Sunshine Desserts was born, a confectionery company where Reginald Perrin is a desk-bound sales executive.

Nobbs knew the book was successful when his agent, Jonathan Clowes, sent him a telegram, the only telegram David ever received from him. It read: 'I didn't get where I am today without recognising a good book when I see one – JC.' He not only recognised a good book when he saw one, he recognised a good catchphrase, too, one that David gave to Perrin's powerful boss CJ (Nobb's agent's initials backwards). Most of CJ's statements begin with the all-purpose introduction: 'I didn't get where I am today ...' followed by any number of declarations from the relatively normal, 'I didn't get where I am today without knowing a favourable report when I read one,' to the downright surreal, 'I didn't get where I am today by selling ice cream tasting of bookends, pumice stone and West Germany.'

There were catchphrases too for some of Perrin's other work colleagues. Executives Tony Webster and David Harris-Jones pepper every conference meeting with simple one-word platitudes – 'Great!' and 'Super!'

Clowes sent David's book to Jimmy Gilbert at the BBC, who commissioned a script. Feeling that his idea needed to be funnier than the book, David filled his script with jokes and one-liners, only to get a bit of a shock when he was invited to a meeting at the BBC:

> They all had long faces and said they didn't like it. 'You've lost the humour of the book,' they said. 'You're forcing the humour with all these jokes. Have faith in the book, have faith in your own writing.' So, I went away and rewrote it and never looked back. [36]

Reginald Perrin is middle-aged and currently going through something of a mid-life crisis, with flights of fancy, mainly revolving around his secretary. It seemed to David the perfect role for Ronnie Barker. Gilbert didn't agree, feeling Barker was doing too many shows at the BBC: *Porridge* was still running and there was *Open All Hours* and *The Two Ronnies*. Gilbert favoured Leonard Rossiter, then a smash hit on ITV's *Rising Damp*. He posted the book to the actor and got it back within three days. Rossiter later told Gilbert that he decided to play the part after reading the first chapter.

Nobbs knew that Rossiter had a reputation for being difficult, and indeed he was made very much aware of this at his first meeting with the actor when he visited the set of *Rising Damp*:

> He was having an argument with the director and went and sat up in the audience seats saying, 'Carry on without me. You don't need me, all you're interested in is your pretty pictures,' and I thought, oh my God. But I have to say he was not like that with us. He was very professional and most of the time he was a joy to work with. He was a perfectionist and couldn't bear it if people weren't doing their job well. I once saw him reduce an actor almost to tears, but we didn't see much of that.[37]

David Warwick, cast as Reggie's son Mark, has just as vivid memories of Rossiter. 'Leonard was brilliant. Working with him was a hell of an experience. The rest of us would be grateful for one decent comedic idea in a situation, he'd have half a dozen and discard five. He was always high octane and energised.'[38]

Rossiter was surrounded by an impressive supporting cast including Pauline Yates as Reggie's loyal wife Elizabeth, Sue Nicholls as his secretary Joan, John Barron, utterly unforgettable as CJ, and Geoffrey Palmer as Reggie's brother-in-law Jimmy, who confronts life through the prism of military operations: 'No food. Bit of a cock-up on the catering front.'

The Fall and Rise of Reginald Perrin went into production with few knowing what a huge impact it was going to have. 'I knew it was solid,' remembers Nobbs:

Leonard had said to me, in a very quiet moment during rehearsal, 'This is very strong, we don't need to force it,' which was very encouraging, so I was pretty confident throughout the recordings. Then when it started going out it was up against some pretty popular stuff and I wasn't sure how well it would go down. Then about halfway through the series I was staying in this hotel in Leeds. I'd had dinner and was waiting for the lift to go back up to my room. I was standing next to these three businessmen when one of them said, 'I'm going to use the stairs. I didn't get where I am today by hanging around waiting for a lift,' and the others went, 'Great! Super!' and they all laughed and went up the stairs, and I wanted to dance. I knew in that moment something was happening with the show.[39]

It did seem that around the country, office workers and executives were identifying with Reggie Perrin. Indeed, the character's appeal was wide ranging, with young people enjoying his anarchic and rebellious side.

For David, the first series remains the best of the bunch, largely because it was self-contained, with a clear beginning and ending, with Reggie, in a last-ditch attempt to preserve his sanity and escape the rat race, faking his own suicide by leaving a pile of clothes on a beach. David truly felt that the story was over. So, when the BBC asked for a second series, he knew he needed to come up with a really good idea to justify it. That idea turned out to be Grot, a shop that Reggie launches dedicated to selling useless things, which to his amazement becomes a massive global success. This was Nobb's little satirical swipe at capitalism and worked quite effectively. However, David felt that the concept for the third series, Reggie's bid to create a self-contained commune in suburbia, didn't quite come up to standards and the series finished.

As a rule, Nobbs didn't always go to the studio to watch filming or even attend rehearsals:

> I can't remember how many rehearsals I used to go to. I don't think I went to as many as I should have. Nobody used to require you to be there. I think it was only from *Reggie Perrin* onwards that I took the decision that because I was responsible for the show by writing it, I should be there as much as I could to help it through its painful birth.[40]

Over time, thanks to repeats, *The Fall and Rise of Reginald Perrin* grew in cult status and reputation, much to the surprise of David:

> I thought, we've got a lovely, successful show, but that would be the end of it. How it's lasted in the nation's consciousness, the catchphrases still existing, and then the papers used to refer to people committing suicide and leaving their clothes on a beach as doing a Reggie, it astonished me.[41]

Indeed, Reggie Perrin was far from finished. An American adaptation was made by ABC in 1983 and Channel 4 produced an off-shoot featuring Geoffrey Palmer's character called *Fairly Secret Army* that ran for two series in the mid-'80s. Then, twenty years after the original show, and despite the fact that Rossiter had been dead for over ten years, Nobbs resurrected his idea. *The Legacy of Reggie Perrin* reunited virtually the entire cast of the original series but it was rather a lacklustre affair and lasted just seven episodes. Faring slightly better was a total reimagining of the original concept that Nobbs co-wrote with *Men Behaving Badly*'s Simon Nye in 2009 starring Martin Clunes as Reggie.

Really, though, *The Fall and Rise of Reginald Perrin* was as near a perfect piece of work as you can get and should have been left alone.

★★★

The final sitcom of what was indeed a busy month, far from reaching the dizzy heights of *George and Mildred* or *Reginald Perrin*, scarcely caused a ripple in the television pool, despite the talents of its two stars, John Bird and John Fortune, who were also the writers. In *Well, Anyway*, Fortune plays a con man who turns up one night outside gullible Bird's Earl's Court bedsit claiming to be his long-lost friend and moves in. Cue an often dark and surreal comedy that seemed ideally suited to its 9 p.m. BBC 2 slot.

Bird later admitted that he was disappointed with the show, although he felt the scripts got funnier as it went along. Any hopes for a potential second series were dashed before Bird and Fortune had even written the opening two episodes when the BBC decided to pull the plug. So dispirited by the experience, Bird didn't return to television writing for two years.

November

Someone at Granada must have thought it was a good idea to produce a sitcom bearing the unfortunate title of *Yanks Go Home* in the year of America's Bicentennial celebrations. Unsurprisingly, there was a ripple of controversy surrounding the show, but it was all light-hearted fun and no one really took offence. The series focused on a group of US Army Air Force pilots stationed in a small Lancashire town during the Second World War. There was a popular wartime slogan about American servicemen: 'Overpaid, over-sexed, and over here,' and this was deliberately played up for humorous effect in the series.

The same theme was used for the feature film *Yanks*, directed by John Schlesinger and released in 1979. Also set in Lancashire, it starred Vanessa Redgrave and Richard Gere. Peter Sallis, who appeared in *Yanks Go Home*, recalls Schlesinger visiting him at the Granada studios:

> We knew each other slightly, and he said, 'What's this series that you're making?' and I said, 'It's called *Yanks Go Home*.' And he was in the process of making this movie called *Yanks*, so in a sort of way we clashed. I think he was obviously concerned that we were going to steal his thunder.[42]

Yanks Go Home didn't quite match the calibre of cast that Schlesinger had at his disposal, with the American contingent headed by Stuart Damon, still best known for his '60s TV spy show *The Champions*, and Bruce Boa, the American guest from hell after the perfect Waldorf salad in the classic *Fawlty Towers* episode.

Obviously, Granada were hoping to attract the same kind of mass audience that tuned in regularly to watch *Dad's Army*, but *Yanks Go Home* proved only moderately successful, lasting just the two series. Perhaps its relative failure was due to a lack of regular writers, with many of the episodes penned by different people, which didn't give the series a consistent style. That, along with the studio-based setting and all too obvious canned laughter, lent the whole enterprise something of a cheap feel.

Chapter Eight

1977

January

The new year started off with a blast from the past, as a 1974 *Comedy Playhouse* episode called 'The Big Job' finally got its own series, entitled *Mr Big*. Devised, co-written and starring Peter Jones, it tells the story of small-time crook Eddie (played by Jones) who rather fancies himself as a criminal mastermind. Unfortunately, Vito Corleone he ain't. Instead of a gang of hardened thugs, he has to muddle through with his immediate family: his light-fingered wife Dolly (Prunella Scales), daughter Norma, played by Carol Hawkins, and her feckless boyfriend Ginger (Ian Lavender).

It was a premise that harked back to those old British comedy crook comedies the likes of the Boulting Brothers used to make invariably starring Sid James. One knows what to expect in the first episode when Dolly walks into the house with two heavy-looking carrier bags. Asked where she's been, she replies: 'Shoplifting for the weekend.'

Each week, Eddie would come up with a daring new criminal plot, such as ripping off a bookie, but always had an uncanny knack for cocking it up. *Mr Big* proved popular enough to merit two series on the BBC but with a cast like this one it didn't do as well as perhaps it might have.

***

With *George and Mildred* successfully spun off from *Man About the House*, writers Johnnie Mortimer and Brian Cooke next turned their attentions to finding a vehicle for Paula Wilcox's Chrissy. When that proved fruitless, they turned to Richard O'Sullivan's Robin Tripp, no longer a catering student but a newly qualified chef keen to open up his own bistro.

Robin lives with his girlfriend Vicky in a flat over a Chinese takeaway in Fulham, only to discover one morning that the tenants have disappeared owing rent to the landlord. It's Vicky's father, not altogether joyful of his daughter's choice of boyfriend, who agrees to come in as a business partner and put up the money to convert the takeaway into a bistro; the 'Robin's Nest' of the title.

Cooke and Mortimer knew exactly who they wanted to play Vicky's irascible father, Tony Britton, in his first regular sitcom role, but casting Vicky presented a few problems. 'Richard had just got back from a theatrical tour and we had him jumping straight away into bed with eight different females that we had lined up,' recalls Brian Cooke.[1] Pretty high up the list was a young actress called Tessa Wyatt, along with Lynne Frederick. 'Lynne happened to be the daughter of the casting director at Thames Television,' says Brian. 'But she was in fact very good, she'd done a few movies and she was very much a contender for the role. But she didn't turn up for the audition and when we spoke to her mother asking what had happened, she said, "Oh, she went off to marry Peter Sellers." And we said, "That's fair enough," and we cast Tessa Wyatt.'[2]

And so, the stage was set for a typically middlebrow sitcom, and yet *Robin's Nest* broke new ground in its depiction of an unmarried couple sharing the same bed, a situation that had never been depicted before in a British sitcom. As Brian recalls, he and Mortimer had to go and see the Independent Broadcasting Authority (IBA) to get the go-ahead. 'Look,' they told them. 'This is a love story because the first words out of his mouth are "Will you marry me?" And she says, "No. Why spoil it, we're doing fine."' The writers continued to plead their case, saying how this kind of thing was quite commonplace and not really frowned upon anymore: 'Now if we're not going to start doing what's happening today in our comedy shows then we might as well go back a hundred years and forget the whole thing.'[3] The IBA remained very edgy about it but in the end the writers managed to convince them that this was OK for early evening viewing.

The fourth member of the team left an indelible impression on audiences. That was Albert Riddle, a one-armed Irish kitchen hand who broke more crockery than he cleaned. The part was played by David Kelly, a television veteran who found unexpected fame when he began to be recognised in the street for the first time:

> The public really believed in that character. People used to hold the door open for me when I went into shops, even though they could see I had two arms, and I got letters saying that Thames were to be congratulated for employing disabled actors.[4]

Kelly loved working on the show. 'We had a great cast and we all got on well together.'[5] There was also the added bonus of working at the Thames studio at Teddington. 'The whole fabric of that place lent itself to success.'[6] Kelly recalled that Morecambe and Wise were working just next door. 'On a couple of occasions during rehearsal we'd find Eric Morecambe hiding behind a sofa pretending to write down our jokes.'[7]

Robin's Nest proved another ratings success and ran until 1981 over six series, although Cooke and Mortimer left by the third series. 'We did it for a year and a half,' says Brian, 'and then Richard, for various reasons, decided that he didn't want to do a book that we wanted to do and we said, "OK we won't do any more for Richard," and we left the show in the capable hands of other writers.'[8]

While *Robin's Nest* turned out to be Cooke and Mortimer's final work of the '70s, they continued writing sitcoms together until the mid-'80s. 'Toward the end Johnnie wanted to stay on at Thames and I didn't,' says Brian. 'We'd been there for years and done all these shows and I wanted to travel around and take up new opportunities, so he stayed there and I moved on.'[9] Johnnie Mortimer died in 1992. For Brian, their partnership had been almost like a marriage. 'Nearly every writer who works with another writer will tell you that it's like a marriage. You see more of him than you do of your wife.'[10] They wrote together in the same room, with two desks facing each other. 'I'd do all the scribbling,' says Brian, 'and Johnnie eventually took it away and typed it out. He was exactly the same as me in many ways. In some cases, I think you have to be, although we had different skills.'[11]

Theirs was a partnership that cut across three decades, writing often to tight deadlines. 'How we planned it,' recalls Brian:

we would do all the storylines so we would know exactly what was happening, and then you've got the opportunity to begin to develop. We would then do the location filming, which we hated because the director instantly went into star mode, thinking this was his great break. I remember in *Man About the House* we had a piano dropped on top of a car and the director said, 'I don't know if we can afford that.' And we said, 'How about a roller skate dropped on a bicycle?' And he said, 'Alright, we'll do the piano.'[12]

April

While Paula Wilcox never got her own spin-off show from *Man About the House*, that show's producer, Peter Frazer-Jones, saw her as ideal casting for Richard Waring's latest comedy offering, playing a young unmarried woman coming to terms with looking after her baby and facing widespread disapproval and prejudice. This was quite a daring subject for a comedy to tackle at the time, and as Elizabeth Jones, Paula Wilcox became British sitcom's first single mum.

That's pretty much where the controversy ended, as *Miss Jones and Son* was a fairly tame and by the numbers show, as we see Elizabeth struggle to make ends meet as a cartoon illustrator on a magazine, watched over by her disapproving middle-class parents. Romance comes in the form of next-door-neighbour Geoffrey, played by Christopher Beeny.

Lasting just the two series, it was deemed successful enough to warrant what turned out to be an even more short-lived US version on CBS in 1979.

★★★

Paradise Island also had an interesting premise: two survivors of a shipwreck thrown together on a deserted tropical island. William Franklyn, then best known for his Schweppes TV ads, played entertainments officer Cuthbert Fullworthy, who immediately plans his escape, while Bill Maynard's puritanical cleric is more circumspect about his plight.

Creator Michael Haley was a design engineer by trade and came up with the idea while on holiday. Brian Cooke, then still at Thames, thought Haley wrote a terrific pilot and he was asked to write more:

> He wrote another episode and it was exactly the same as the first one and we thought, oh dear. Then he wrote a third one, which again was almost identical, there was no real story difference and we thought, Oh Christ. But by then we were already committed.[13]

In the end Brian wrote one of the episodes himself and farmed the others out to writers such as Vince Powell and actor John Junkin. Not surprisingly, only one series was made.

***

A little more promising was *Backs to the Land*, written by David Climie, whose credits went all the way back to *The Army Game*. It was produced for ITV by Anglia, one of the very few sitcoms the franchise holder ever made. Set in Norfolk, this gentle nostalgic trip back to 1940 is about three young girls who volunteer for the Women's Land Army to carry out the farm labouring work formerly done by men who have gone off to fight in the war. It was an interesting subject for a comedy, an aspect of British history few people knew much about, and that included the cast, who had to do a bit of swotting about it. 'We also had some of the real land girls come to the set and tell us about their experiences,' recalls Philippa Howell.[14]

Philippa had just appeared in *Softly Softly: Task Force* as a young policewoman, so *Backs to the Land* was a nice change of pace. She plays Shirley Bloom, a sensible Jewish girl, alongside Marilyn Galsworthy's ditzy debutante Daphne Finch-Beauchamp. 'The ironic thing was,' says Philippa, 'Marilyn was Jewish and I was the deb. Often you just get cast on how you look and what you can play rather than what you really are.'[15]

It was an interesting mix of characters, with Terese Stevens completing the trio as the always cheerful cockney Jenny Dabb. Terese was actually a singer and this was her first television acting role. 'Marilyn and I got on really well,' recalls Philippa, 'we shared rooms and everything, but Terese was a bit of a wild card.'[16] She had a manager at the time who not only got himself banned from the set but ultimately banned from Norwich because he was such a nuisance.

Much of the location shooting took place in and around the Norfolk village of Heydon, 'which was a bit of a time warp,' recalls Philippa. 'There was no sign of any television aerials or anything modern.'[17] The crew would always film at the height of summer for the best weather, 'and it was fantastic fun to make,' confirms Philippa, 'so idyllic, with lots of outdoor filming and working on the farm. And everything was done for real, we made the food, we churned the cheese, we used all the equipment that was actually from the 1940s.'[18]

Things went wrong, of course. Philippa recalls accidentally backing a tractor into a ditch:

We were doing another shot outside and there was a donkey in the background who was unfortunately feeling extremely frisky. The director had to say, 'Cut, somebody pour a bucket of water over the donkey,' because he was standing there stealing the scene with a huge erection![19]

Backs to the Land turned out to be a popular hit, running for three series, during which the girls share several misadventures and a bit of romance, along with a hasty education in agricultural matters, determined to prove to the cantankerous farm owner that they can do the work of any man. The series almost certainly inspired David Leland's 1998 film *The Land Girls*, starring Rachel Weisz and Anna Friel.

Backs to the Land also featured a theme song performed by Anne Shelton, who provided inspirational songs for soldiers both on radio broadcasts and in person at British military bases during the Second World War.

June

Middlemen must rank as one of the more interesting sitcoms that posterity has seen fit to ignore, if not totally forget. That's despite it coming from the esteemed pen of Alan Plater. It's a quirky and almost surreal look at a middle-aged, middle-class, middle-management man George Livingstone, whose life is turned upside down when he is made redundant. He falls into partnership with fellow businessman Stanley Binns and together they dream up money-making scams and absurd enterprises, such as inventing and trying to sell a new religion.

Plater said he came to write the series as a vehicle for two actors he particularly liked and wanted to work with, Frank Windsor and Francis Matthews. Unfortunately, critics and audiences didn't take to it and only six episodes were made. 'I think it's fair to say it was pretty well blasted out of the water by the press,' lamented Plater.[20] Only Joan Bakewell, then television critic of *Punch*, admired it, as did many within the BBC itself. Shaun Sutton, the network's Head of Drama, commented that it was, 'well worth watching for the writing alone'.[21]

★★★

No Appointment Necessary saw the likeable Roy Kinnear in his first sitcom lead for almost ten years. He plays Alf Butler, a green-grocer who decides to expand his business interests by buying a lady's hairdressing salon. Alarmed by the fall in trade, he hires an efficient and experienced manageress, played by Josephine Tewson, whose efforts to bolster the business bring her into conflict with everyone. It was the kind of situation that seemed perfectly suited to the comedic talents of Kinnear, but only one series was made.

It was produced at the BBC by Harold Snoad, who was disappointed the show never found its audience, although it did over-rely on crude seaside postcard innuendo. This was in spite of the fact it adhered to what he saw as a set formula that every sitcom had to follow:

> It was well known that the viewing public liked to see shows based round normal everyday life situations that they could relate to: dating, marriage, employment, moving home, holidays etc. Sadly, nowadays, this sort of thing is regarded as 'old fashioned' and is known as 'traditional sitcom' – a term that seems to be used in a derogatory fashion. In my day, sitcoms had to be funny – nowadays it seems more important for them to be different.[22]

July

Granada's *Devenish* was another workplace-set comedy, created and written by Anthony Couch, and starring Dinsdale Landen as Arthur P. Devenish, who works in middle management in a company that manufactures board games. Full of grandiose business plans, and with an overinflated sense of self-importance, Devenish has his sights firmly set on a seat on the board and is jealous of anyone who gets in his way.

With *Devenish* Granada tried something new. Instead of the traditional one week of rehearsal, two weeks were set aside, which ended up being far too much time. In the end actors including Terence Alexander and Geoffrey Bayldon found themselves bumping into each other in Marks and Spencer or other shops on the high street, just killing time.

By the second series there was a distinct impression among the cast that the scripts were not quite right. 'We would all sit in the hotel and talk about it,' recalls John Kane, who played Landen's assistant in the series. 'And these were very experienced comic performers and they all knew there was something wrong with the scripts.'[23] John took it upon himself to call the producer John Temple to voice everyone's concerns. Temple reassured him that the scripts had been worked on and were perfect.

One day in the rehearsal room, they were working on a scene and Landen walked over to where John was standing and gave him a nudge. 'There's something wrong with this, isn't there.' Because John was perhaps the most outspoken of the group in his criticism of the scripts he wasn't going to disagree and went on to explain exactly why he thought the scene wasn't working. 'Yeah, I think you're right,' said Landen. When the director came into the room John recalls,

Dinsdale said to him exactly what I had told him about why the scene wasn't working and the director replied, 'No, it's alright,' and went into the reasons why, and then Dinsdale turned to me and said, 'You see, John, you're worrying about nothing,' and put me right in the shit.[24]

Audiences, however, agreed with John and *Devenish* did not return.

August

Michael Green was a Leicester journalist and humourist whose love of amateur dramatics and rugby inspired the books *The Art of Coarse Rugby* and *The Art of Coarse Acting*. This bestselling series expanded to include further sports and, in *The Art of Coarse Moving*, a funny account of one man's battle to sell his house. This idea was picked up by Barry Took and turned into the BBC sitcom *A Roof Over My Head* starring Brian Rix and Lynda Baron as the hapless couple encountering all manner of pitfalls as they endeavour to move. Such a premise, though, just didn't have the legs and only seven episodes were made. Green made a cameo appearance.

September

Mining a richly comic terrain that would be revisited a decade later in *Waiting for God*, Yorkshire Television's *You're Only Young Twice* starred the much-loved duo of Peggy Mount, renowned for her formidable battleaxes, and Pat Coombs, who specialised in more timid characterisations. Both are residents at Paradise Lodge – a superior residence for retired gentlefolk. It's quite obvious from the first episode that Peggy's Flora Petty rules over the other inhabitants, especially her subservient sidekick Cissie, played by Pat Coombs, of whom she demands, 'unquestioning obedience'. This manifests itself in helping with Flora's numerous attempts to thwart the long-suffering staff, although invariably these schemes backfire.

Despite the limited scope of the storylines *You're Only Young Twice* still managed to run to more than thirty episodes and two Christmas specials over the course of four years.

***

When a comedy set in a police station works you have something like *The Thin Blue Line*, when it doesn't, I'm afraid you get *The Fuzz*, which is rather a disappointment coming from veteran playwright and author Willis Hall, whose most famous creation was *Billy Liar*, co-written with Keith Waterhouse.

Colin Jeavons, who returned to the constabulary as Inspector Lestrade in the Jeremy Brett Sherlock Holmes TV series, is Superintendent Allardyce, in charge of a small provincial police station. Michael Robbins is Detective Sergeant Sidney Marble, in charge of CID, but spends most of his time picking up the pieces left behind by the station's bumbling PCs; while everyone is frustrated in their pursuit of the chaste WPC Pamela Purvis, an early TV role for Lynda Bellingham. Lynda was fairly derogatory of the show in her memoirs: '*The Fuzz* was pretty dire but it paid the mortgage.'

It wasn't just that the jokes were weak, but the plots were rather tired, too – stuff like burglaries at the local chippie, washing line panty pilferers or a bid to stop a notorious handbag snatcher requiring one of the detectives to dress up as a woman. As a result, this Thames comedy didn't go beyond one series.

***

Back in the early '60s, *The Rag Trade* was a big hit for the BBC and for writers Ronald Wolfe and Ronald Chesney. A groundbreaking comedy series that had its roots in the Peter Sellers satire of British trade unionism *I'm All Right Jack* (1959), Peter Jones starred as Harold Fenner, the much put upon proprietor of Fenner Fashions, a London East End sweatshop. Miriam Karlin was the chain-smoking militant shop steward Paddy, with her catchphrase of 'Everybody out!' And Reg Varney played the foreman trying to mediate the conflict between employer and employee. There were also early television roles for Sheila Hancock and Barbara Windsor.

When the writers decided to revive the show, they took it back to the BBC, who produced a pilot episode that was never transmitted. Ultimately the BBC passed and it was taken up instead by LWT. Both Jones and Karlin revived their original roles, along with new cast members including Christopher Beeny and Anna Karen, playing a character called Olive who to all intents and purposes is the same Olive from Wolfe and Chesney's *On the Buses*. There was also an early role for Gillian Taylforth, who went on to fame as Kathy Beale in *EastEnders*.

While the decade had changed, things were very much as before at Fenner Fashions, with most of the drama and storylines revolving around the conflicts between management and worker. Indeed, some of the 'new' scripts were directly recycled from the BBC originals. The show still managed to impact on the public, though. When fifteen girls were sacked by an electronics firm in Derby, the stewards ordered an all-out strike.

Asked by reporters to make a comment the firm's boss said: 'I think this is a case of the girls watching too much *Rag Trade*.' Despite all that, the new *Rag Trade* failed to emulate the success of the original BBC episodes and after two series it was dropped.

***

The Upchat Line was a humorous and playful sitcom especially written for John Alderton by *Billy Liar* creator Keith Waterhouse. In it he plays loveable rogue Mike Upchat, of no fixed abode – he keeps his belongings in a left-luggage locker at Marylebone Station – or fixed profession. Nobody quite knows what he really does for a living; sometimes he says he's a writer but at other times he claims to be anything from a psychologist to a piano tuner, anything to get a girl into bed (his conquests included Wanda Ventham, Liza Goddard, Sue Lloyd and Gabrielle Drake) along with a roof over his head for a few days.

On the strength of Alderton's name, *The Upchat Line* was a rating's winner for Thames. Alderton gives a real star performance, proving he was one of the best light comedy actors around at the time. After seven episodes he decided not to make any more and his address book of willing females was handed over to Robin Nedwell for 1978's *The Upchat Connection*.

October

During a production hiatus of the seemingly never ending *Are You Being Served?*, John Inman personally approached Vince Powell to come up with a suitable sitcom vehicle for him. After much cogitation, Powell's scenario saw Inman as Neville Sutcliffe, the owner of a Blackpool fish and chip shop, who relocates to the Sussex coast where he has inherited his late father's struggling stick of rock factory, along with his less than welcoming stepsister. Powell took the concept to Philip Jones at Thames, who liked the idea and commissioned a series to be called *Odd Man Out*.

Produced by Carry On veteran Gerald Thomas, Powell quickly realised that it wasn't working, that he'd gone way over the top with Inman's character. 'He was far too camp and there were too many gay jokes.'[25] Indeed, Inman's performance is such that you half expect him to say 'I'm free' at any moment. Powell also thought that Inman made a greater impact as part of an ensemble like on *Are You Being Served?*. With *Odd Man Out* he was the star and hardly off the screen: 'It was just too much for the viewers to take and the show sank with hardly a trace.'[26]

November

Part of Dennis Main Wilson's day at the BBC in his capacity as a producer was to nip over to the Light Entertainment bar on the fourth floor of BBC Television Centre, sink a couple of drinks, have a natter to whomever was there, and get back to his office before one o'clock. Wilson was in the bar one day when a young chap introduced himself and explained that he was a scene shifter at the BBC and had written a script, would he take a look. Wilson had a reputation for reading scripts, no matter where they came from. Wilson took the script, sat at a table and began to read. After just fifteen minutes he expressed a desire to buy it and immediately bounded in to see Jimmy Gilbert, the BBC's Head of Comedy. 'This is wonderful. You must read it,' he said, throwing the script on Gilbert's desk. 'I'll be in the bar.'[27] Gilbert duly read it and asked Wilson and the writer to come and see him straight away in his office. The decision was made there and then to get a pilot done. The writer was John Sullivan, the script was *Citizen Smith*.

Sullivan had got a job at the BBC with the express intention of watching how TV programmes were put together, as well as picking up the odd script that was left behind to take home and study. A cockney lad, Sullivan left school at 15 and was still living in a council flat in Balham with a new-born baby when he wrote *Citizen Smith*. It was his big breakthrough and he went on to write '80s comedy hits *Just Good Friends*, *Dear John* and, of course, *Only Fools and Horses*.

Citizen Smith followed the activities of aspiring Marxist Wolfie Smith, who is the idealistic figurehead of the Tooting Popular Front, a feeble misfit band of would-be revolutionaries, the goals of which are: 'Power to the People' and 'Freedom for Tooting'. The character was based on a loud-mouthed yobbo that was a regular in Sullivan's local pub in the late '60s and spouted all the cliché jargon of a revolutionary but never actually did anything about it. Back then it was a trendy thing to be part of some Marxist, anarchist, neo-communist group and no right-minded student was seen without a poster of Che Guevara on their bedsit wall.

The role of Wolfie Smith propelled Robert Lindsay to TV stardom. Sullivan had seen him in *Get Some In* and it was his suggestion that he play the role. At the time Lindsay and Mike Grady were writing scripts together that weren't going anywhere. They also shared the same agent, 'and we were often sent to auditions together,' recalls Mike. 'Somebody had said, "Oh they would make an interesting double."'[28] When Lindsay got the lead in *Citizen Smith*, he called Mike and it turned out he was up for a part on the show, too. Mike plays Ken, one of Wolfie's followers, along with Tony Millan as Tucker, who spend most of their time cooking up various half-baked revolutionary schemes. Meanwhile, in the real world Wolfie has problems with his girlfriend Shirley (played by Lindsay's then wife Cheryl Hall), her not very understanding parents, a lack of money, and the frequent misfortunes of his football team, Fulham.

As an ensemble everyone bonded quickly and had a great time making the show. 'All of us had come out of the theatre,' says Mike:

> Bob had been at Manchester and Exeter, and I'd come out of the Royal Court, so we were used to improv and we could see opportunities between the dialogue to do little gags. You never messed with John's lines, but you would say, 'Could we set the scene over here?', or 'Could I be doing this while we're doing the scene, could I be playing the guitar or something else?', just to take the edge off of it being two blokes sitting in a room talking.[29]

When the *Citizen Smith* pilot met with a good response Jimmy Gilbert commissioned a full series. For Gilbert it was the first time he ever recalled an unsolicited script turning into a successful sitcom. Dennis Main Wilson took the directorial reins on the first series. Mike and the rest of the cast liked Dennis but admits he was something of a force of nature:

> Working with him you were challenged a lot. He was forthright and a famous presence within the BBC. And he was of a generation of producers at the BBC all of whom had seen action in the war. These men were a breed apart and they didn't take any shit from anybody, and they certainly didn't take any shit from the sixth floor.[30]

In one episode Sullivan wrote a sequence where Wolfie and his gang steal a tank and drive it around the streets of London. Mike recalls that the BBC boffins reacted with incredulity, that there was no way it could be done, it wouldn't be allowed:

> Dennis was on the phone immediately to some Military of Defence chap, told them what he needed, they said, 'Of course, we'll arrange it,' and he got it done.[31]

From series two onwards Dennis moved over to producer and Ray Butt took over as director, forging a significant association with John Sullivan. Indeed, it was during filming on *Citizen Smith* that the two men, having one of their many chats, discovered both had worked in street markets. Each of them agreed that the most colourful characters of any such market were the fly pitchers, men who showed up and sold dodgy goods out of a suitcase. Sullivan went away, played around with the idea and came up with *Only Fools and Horses*, which Ray not only helped launch but produced until series five, directing most episodes himself.

Mike Grady recalls he and Robert Lindsay sitting with Sullivan during a break when he told them this story about some workers who had to move these chandeliers, but there was a mix-up and the wrong one was undone and smashed. 'We begged him to write it for *Citizen Smith*,' says Mike. 'We begged him. We said, "Let us have that story," and he said, "I'm saving it, I might get round to it one day, I dunno." And, of course, he put it into *Fools and Horses*. It was a true story. It actually happened to his dad.'[32]

Mike admired and liked Sullivan very much. He was reassuringly down to earth and although he didn't really fit in with the BBC stable of writers, he was respected and knew about comedy. 'He wasn't very good at time keeping though,' says Mike. 'His episodes ran for forty minutes, so you'd often get a call going, "You know that great scene, you were so funny in that, well we've cut it." And it never came back in another form; we'll use it somewhere else they said, but it never happened.'[33]

The enormous success of *Citizen Smith* came as a surprise to many, not least Robert Lindsay himself, who suddenly found that he was recognised everywhere he went; people took to shouting, 'power to the people' at him in the street. As he recalled, 'It got to the stage where I couldn't go anywhere without being mobbed. I'd stop at a supermarket and bring the place to a standstill.'[34] It was tough to deal with, along with the feeling that being in a sitcom conflicted with his desire to be seen as a 'proper' actor. 'And so,' recalls Mike, 'after four series and thirty episodes Bob suddenly went, "I think I need to move on. I don't want this to be on my gravestone." And he was quite right.'[35]

***

Having got on so well with Richard Briers on *The Good Life*, Bob Larbey and John Esmonde were keen to do something else together, as were the BBC, but what they came up with wasn't at all what anyone expected. In *The Other One* Briers plays Ralph Tanner, a brash, compulsive liar, determined to be seen as a man of the world, but in reality he's really a sad loner, totally vacuous. 'He was all bluff and bluster,' says Richard. 'Or as my grandfather used to say, all talk and no trousers.'[36] At an airport en route to a package holiday in Spain he meets the gullible, timid Brian Bryant, played by Michael Gambon: 'The most boring man in the world,' says Richard. 'He had nothing in him either; they were two hollow men. Both failures.'[37] Perhaps sensing this in each other, both strike up an unlikely friendship. 'The basic idea was that two very different characters somehow needed each other to get along,' according to Bob Larbey. 'Two sides of a coin if you will.'[38]

Much of the story was set in Spain, with Ralph exuding confidence and Brian following behind, invariably into misadventure. 'But by the end of the series Gambon's character became stronger than me,' says Richard. 'I'm saying things like, "Come on, you've got to get in the fast lane of life. And will you stop being a full stop. You've got to be more like me, be an exclamation mark!" Then by the end he was the one supporting me.'[39]

Public reaction was muted and ratings poor. Everyone expected it to be cancelled. Richard recalls how John Howard Davies, who directed it, reacted, 'Sod them, I love it and I'm going to commission seven more.'[40] Series two sees Ralph seek out Brian once they get back to England and they team up as travelling salesmen. The public reaction was much as before, they didn't like it. 'The audience never quite accepted Richard as a not too likeable character,' claims Bob Larbey. 'Whether he liked it or not, he had a loveable appeal. Shame, because he loved the idea of playing an empty braggart like Ralph, and it remained one of his favourite series.'[41]

Briers also liked working with Gambon, 'He had a great sense of humour. And we both loved that series. It was so dark and so bleak. John Esmonde had a very bleak view of the world sometimes. Out of the writers he was the darker of the two, Bob Larbey liked the happier side.'[42]

When he looks back on *The Other One*, Briers thinks maybe it would have benefitted from a third character for Gambon and himself to bounce off. 'It was perhaps a bit true to life. In other words, a bit too miserable.'[43]

December

Vince Powell had hired a French au pair girl to look after his young son. The girl, whose handle on English was tenuous at best, attended a language school and sometimes brought back some of her students to the house. 'Their efforts at English were often hilarious and I began to wonder if there wasn't an idea for a sitcom about a class of foreigners learning English.'[44]

No longer contracted to Thames but a freelancer, Powell spoke to Michael Grade over at LWT. At the time Grade wanted Powell to write a sitcom for Larry Grayson, but he liked the new idea and commissioned a series, putting it into the capable hands of producer/director Stuart Allen, whose numerous credits included *On the Buses* and *Love Thy Neighbour*.

Mind Your Language saw a welcome return to television for Barry Evans, who had virtually vanished from the nation's screens after leaving the Doctor series. Working at LWT was Humphrey Barclay, who was delighted that Stuart Allen had decided to bring Barry back into the fold, 'because he had left the Doctor series under a tiny cloud, not signing his new contract, but he was terrific in *Mind Your Language*'.[45]

Evans plays Jeremy Brown, an English teacher at a London College of Further Education. In his evening class is a motley group of foreign students from China, France, Germany, Greece, India, Italy, Japan, Pakistan, Spain and Sweden. Much of the humour of the show derives from the numerous linguistic misunderstandings and what some critics found to be crude national stereotypes. However, it must be said that never before had so many multi-racial actors been seen in a British sitcom.

Notable among the class is Danielle Favre, a role that was written expressly for French/Mauritian actress Françoise Pascal, 'even though that character was nothing like me because I'm quite insecure in my own self.'[46] Françoise recalls that she was given plenty of freedom to play the character in the way she wanted. 'But Vince used to come up to me and say, "Be sexier, be more French," and I'd say, "Oh God, how more French do you want me to be?"'[47]

It was a happy set and everyone in the cast bonded and got on well. Françoise remembers Barry Evans as friendly and always interesting to talk to. 'But he was very shy and in many ways was a lonely man. He didn't feel comfortable among strangers, he preferred being with friends, people that he knew.'[48] At the time Françoise was in a long-term relationship with the actor Richard Johnson and invited Barry to a dinner party at their house with the likes of Albert Finney and Diana Rigg, 'and he stayed in a corner and did not say a word to anyone'.[49]

From the word go *Mind Your Language* was a huge success, attracting audiences in the region of 18 million, and even on a couple of occasions knocking *Coronation Street* off its perch at the top of the national ratings. Such was its popularity that Françoise was sometimes stopped in the street by men asking if she could come and au pair for them and their kids. It did well in other countries, too, in spite of the cries of racism levelled against it. At one point it was making more money for LWT in overseas sales than any other show.

All that came to an end in the most unexpected way: 'It ultimately fell foul of the left-wing thinkers,' says Humphrey Barclay.[50] Michael Grade had moved up to being Director of Programmes at LWT and appointed Barclay his head of comedy and together they attended the Edinburgh television festival. One afternoon they were guests at a panel discussion about the portrayal of ethnic minorities on television, 'and from the back of the hall,' recalls Barclay:

somebody said to Michael, in so many words, 'When are you going to get rid of that racist rubbish *Mind Your Language*?' And Michael said, 'Well, that's a very interesting point, and as it happens my head of comedy is here, so Humphrey what do you think?' Thanks a bunch, Michael. I'd only been in the job a week and had nothing whatsoever to do with this programme, but I had to stand up and say, 'If we are getting something wrong with the show then we will seriously have to think about it.'[51]

It wasn't very long after this event that Grade took the decision to cancel *Mind Your Language*, 'because he saw that it was guilty as charged,' says Barclay:

It wasn't written with sufficient intellectual rigour. It was innocent in a way but it was guilty of perpetuating rather simplistic portrayals of Johnny Foreigner. In Vince's hands it had a certain style of humour and when that style of humour, which was fine for things like *On the Buses*, met different races then there was trouble. And Vince, many conversations later on could never really understand what was wrong with his approach. But it was all part of my learning curve that eventually got me to making a show like *Desmond's* [the late '80s Channel 4 sitcom set in a Peckham barber shop featuring a predominantly black cast], where we got it right. So, from that point of view it was a very interesting experience.[52]

The irony of cancelling *Mind Your Language* meant that a lot of actors from ethnic backgrounds lost their jobs. There was, however, a feeling among some of the cast, including Evans and Françoise, that after three series the show had pretty much run its course. Then again, it might have been nice to have done one last series and left on a high. As it was, in 1986 *Mind Your Language* returned, made independently of LWT. The new series was not screened nationally, with only a few ITV regions picking it up. The reason was obvious, Vince Powell's scripts were terrible. Françoise, then living and working in LA, made the right decision in turning it down:

> I had grown out of it to be honest and I really didn't want to do it. But I came back to England and went to the rehearsals and read the script and said, 'No thank you. I'm not doing it. I'm going back to LA.'[53]

Only about half the original cast returned, including Evans, who again was finding work hard to come by. It was to be his last television credit. By the mid-'90s Evans was working as a minicab driver in Leicester, trying desperately to resurrect his career but finding nobody willing to hire him. Tragically, in 1997 he was found dead in the living room of the flat where he lived alone with high levels of alcohol in his system. He was only 53.

Humphrey Barclay was particularly upset when he learned of the death:

> Barry was a charmer, I loved him very much. He was a very serious worker, but very quiet. He was an unhappy person in himself. Having been abandoned as a baby [as an orphan he was brought up in a Dr Barnardo's home], I think he battled with the fear of rejection throughout his life and eventually that's what probably got to him.[54]

Chapter Nine

1978

January

When Humphrey Barclay first got the script for *Maggie and Her*, about a 30-something divorced schoolteacher living alone in a flat, with an interfering but well-intentioned elderly neighbour, the first actress that popped into his mind was Judi Dench. 'When I approached her,' recalls Barclay, 'she said, in so many words, "I don't think I will ever do sitcom." I'm glad to say when I approached her a few years later with *A Fine Romance* she had changed her mind.'[1] Instead, Julia McKenzie, better known as a musical theatre actress, was cast as Maggie, along with veteran comedy actress Irene Handl.

Barclay liked the premise of the show: 'Here is a woman, uncertain about her place in the world and her future life and her romances, who finds an ally and friend in her chatty neighbour across the hall, in the same block of flats, and her liking for this amusing character was tinged with a dread of turning into her.'[2] Unfortunately, Barclay thinks it ultimately fell short.

'We didn't make the scripts successful enough to make the series work.'[3] The writer in question was Leonard Webb, who hadn't done very much before, and did next to nothing afterwards. Still, Barclay saw it as his duty to collaborate with the writer and try to make sure he did the best quality work that he could:

> I learned the lesson that everything starts with the writer and is owed to the writer. The producer has a responsibility in two directions, between the management who is expecting the producer to deliver and the writer who is hoping the producer won't f*ck up his work. And I like to think that I always championed the writer.[4]

In the end *Maggie and Her* ran for two series. The theme tune, written by Laurie Holloway, was sung by Julia herself.

February

Following David Jason's success in *Open All Hours*, writer Ronnie Taylor fashioned a comedy vehicle for him over at ATV called *A Sharp Intake of Breath*. This would prove to be Jason's biggest solo success before *Only Fools and Horses*, running for four series. It began life in the summer of 1977 as part of ATV's *The Sounds of Laughter* strand that showcased six potential sitcom pilots. *A Sharp Intake of Breath* was the only show that went on to a full series.

Jason plays Peter Barnes, an ordinary bloke seemingly thwarted at every turn by authority, petty officialdom and bureaucratic obstruction. The series played on Jason's skills as a physical comedian and also made him break the fourth wall by addressing the viewing audience, usually with an exasperating look. Another interesting feature was the casting of Richard Wilson and Alun Armstrong playing different characters in each episode, usually professionals and jobsworths that make Barnes' life a perpetual misery, be it doctors, solicitors or bank managers. It's especially interesting today to see Jason and Wilson share scenes together, the future Del Boy and Victor Meldrew.

Tragedy struck during filming of the third series when Taylor was rushed to hospital with acute inflammation of the brain. After two weeks in intensive care he died, a huge shock to the whole cast and crew, and that series was abandoned after just three episodes. Vince Powell took over script duties on series four, but the dynamic of the show just wasn't the same. Both Wilson and Armstrong were missing, too, which didn't help.

An American adaptation, titled *Harry's Battles*, was screened as a pilot by ABC in 1981. Dick Van Dyke starred alongside Connie Stevens as Harry Fitzsimmons, a supermarket manager in Pittsburgh who struggles to keep his cool while cutting through the red tape of everyday life. No series followed.

★★★

In 1977, Ronnie Barker said goodbye to making another series of *Porridge*, but that didn't mean the end for Norman Stanley Fletcher. In *Going Straight* Dick Clement and Ian La Frenais came up with the concept of Fletcher being released on parole from Slade prison and watching him deal with life on the outside. 'The idea of the show was to see whether he could stay on the straight and narrow, whether he could adapt,' says Dick. 'It was a good theme because so many people coming out of prison can't get a job, people don't want to know and eventually they go off the rails.'[5]

Richard Beckinsale's Lennie Godber was also out of prison and working as a long-distance lorry driver. A further echo to *Porridge* occurs in the opening episode when Fletcher shares the train journey back to London with his old nemesis Mr Mackay, who has just retired from the prison service, and the two men share a few drinks and memories together in the buffet car. 'I'm fond of that episode,' says Dick. 'There's something about the change in their relationship. Mackay is going down south looking for a job and Fletcher is saying, "You're the same as me now." It was a nice dynamic because Fulton was a wonderfully three-dimensional actor.'[6]

All the ingredients were there for another success, and while the ratings were high, and it won a BAFTA for Best Situation Comedy, it's true to say that the public didn't really take to *Going Straight* in the way they had with *Porridge*. Maybe audiences preferred to see Fletcher in what they considered to be his 'natural' habitat, in a prison cell, fighting the screws and sticking two fingers up to the establishment. 'That was the problem,' recalls Ian. 'People said, I love Fletch but I wish he was back in the nick.'[7]

In *Porridge* it worked so well because Fletcher was trapped, whereas once he was free somehow it lost that pressure that he was under. In *Going Straight*, he's under a different kind of pressure as he struggles to find a steady job amidst rampant unemployment and the stigma of being an ex-convict. Things aren't any better at home in Muswell Hill either, where his wife has done a bunk with a fella. Barker's one and only condition about returning to the role was that he didn't want to have a wife. He didn't want to get stuck in that sitcom rut of domesticity. So, he's been left in sole charge of a teenage son Raymond, played by Nicholas Lyndhurst. 'And he was a lovely foil for Fletcher,' says Dick, 'that generation gap. And he was a lovely actor Nicholas.'[8]

Then there's Godber, dating Fletcher's daughter Ingrid, played again by Patricia Brake, who was delighted to be back working with Barker and Beckinsale:

> The amazing thing about Ronnie was he was able to grow what he was given. Watching him play with the script was wonderful. He could develop a joke so that it went on much longer because he was just so clever at it. And what I loved about Richard was his total reality. He didn't change at all when the camera started, there was no feeling that anything had changed. He was who he was and that's the way he played it. He wasn't theatrical or actorly in any way. He had a lot of charm.[9]

Despite impressive viewing figures, only one series of *Going Straight* was ever made. For some reason there was no great desire from the high-ups in the BBC to continue with it. Besides, Barker was busy on other things and Dick and Ian were spending more of their time in America. '*Going Straight* tends to be overshadowed by *Porridge*, understandably,' admits Dick. 'But there's some lovely things in it, particularly the last episode when Godber marries Fletcher's daughter. There's something very satisfying about that episode.'[10]

March

Mixed Blessings was another hit for Humphrey Barclay at LWT. The script was brought to him by Michael Grade and had come in from Grade's old buddy Sid Green, who used to write for Morecambe and Wise. The story centred on a newly married couple, Thomas Simpson, played by Christopher Blake, and

Susan, played by Ghanaian-born Muriel Odunton, both university graduates. Thomas is white, though, and Susan is black, and the two sets of parents don't like it one little bit, or each other for that matter. 'It was very unusual and fresh,' recalls Barclay,

> in that surrounding a daring, if you like, but unsensationalised black and white romance between a young couple, the comedy was about the fact that black people can be just as prejudiced as white people. So, it was purporting to speak from a black point of view, as well as from a white.[11]

Barclay liked the idea a lot and gave the show to director Derrick Goodwin, who had worked on everything from *Z Cars* to *Doctor Who*. Goodwin said he would love to do it provided he could make the black family as white collar as the white family. 'I remember we enjoyed symbolising this fact by having both families owning the same tea service,' says Barclay:

> That was a most important step because it wasn't so far away from that time when someone else was saying to me, 'When we see a black face on screen, why is it always a bus conductor?'[12]

Of course, viewed by a contemporary audience, for whom inter-racial marriage barely raises an eyebrow, *Mixed Blessings*, despite the ambiguous title, was something of a breakthrough. 'I was told at the time it couldn't be done in America,' Barclay claims.[13] In the first series Thomas and Susan have to honeymoon in secret and then live for a while at the home of Thomas' Aunt Dorothy (*Fawlty Towers*' Joan Sanderson) before finding a place of their own. By the end of the second series Susan becomes pregnant, carrying the child through most of series three.

By the close of the third series Barclay felt the show was getting a little tired:

> The prejudice joke was running a bit thin because these two families were rather human people, and likeable, they weren't Alf Garnetts, so you couldn't go on banging the same drum because actually they had begun to quite like each other. Unfortunately, the writing wasn't ingenious enough to deal with that development.[14]

Barclay knew the reason for this was partly because Sid Green was white and couldn't really write for the black characters. Back then there were hardly if any black comedy writers around, and for a long time afterwards. This realisation, that even with the best intention people would not write decently for people other than those from their own culture, eventually led Barclay and others towards hiring better voices, and better representation.

June

In Yorkshire Television's *Life Begins at Forty*, Derek Nimmo and Rosemary Leach play a quintessentially comfortable middle-class couple, married for seventeen years, who suddenly have to face up to parenthood. Cue lots of typical Nimmo dithering and flapping. The baby arrives in the last episode, so inevitably there was a second series.

As it turned out, this was Nimmo's final sitcom of the '70s. *Life Begins at Forty* writer Jan Butlin did create two more comedies for him in the early and mid-'80s before Nimmo virtually disappeared from our television screens. He returned to the London stage and also concentrated on his own theatre company, which took productions with star casts to countries including Australia, New Zealand, Singapore, Hong Kong, Thailand and Dubai. 'That was a marvellous business,' remembers David Kelly. 'But I'm afraid a lot of the money went on the bookies.'[15]

David remembers one year being a very early tourist to Dubai, before the resort became popular. 'I went there to get away from actors and theatre and everything else. But who the hell was staying at the same hotel but Tony Britton doing the farce *Move Over Mrs Markham*; it was the Derek Nimmo dramatic society! And Tony said to me, "Sweet God, do you mean you paid to come here!"'[16]

Nimmo eventually had two companies doing these tours and turned the basement in his west London home into an office. Kelly remembers a conversation he had with Tony Britton about this office, which was very nicely designed, with these elegant stairs going down, but Britton was concerned that they didn't have a banister. Kelly thought that an odd thing and the next time he met up with Nimmo raised some concerns:

> I said, 'Derek, please get some banisters put in, you're not young anymore, it's dangerous.' And he said, 'Oh no, we can't interfere with the design.' And he didn't interfere with the design and he did fall one day and never recovered. It was a sad way to go.[17]

Derek Nimmo died in hospital aged 68, two months after that fall in 1999.

July

David Roper was sitting in an apartment overlooking the Indian Ocean in Durban, South Africa, when a phone call came through from his friend John Temple, producer of *The Cuckoo Waltz*. David was in South Africa at the time helping out one of his in-laws, who was managing a gold mine near Johannesburg, but Temple's call didn't find him in good spirits, recovering as he was from being stung by a Portuguese man-of-war. 'Thanks to the lifeguards, who applied vinegar to my wounds, I survived, but felt quite "woozy" for several hours.'[18]

David didn't really need much persuading though to accept the lead role in another Granada sitcom, *Leave it to Charlie*, playing a happy-go-lucky insurance salesman starting a new job in a northern town. It was created by one H.V. Kershaw, better known for his long association with *Coronation Street*, for which he started as the soap's first script editor, then producer, and finally as scriptwriter, contributing 299 scripts, his last broadcast in 1988. The director of *Leave it to Charlie* was Eric Prytherch, a committed left-winger. 'He was always having friendly sparring matches with H.V. Kershaw,' David recalls, 'who was an equally committed right-winger. Eric was great company and was forever rabbiting on about something or other. His secretary knew of Eric's propensity for chatting at length and would answer the phone by saying, "Eric Prytherch's office. Who would like to listen to him?"'[19]

Playing Charlie's boss was Peter Sallis. 'Peter was great to work with,' says David:

and was always good for a bit of sensible advice. I remember coming into rehearsals one morning with one of those hangovers that make you wonder what kind of a fool you made of yourself the night before. I said to Peter, 'When will I reach the age of discretion, Peter?' 'You never will, David, but you'll soon reach the age of being discreet,' he replied as he pulled a bottle of Scotch from his briefcase – it was half-empty.[20]

Leave it to Charlie proved popular enough to run for four series. Even so, not everybody was happy with it. The Head of Comedy at Granada at the time was Brian Armstrong. One December he received a letter from an irate viewer, who launched into a vicious attack on what he considered to be the rubbish that Granada was dishing out as comedy. 'The letter was riddled with swearing,' David recalls, 'culminating in calling Brian by a somewhat gynaecological name.'[21] Armstrong showed David a copy of his brilliant reply:

Dear Sir,

Thank you for your letter. I was sorry to read that you disap-prove of our comedy output and I assure you that I will pass on your forceful opinions to the appropriate departments. We always welcome advice from the public and take any criticism extremely seriously.

Thank you again for getting in touch, and may I take this opportunity to wish you a Happy Christmas and suggest that you stick your head up a dead bear's arse.

Yours faithfully,

Brian Armstrong

'It was at that moment I realised why Brian was Head of Comedy,' says David.[22]

★★★

After their enormous success with *Are You Being Served?*, David Croft and Jeremy Lloyd sat down to write another sitcom together. Such was Croft's standing within the BBC at the time that he got the go-ahead to make a pilot without revealing to his bosses what his new show was even about.

This time, however, the BBC's faith in Croft was misplaced by giving *Come Back Mrs Noah* its own series, given how it is cited by some as one of the all-time worst sitcoms. The year is 2050 and the UK have established a space exploration complex in Pontefract. As first prize in a cookery competition, Mollie Sugden's housewife Mrs Noah is given a guided tour of the facility, only to be accidentally blasted off into space along with the crew of a new space station.

Comedies set in outer space are few and far between, and rarely work. *Come Back Mrs Noah* certainly had the ingredients to succeed and it's hard not to love a series that sends Mollie Sugden into orbit. The show featured a veritable repertory of Croft regulars: besides Mollie there's Donald Hewlett and Michael Knowles from *It Ain't Half Hot Mum* as a pair of snooty space officers, Ian Lavender from *Dad's Army* playing a TV reporter and there's an early role for future *'Allo 'Allo!* star Gordon Kaye as the host of a news special with updates on the ongoing attempts to bring Mrs Noah back to earth. As it turned out by the final episode, and there were to be no more than six altogether, Mrs Noah and Co. are still stranded in the outer reaches of the Universe, and for many viewers it was the best place for them.

Croft considered the show, 'very funny indeed', and one of the best things he did; innuendo is in plentiful supply but there is an over-reliance on crude slapstick. He also admitted that the technical challenges were not met by the BBC special effects crew. As for the low ratings, Croft blamed it on being scheduled opposite the popular Kenny Everett show on ITV. Not to be outdone, Croft, along with Jimmy Perry, bounced back in 1980 with *Hi-de-Hi!*

September

Within a year of *Dad's Army* coming to rest, Arthur Lowe swapped the military uniform of captain Mainwaring for the priestly robes of Father Duddleswell in LWT's *Bless Me, Father*. Set in the fictional parish of St Jude's in suburban London during the 1950s, Lowe saw this laconic Roman Catholic priest as a welcome change from playing a lot of bumbling middle-aged Englishmen and counted it as one of his favourites.

At the heart of the comedy is a charming, almost fatherly relationship between Duddleswell and a newly ordained young priest, played by Daniel Abineri. Just a year earlier Daniel had played another young priest in a television play by Christopher Fry called *The Best of Enemies*, a performance that no doubt brought him to the attention of the producers. 'I was asked to do a screen test with Arthur Lowe at London Weekend studios,' says Daniel:

I remember I was very nervous to be playing opposite Arthur, who was by now a huge star. I also was nursing a bad bout of flu. So, I have to say I was astonished to be offered the role. I heard later that the producers were originally going to offer Father Neil to John Alderton, until someone pointed out that he was perhaps a little too old for the part.[23]

Daniel found Arthur great to work with:

He was very supportive and would quietly give me tips on delivery and timing. He was obsessed by physical comedy and was a huge fan of W.C. Fields. Personality wise, Arthur was very much like his Captain Mainwaring character. Easily irritated by incompetence and slightly bumptious![24]

Lowe brings a mischievous quality to Father Duddleswell, along with a gentle Irish brogue, and is outstanding in the role. Father Duddleswell has some rather dubious ways of raising money for the parish church. There's the time he comes up with the almost Del Boy-like scheme of selling bottled holy water.

Amusingly, during breaks in the studio recording Lowe used to sneak under the raised seating and eavesdrop on the audience. 'One particular day,' recalls Daniel:

he came back on set and sat down with me while the crew were fiddling with the lighting. He quietly said to me that he couldn't believe the asinine conversations he'd overheard from the audience and what a bunch of idiots he thought they were. I remember noticing that the chitter chatter of the crowd quietened all of a sudden to horrified silence. It was then that I noticed that we were on camera and the mic boom was dangling over us. I have to say that Arthur handled it brilliantly. He turned to the audience with a big cheeky smile and said, 'Ha ha I tricked you all. Just making sure you were all awake and listening!' Thankfully the crowd bought it and roared with laughter.[25]

Bless Me, Father was written by Peter De Rosa, who had previously been a novice curate himself, and proved popular enough to run for three series. However, by the time of the third series in 1981 Lowe was seriously ill. He never revealed what was wrong with him but rumours began swirling around the set. 'It became obvious that something was wrong as he started going to sleep in the middle of scenes when it wasn't his line,' recalls Daniel. 'It was very disconcerting to act with as he would go to sleep as Duddleswell and then when nudged by the floor manager, wake up as Captain Mainwaring!'[26]

Plans were under way for a possible fourth series. Daniel was in Australia by this time playing Frank N Furter in an Australian tour of *The Rocky Horror Show* and was intending to come back to England if LWT picked up the option to do another series:

I was playing in Melbourne when I got a call from my London agent at the stage door informing me that Arthur had collapsed in his dressing room on tour and later died. It was upsetting as he was relatively young, just 66. But I have very fond memories of *Bless Me, Father*. It shot me from a practically complete unknown to being seen by 16 million viewers a week and led to other good roles. And to work with such a comedy legend as Arthur was indeed a rare privilege.[27]

October

Back in 1953, Frank Muir and Denis Norden teamed up for the classic BBC Radio sketch series *Take it from Here*. By far its most famous creation was the Glums, featuring Jimmy Edwards as the boorish Pa Glum, a character Johnny Speight later admitted was partly the inspiration behind Alf Garnett, Dick Bentley as his gormless son Ron and June Whitfield as Ron's dowdy fiancée Eth. Such was its popularity the Glums remained a regular fixture on *Take it from Here* until the show ended in 1960.

Fast forward to 1978 and LWT were putting together *Bruce Forsyth's Big Night*, a prime-time Saturday variety show. For one of the segments Muir and Norden were invited to adapt some of their old Glums radio scripts into ten-minute sketches. Jimmy Edwards was asked to reprise the role of Pa, with Ian Lavender and Patricia Brake taking over the roles of Ron and Eth. At first Patricia did feel a little apprehensive stepping into the shoes of June Whitfield:

> As it turned out she was so nice about it when I met her. I said, 'Gosh, I feel really embarrassed.' But she was so lovely, she just said, 'I'm too old to do it on the telly.'[28]

Patricia found Jimmy Edwards enjoyable to work with and they got on well. To her surprise he took to sending her postcards from wherever he was abroad. 'He was either hated or loved, Jimmy, there were no half measures with him. And, of course, he did like the bottle. It was always better working with him in the morning.'[29] Some people found him a bit too larger than life, but behind closed doors he was a very quiet man. 'I think his bombastic persona was a front that was probably covering a whole multitude of worries and problems,' says Patricia. 'I liked him a lot but he could be incredibly rude.'[30]

Ironically, Bruce Forsyth's 'big night' bombed but the Glums got their own series in 1979 with Muir and Norden again adapting their original radio scripts, this time into a half-hour format. The television revival never recaptured the glory of the old radio episodes and *The Glums* only lasted for one series of eight episodes. 'But I loved doing that,' says Patricia. 'Some of the scenes were very funny. I'll never forget the scene where Jimmy gets his toe stuck down the plughole of the bathtub. I have never heard laughter like it in a studio.'[31]

★★★

Rings on their Fingers was another domestic comedy from Richard Waring and starred Martin Jarvis and Diane Keen as Oliver Pryde and Sandy Bennett, a couple who have lived together for six years. Sandy is forever trying to encourage Oliver to agree to tie the knot. He, however, is quite happy with the way things are. But by the end of the first series wedding bells are in the air.

Diane had just come off the hugely popular *Cuckoo Waltz*, while this was Martin's first sitcom experience, having appeared in quite a few comedies in the West End and regional theatre. 'So, I was able to learn from her and share the fun, but it was hard work, learning and recording a new episode every seven days.'[32]

Rehearsals took place at the Acton Hilton, where the measurements of the set were taped out across the floor, with pretend doors and kitchen furniture to help the actors get the feel of the action. Then, a day before the actual recording, the technical crew turned up for a final rehearsal of that week's episode. 'During the run-through Di and I paid careful attention to where and when the crew laughed, and where they didn't!' says Martin. 'Helpful guidance for when we performed next evening in front of the "live" audience.'[33] That could be tricky too, especially when the show had to be halted due to a technical glitch or an actor fluffing his lines, as Martin recalls:

> Occasionally we would say to the audience: 'Do you remember how much you laughed at that moment? When we do it again, would you mind laughing again, even though you know what's coming?' Sometimes they almost fell out of their seats in their eagerness to be part of the show.[34]

Rings on their Fingers was a big hit for the BBC, 'probably because there were quite a lot of people out there who were in a similar position', believes Harold Snoad, who produced the show.[35]

At times it was getting something like 15 million viewers. For Martin a lot of that success was down to Richard Waring's acutely observant writing. 'He was a master of relationship comedy. And Diane, a brilliant actress, also added enormously to the popularity of the show.'[36]

Waring really was one of the unsung heroes of British television sitcom. His sense of the comedy (and absurdity) of life was remarkable. It seemed that so many viewers recognised the characters' behaviour and their to-and-fro comic exchanges – if not directly in themselves then certainly among friends, neighbours, workmates or family members. 'Richard was a large genial man with, as you might expect, a bubbling sense of humour,' Martin recalls. 'He chortled continuously during rehearsals, often laughing louder than anybody at his own scripted words.'[37]

Having been an actor himself, Waring was sympathetic to the way each performer approached rehearsals and recordings. 'Both Martin and I felt that it should be as real as you could get it,' says Diane. 'And Richard was happy for us to play around with the script and try a few things. He trusted us.'[38]

Waring was also the 'warm-up' man for the show in the studio. 'He loved chatting to the audience between scenes and keeping the jolly atmosphere going,' recalls Martin. 'I think his chief delight was in performing magic tricks for them, and hearing their amazement and applause!'[39]

A few years later Martin began working with Alan Ayckbourn on a series of his plays. Ayckbourn revealed to Martin that he admired Waring's work enormously and had been influenced in his own writing by his early '60s television comedies, *Brothers in Law* and *Marriage Lines*. 'When I told Richard what Alan had said, he was thrilled, modestly surprised, and beamed from ear to ear.'[40]

Rings on their Fingers went into a second and third series, showing the couple adjusting to married life and then the discovery that Sandy is pregnant. Although a proposed fourth series would have concerned them adapting to parenthood, it was never made.

★★★

After John Alderton passed on making a second series of *The Upchat Line*, Keith Waterhouse came up with a brilliant ruse to keep the whole thing going. Before emigrating to Australia, Alderton's Mike Upchat raffles off the key to his left-luggage locker at Marylebone Station, the winner inheriting his personal effects and his prized address book. The winner turns out to be Robin Nedwell, who duly takes over the mantle in a new series of adventures entitled *The Upchat Connection*.

Nedwell was one of those actors who was perfect for sitcom. 'He just relaxed into it,' recalls co-star Susan Jameson, 'and made it all seem effortless.'[41] And he was a good fit for the new Mike Upchat, someone who was a bit of a rogue. 'Somehow Robin could get away with more because of the charm he had,' says Susan. 'And the slightly self-deprecating manner that he brought to the performance.'[42]

Susan had been in an episode of *The Upchat Line*, but returned as a new character, Maggie, for *The Upchat Connection* and appeared in all seven episodes. 'There was no romantic involvement between Maggie and Mike,' she says. 'I was more of his mate, someone that he would come back to and relate what he had been up to.'[43] In one scene in a pub, Mike tells Maggie he lives on Park Lane and proceeds to take her there only to proudly show off a park bench.

Produced once again by Thames, Susan enjoyed working with Robin and loved doing the show:

> It was one of those jobs where you got up in the morning and jumped on the tube or got the bus with a smile on your face because you knew you were working with lovely people.[44]

Sadly, *The Upchat Connection* lasted just the one series. And by the early '80s television jobs had begun to dry up, too, for Nedwell. Instead, he gravitated more towards the theatre, working mostly in light comedy, often on foreign tours for Derek Nimmo's company. Tragically, Robin died of a heart attack in 1999. He was just 52. Ironically, given that he rose to fame playing a medical student in the Doctor series, Robin collapsed and died during a visit to a doctor's surgery near his home in Southampton.

November

Riding high on his success as Rigsby and Reggie Perrin, Leonard Rossiter was hoping renowned journalist and satirist Alan Coren might provide him with another hit comedy vehicle in *The Losers*. Alas the show got a roasting from the critics and is all but forgotten today.

Rossiter plays Sydney Foskett, a low-rent, manipulative wrestling promoter who comes across the gentle but dim-witted Nigel, a young wrestler played by Alfred Molina in his first television role. Sydney trains Nigel up, only to see him lose badly in his first fight. Realising there might be more money to be made promoting a great loser, Sydney sets out to sabotage Nigel's attempts for a successful career in the ring by negotiating defeat in a series of rigged matches. Nigel is, of course, too naïve to realise what's going on.

Molina, who later made a name for himself in British and Hollywood movies, recalled how he was completely in awe of Rossiter and watched him like a hawk during rehearsals:

> He was a big part of helping me learn. One's tendency is to perhaps try a bit too hard when you're young. You want to make an impression, and you kind of throw yourself into it with a lot of enthusiasm. And he was experienced enough to just know that you can take it easy, you don't have to crack all your eggs to make an omelette. You can be a bit more judicious. So, I learned about restraint and I learned about timing from him. It was a great experience.[45]

Both Rossiter and Molina give excellent performances, but it wasn't enough to save this ATV series. Arriving as it did hot on the heels of *Rising Damp* and *Reggie Perrin*, *The Losers* was inevitably, and perhaps unfairly, compared to both.

★★★

As *The Liver Birds* began to wind down after almost a ten-year run, its writer Carla Lane was moving on to a new challenge. Carla had always seen herself as predominantly a serious writer rather than a comedy one. 'And I wanted to try something a bit more serious, but with comedy to help it along.'[46] The result was one of the most accomplished sitcoms of the decade, and arguably Lane's greatest achievement – *Butterflies*.

Wendy Craig, of *Not in Front of the Children ... And Mother Makes Three/Five* fame, plays a very different kind of suburban housewife in Ria Parkinson, an attractive woman approaching middle age and worrying that she has not made the most of her life. 'Like everyone she has her dreams,' says Wendy. 'She was a housewife who was lonely and bored. Her husband Ben was a lovely man, a good husband, but he wasn't fulfilling what she needed at that time.'[47] Played by Geoffrey Palmer, Ben is a dentist and a collector of butterflies, but essentially a bit dull. All of which opens up Ria to the temptation of adultery, when she is wooed by a wealthy businessman called Leonard, played by Bruce Montague. 'It was a case of the grass is greener, I think,' says Wendy. 'If Ria had gone off with Leonard she might have soon be wistfully looking back on her marriage.'[48] It's for this reason, along with Ria's natural timidity, that makes it impossible for her to consummate the relationship. 'Nothing happened,' says Wendy. 'And it's just as well it didn't because I think she would have got bored very quickly. It was the thrill of being chased. Also, somebody was paying a lot of attention to her, and she loved it.'[49]

The series' bittersweet nature and sometimes downbeat atmosphere set *Butterflies* apart from most other sitcoms. Indeed, the BBC initially didn't want to do it. 'I had a huge problem with them,' reveals Carla. 'They said, "It's not that we want people to fall about laughing all the time, but it's just not funny."'[50] In the end the BBC hedged their bets by putting it out at 9 p.m. on BBC 2. 'They really were quite edgy about it,' Wendy confirms.[51]

Carla had her own concerns, too; would the dramatic undertones of the scripts alienate the audience? 'I thought they'd hate Ria for treating her husband like that and hate me for encouraging people to go out and have affairs. In fact, I was terrified when the first episode went out but I was surprised by the reaction.'[52] Very quickly *Butterflies* won huge admiration from public and critics alike. Wendy wasn't at all surprised by its success. 'When I first read it, I thought it was very beautifully written and knew that it was going to be something a bit special.'[53]

The casting was also excellent. Palmer gave a fine, under-stated performance as Ben. A lot of actors might have thought, I'm going to be disliked in this part, so I'd better play it for sympathy. 'Geoffrey didn't compromise in any way,' says Wendy. 'Consequently, because he was so honest people grew to like that character because they could see he was a straight-forward guy.'[54]

The couple's work-shy, womanising teen sons, Russell and Adam, were played by Andrew Hall and a fresh-faced Nicholas Lyndhurst. As Adam, Lyndhurst had a particularly affect-ing relationship with Ria. 'Adam was very sympathetic to his mother,' says Wendy. 'And they did have long chats together where he tried to ease his mother's pain. I thought that aspect was so lovely, that kind of wisdom from a teenage son, who knows more about the world than his mother does, and is able to put her mind at rest.'[55]

Butterflies did contain some traditional sitcom elements amidst the soul searching, notably Ria's appalling culinary skills and her family's reaction to her latest domestic disaster. 'And that was Carla's little joke,' says Wendy, 'because she was absolutely hopeless herself in the kitchen.'[56]

And Carla was always around, during rehearsals and record-ing, which suited Wendy fine because she could always go to her and ask, 'Am I doing this right?' or 'Is there any way I can improve on it?' And while actors were not discouraged from making their own suggestions, Carla knew exactly what she wanted and rarely submitted to any changes to her scripts.

After four series the plug was pulled on *Butterflies*. The last episode went out in October 1983. 'I think the story had been told,' says Carla. 'There was nothing else to say, really.'[57] Wendy too felt enough was enough. 'I was very sad but I understood how it could not really continue in the way it was going. It had to end. There is a time for everything and it was the right time for it to finish.'[58]

True to Carla's instincts as a writer, the story is left unresolved. Ria was a butterfly trapped under glass. Should she stretch her wings and fly away? That question remains unanswered, really. 'I thought that was the best way to do it,' says Carla. 'I didn't want a beginning and an end. I always like to leave things drifting for people to think about. Life doesn't get itself right, it goes on and on trying to.'[59]

In 1979 the format of *Butterflies* was sold to the US and Carla was flown over to Los Angeles to work on the script. It was not an experience she enjoyed:

> I had a good time, they treated me beautifully, and they paid me endless money, but quite honestly I didn't know what was happening to me, it all happened so suddenly.[60]

The American television method of writing sitcom by committee, with a room full of writers working together, just didn't suit Carla at all. A pilot episode was screened by NBC but it failed to graduate to a full series.

In November 2000, the main cast of *Butterflies* reunited for a special episode broadcast for Children in Need. 'It was wonderful to see everyone all together,' Wendy remembers. 'The boys were so grown up, but it just quite naturally fell into place again as if we'd never been apart.'[61]

Chapter Ten

1979

January

Thames Television had bought an idea from the head waiter at the Royal Lancaster Hotel in London. To actually put the show together, they turned to Jimmy Perry, who for the very first time in his career agreed to write something that was not his own idea. It proved to be a big mistake.

For starters, Perry knew next to nothing about the goings on at a hotel, so over the course of two weeks he went to work at the Royal Lancaster as a room service waiter. He picked up plenty of knowledge and out of the experience came *Room Service*, set in a fictitious five-star London hotel and revolving around the 'hilarious' complications and domestic disasters that beset a team of room service waiters.

The department was managed by the formidable Mr Spooner, played by Bryan Pringle, and there's the usual motley bunch among the staff, including a young Matthew Kelly in one of his earliest television appearances and his first sitcom. Matthew had previously done a sitcom pilot called *Sidney, You're a Genius*, by Raymond Allen, co-starring with Maria Aitken and Ronald Lacey. However, it was binned by the BBC. Matthew had also appeared in the West End in a play called *Funny Peculiar* with Richard Beckinsale and Julie Walters. And it was here that he was spotted by Jimmy Perry and cast in *Room Service*. And it was an odd feeling walking on to the set for the first time, 'because it was very like how I remember the kitchen at the Hotel Piccadilly in Manchester where I used to wash dishes in the '60s'.[1]

Originally Derek Newark played the boss Mr Spooner. Newark was often cast as tough guy characters; he memorably played the role of Spooner, an ill-tempered former Red Devil turned professional wrestler, in several episodes of *Rising Damp*. In real-life Newark had a bad boy reputation and was known around the pubs and private drinking dens of Soho as a bit of a boozer. Following the recording of the first episode, the decision was taken not to press ahead with Newark in the role – perhaps the warning signs were there for all to see – and he was paid off for the entire run. He was replaced by Pringle, 'who was a very sweet man,' recalls Matthew.[2]

Matthew found the entire cast great to get on with and there was a nice spirit of camaraderie on the set:

> There was a lovely chap called Freddie Earlle who really took me under his wing. He was very kind to me and very encouraging because I was very frightened because I didn't know anything about telly. I didn't know how it all worked.[3]

Besides the regular cast, each episode saw a special guest arriving at the hotel, the likes of Peter Sallis, Sarah Douglas, who had just come off doing *Superman*, and Frank Williams of *Dad's Army* fame. There was also Janet Webb, an actress best known for gate-crashing the end of *The Morecambe and Wise Show*. The series was directed by Michael Mills, the former BBC Head of Comedy, and it was customary after the recording of each episode to meet in the bar for a few drinks. 'And we were all standing at the bar,' recalls Matthew:

> And Michael Mills was a very small man and Janet was quite tall and had this massive bosom. And Michael suddenly said, 'Do you know I've always wanted to do this,' and he buried his head in Janet Webb's tits and went, 'brrrrrrr'. I was really shocked.[4]

Unfortunately for Matthew, *Room Service* was not taken up for a second series. 'And that was a crushing disappointment. But it was a great start for me and a wonderful learning curve.'[5]

★★★

Thames didn't do much better with their next offering, *Feet First*, from the usually reliable team of Bob Larbey and John Esmonde. It was set among the heady atmosphere of top flight domestic football when young motor mechanic Terry Prince, played by newcomer Jonathan Barlow, is talent spotted playing for his local team and given the chance of a lifetime in the professional First Division. 'The story was about the seduction of a young footballer who was talented but not very bright,' says Bob Larbey:

> and how he and his young wife were manipulated by his club and his agent. We also wanted to say something about the corrupting of the game. We had a scene of the players in

training being taught how to fake an injury convincingly. A little before its time maybe? Just watch any Premiership match now and judge for yourself.[6]

Looking back, Larbey's main memory of the show was all the wise arses saying that a sitcom about sport would never work and then finding out that they were right! 'That's one reason why it only ran one series. The other one was that the scripts were far from the best John and I ever wrote.'[7]

★★★

Next it was the turn of Granada to fall at the first hurdle when their new sitcom *Take My Wife* ended after just six episodes. This was a comedy vehicle for Duggie Brown, a popular cabaret artist who came to prominence earlier in the decade in the comic stand-up show *The Comedians*. Duggie had also done quite a bit of acting and a couple of sitcom guest spots in *For the Love of Ada* and *My Brother's Keeper*.

'I knew the producer John Temple from when we were shooting *The Comedians*,' recalls Duggie, 'and he chatted to me about doing something for Granada and came up with the idea of doing something about the domestic home life of a club comedian.'[8]

Duggie plays struggling northern stand-up comic Harvey Hall, with Victor Spinetti as his agent who can't seem to land him a break. Things aren't too great at home for Harvey either, where his wife can't understand his ambitions and his upper-class mother-in-law is none too impressed either. 'It was so much fun to do,' says Duggie, 'because I also did the warm-ups and so I got to know the audience before falling back into the show and that made it a little easier for the comedy because I had broken the ice.'[9]

In the role of Harvey's much put-upon wife Josie was Elizabeth Sladen, fresh from her adventures with Tom Baker's *Doctor Who*:

> Liz was a dear to work with, always fun but very professional, and always on cue. And Victor Spinetti was one of the most endearing and interesting people I have ever worked with. Gordon Flemyng was a very good director, and had great comic timing, and came up with ideas that enhanced the series. He laughed really loud at my ad-libs, and gave me expert advice.[10]

In one episode the improbably named Bubbles Boutique, played by former nude model Fiona Richmond, causes a bit of a stir in the Hall household. 'Working with Fiona was the first time I had met or worked with a glamour girl,' recalls Duggie. 'But she was good and very shrewd in what she could bring to the show.'[11]

Ratings for the series were pretty good and the cast were hopeful of a second series to follow, but Gordon Flemyng had an offer from the States and then Duggie went off to do a detective series for the BBC called *The Enigma Files*, and nothing more was heard.

February

Yorkshire Television's *How's Your Father* saw the welcome return of Harry Worth to television after a break of five years. In this series, created by the same team behind *You're Only Young Twice*, Worth was cast as a recently widowed middle-ager, Harry Matthews, left with the problems of raising two teenage children, Shirley, a precocious schoolgirl, and Martin, played by future Conservative MP Giles Watling.

This rather thin premise managed to stretch to two series, after which Worth appeared in the short-lived Jeremy Lloyd/ David Croft penned sitcom *Oh Happy Band!* in late 1980. Sadly, by this time Worth was forced by health problems to retire early, although he continued to make the odd radio and television guest appearance until a few months before his death in 1989.

March

Before his untimely death, Arthur Lowe left us with another wonderful sitcom character in Roy Clarke's *Potter*. As the head of a family firm of confectioners, the incorrigible meddler Redvers Potter enjoys his standing as a captain of industry. But when he is forced into retirement, he soon becomes bored stagnating in the leafy suburbs of south London and so keeps himself occupied by interfering in other people's business.

This series had its origins in Roy Clarke's friendship with a married couple, the husband of which used to order his wife around all the time. 'He was a mate of mine, but he never realised what a martinet he was, so I couldn't resist doing something on him and he became this character called Potter. And I was damn lucky to get Arthur Lowe in it.'[12]

Potter is a bombastic man, set in his ways and generally at odds with those he is trying to help. Lowe's wife Joan was once asked which of the characters her husband played over the long course of his career most resembled the real person. She answered by saying that she always used to see signs of Captain Mainwaring, but after watching him in *Potter* that was much more like the real Arthur.

The series co-starred Noel Dyson as Potter's wife Aileen, who has no choice but to put up with his eccentricities, and John Barron as the local vicar. Making a welcome return to sitcom, his first since *Steptoe and Son*, was Harry H. Corbett, who popped up as a comic ex-villain in a few of the later episodes.

When Arthur Lowe died in 1982, the BBC were preparing to go into production on a third, and as it turned out, final series of *Potter*. Instead of cancelling, the lead role was taken over by Robin Bailey, who'd memorably played Uncle Mort in *I Didn't Know You Cared*. Someone else missing was Harry H. Corbett, who'd died just a few weeks prior to Lowe.

Roy Clarke would continue his winning run of sitcoms into the '80s and '90s, especially with the creation of Hyacinth Bucket in *Keeping Up Appearances*. He admits to always feeling a little nervous when a new show of his makes its debut:

Sitting down in front of the telly at the same time millions of people may be watching, that's indecent exposure and I hate it. The only shows of mine I enjoy are repeats because you've had your thrashing or whatever it might be and you can just look at it and perhaps see where things went wrong. And I don't want to be with anybody when I'm watching new stuff either. I agonise quietly alone.[13]

★★★

Humphrey Barclay was relaxing in his office at LWT one morning when the script reader came in with a carrier bag stuffed full of scripts. He pulled one out and told Barclay that he really ought to read it. The story concerned an American mother running a sex shop in Soho. 'It had bite and it was fun and outrageous,' Barclay recalls. 'But, of course, there was no way we could do it.'[14]

Intrigued, Barclay sent for the writer to come and see him anyway and in walked this gangly Californian called Len Richmond and they settled down to talk. 'You know we can never produce this,' Barclay opened with. 'Why did you send it in?'

'Well, I had to write that,' Richmond answered, 'because that's my mother. That's what she does.'

'OK, now get real,' said Barclay. 'What do you want to write that we could use?'[15]

It turned out that Richmond was good friends with Anna Raeburn, the broadcaster and journalist, and they wanted to write a comedy series about an agony aunt. 'You got it,' said Barclay. 'Let's do it.' The result was *Agony*.

For Barclay, this seemed an ideal vehicle for Elaine Stritch, now that *Two's Company* had finished. 'But when the script came in it was clear that it wasn't Elaine and I quickly got the idea that it was Maureen Lipman.'[16] Barclay had seen Maureen perform at the Edinburgh fringe in a play years before, 'and I'd not forgotten her.'[17]

Just the previous year, Lipman had made a bid for sitcom fame in *A Soft Touch*, playing a hard-working young wife saddled with a daydreaming, lazy husband trying to break into showbiz. It lasted just one series and was swiftly forgotten. In *Agony* Maureen plays Jane Lucas, a successful radio call-in host on a local London station and the author of an advice column for a magazine. Ironically, it's her own marriage and personal life that is a complete disaster. Simon Williams played her unreliable psychiatrist husband.

Agony was entertaining, bold and sometimes controversial. 'And because it was about an agony columnist and we were on late you were going to have to talk about sex and all that kind of thing,' says Barclay.[18] There was also the taboo-busting portrayal of a homosexual couple that lived next door to Jane and were just about the only people to offer her genuine warmth and comfort. Far from being the screaming gay caricatures of sitcoms past, this couple are shown as sensitive, intelligent, witty and generally happy with life; it was a notable first for a British sitcom.

The first series of *Agony* met with positive reviews, only for Barclay to receive a bombshell when Richmond announced he was going back to the States:

> This unknown Californian, I'd got him his own series on the air and when it was over he said, 'I'm going back to California now.' And I said, 'We're doing another series. When will you be back?' He said he wasn't coming back. What! It turned out the sex life was better in California than in London. He was that rampant. So, it left me totally high and dry trying to find new writers for a smash hit.[19]

Anna Raeburn, who had given the show some invaluable authenticity, also departed and Barclay brought in two young writers in Stan Hey and Andrew Nickolds. Following two more successful series, Barclay faced more problems, this time from Maureen:

> She said she wouldn't do any more unless LWT stopped f*cking around with the transmission time. We kept being displaced for snooker. And Maureen said, 'If they don't stop that they can whistle for it.' So, we stopped. Despite that, *Agony* is one of the series I'm most proud of.[20]

In 1995 Maureen returned one more time to play Jane Lucas in *Agony Again*, this time on the BBC and with Humphrey Barclay producing. It lasted just the one series.

April

Back in 1977 Robin Hawdon won a leading role in a half-hour play for Thames titled *Spasms*. It was a funny script by Alex Shearer about two disparate husbands waiting nervously in the waiting room of a hospital maternity ward, while their respective wives were giving birth next door. Playing the other husband was an up-and-coming actor by the name of Jonathan Pryce. 'Jonathan and I got on well,' recalls Robin. 'And we had fun making the show. It received very complimentary reviews, but then we went off and thought no more about it.'[21]

A few months later Michael Mills, a producer at Thames, rang Robin with the news that ITV wanted to make a comedy series out of the show. Shearer had been commissioned to write six episodes and they wanted Hawdon and Pryce to repeat their roles. This was great news. But Robin's elation was punctured when Mills phoned him again with the news that Pryce didn't want to do it. He was too busy with the Royal Shakespeare Company. 'However,' said Mills, 'what do you think of the idea of Michael Crawford?' Robin was unconvinced Crawford would do it, given his star status. 'Well,' said Mills, 'since I directed *Some Mothers*, and I know he's looking for something different, I think I might be able to persuade him.'[22]

The premise of *Chalk and Cheese*, as the series was called, was that of two incompatible men, and their wives and new-born babies, who, after the first episode (a repeat of the maternity ward play), find themselves neighbours in a genteel middle-class London street. Robin Hawdon was cast as Roger Scott, a marketing director, while Crawford played the uncouth bearded cockney Dave Finn, who had turned his home into an unkempt slum, in contrast to Scott's pristine domestic abode. It was a character a million miles away from Frank Spencer.

Hawdon had an excellent working relationship with Crawford:

Michael and I got on fine, which was just as well since he could be very intolerant of people he didn't consider up to the job. He was the archetypal actor – obsessed with his current role, extremely egotistical, but at the same time very lively and entertaining when in company.[23]

The early reviews were largely positive, though a few critics were thrown off slightly by Crawford's new television persona. As for the viewing figures, they were far from spectacular. Mills was adamant that the ratings would improve with a second series, which was usually what happened after audiences had grown familiar with the characters. Things looked good.

Then, many months later, when the writer was well into the scripts for the next series, Crawford announced that he did not want to return. He later admitted that part of the reason was the adverse reaction to the character from some of his fans, especially his grandmother who refused to watch the show; indeed, when it came on, she'd turn her back to the television set.

***

Lovely Couple is another of those sitcoms that came and went and then simply vanished from the public's consciousness. Written by Christopher Wood, in between his two screenwriting assignments for James Bond, *The Spy Who Loved Me* (1977) and *Moonraker* (1979), the couple in question are David Mason, a lowly clerk, played by Anthony O'Donnell, and June Dent, played by Elaine Donnelly, whose family live slightly further up the suburban social scale. In order to get parental permission to holiday together, the couple announce their non-existent engagement, only June's mother swiftly latches on to the idea of a wedding and like a dog with a bone won't let it drop.

One series of thirteen episodes was made and there is much ribald humour, not a surprise really given the fact that Christopher Wood, under the pseudonym of Timothy Lea, wrote the popular Confessions series of novels and films.

May

During his time as a lieutenant commander in the Royal Navy, Ian Mackintosh began to dabble as a writer, first as the author of thrillers and then a scriptwriter when he managed to persuade the BBC and the Navy to co-operate for the drama series *Warship* (1973–77). Attracting a weekly audience of 12 million, the success of *Warship* led to an invitation for Mackintosh to work for Yorkshire Television.

Thundercloud was Mackintosh's less than successful attempt at a sitcom. Drawing on his naval background, it depicted the goings on at a small naval base on the Yorkshire coast during the Second World War. Due to an administrative error, the base, curiously named HMS Thundercloud, is classed as a destroyer and continually sent vital equipment, which some of the crew are only too happy to sell off on the black market.

Former film actor John Fraser plays Lieutenant Commander Morgan, who tries his best to keep order, and Sarah Douglas, then best known as the villainous Ursa in the *Superman* films, is the vicar's attractive but naïve daughter Bella who has the hots for the commander.

Tragically, by the end of the series, Mackintosh was involved in an accident flying over the Gulf of Alaska in a light aircraft.

The plane sent out a distress signal, which was picked up by the United States Coast Guard, but after a search no wreckage was ever found, and Mackintosh, along with two colleagues, was never heard of again.

★★★

A few years before landing the big time with *Just Good Friends*, Paul Nicholas starred in the ill-fated *Two Up, Two Down*, which also marked the television debut of Su Pollard, soon to achieve fame as Peggy in *Hi-de-Hi!* Sue had never done any telly before when her agent sent her up for the show:

> I went along for a chat and Paul Nicholas was there. He'd already been cast and they wanted to see if we gelled a bit. We read a few pages of the script and then later my agent called to say I'd got the part. I was extremely lucky.[24]

Paul and Su are Jimmy and Flo, two revolutionary squatters who take over a terraced house in Manchester, much to the annoyance of the nice middle-class newlyweds Stan and Sheila who have just moved in. With the law moving at a snail's pace to evict them, Stan and Sheila have no choice but to co-habit with the two young dropouts and to confront their alternative way of life.

A sitcom about squatters was certainly a novel idea, and a first, but maybe not enough planning or thought had gone into it. 'Jimmy Gilbert, who was Head of Light Entertainment at the BBC, came to see it one day,' recalls Su. 'He said he really liked it but he didn't know whether it was a comedy or a drama.' And therein lay the problem, the show never really managed to find an identity, falling as it did between two stools. Nevertheless, Su enjoyed the experience:

I learnt such a lot. I got talking to the cameramen, I kept saying, 'Can I look through that lens there?' and asking questions, and they were very encouraging. I wanted to get as much experience as quickly as I could so I didn't waste anybody's time. And I was very grateful for that, it was a marvellous grounding. Although people are patient with you if you haven't particularly done a lot, you don't want to be the dunce at the back of the class. You've got to try and take it all in.[25]

Su got on well with the rest of the cast. 'Paul was fabulous. He always used to say, "Have you got my best side, darling?" He was very professional.'[26] Su became especially close to Claire Faulconbridge, who played Sheila, forging a long friendship. Claire had only recently returned from doing television in America as a regular performer on the comedy show *Laugh-in*, which helped launch the career of Robin Williams. 'Claire was extremely helpful and gave me lots of tips. This being my first TV, I was kind of in awe.'[27] The nerves really hit home on the day of that first studio recording:

You like to think that you've gone through it with a fine-tooth comb and that you've rehearsed and rehearsed within an inch of your life. Even so, you've still got that awful fear. Then you have to give yourself a talking to: Su, they've asked you to do the part, they must have faith, don't doubt yourself, get on and do it to the best of your ability.[28]

Two Up, Two Down was filmed at the BBC studios at Pebble Mill in Birmingham, and overseen by Tara Prem, a young television producer who in the 1970s was instrumental in writing and commissioning British multicultural TV drama. Unfortunately, she could do little with *Two Up, Two Down*, which didn't have the satirical edge to satisfy either audiences or critics, and just six episodes were made. 'We were all disappointed we didn't get to make any more,' says Su. 'But I was very grateful to learn what I did on that show. It was real fun and great friendships. They were lovely times.'[29]

July

By 1978 the great writing partnership of Galton and Simpson was no more when Alan Simpson decided to more or less retire from scriptwriting to concentrate on his business interests. He also spent a lot of time driving in his Rolls-Royce around France, exploring restaurants and vineyards.

Ray Galton continued to work and joined forces with that other titan of comedy, Johnny Speight, for *Spooner's Patch*. After his long association with Simpson, it took Ray a little while to get into a new groove with Speight:

Alan and I used to have great long pauses of silence while we were thinking. We always did this. When I started working with Speight, I think on the first day, I hadn't said anything for about five minutes and John was terribly worried and asked what was the matter. I said, 'What about?' He said, 'Well, you haven't said anything.' I said, 'I'm thinking.' He said, 'We haven't got time for that!'[30]

Very much echoing the Will Hay comedies of the past, *Spooner's Patch* takes a wry comic look at the daily life in a small police station in a fictitious London suburb. Ronald Fraser starred as Inspector Spooner, who lives above the station and isn't averse to engaging in various dodgy ventures. His force is not much better, including *Please, Sir!*'s Peter Cleall, who drives around in a Ford Anglia painted in the same red and white colour scheme as Starsky and Hutch's famous Ford Torino.

Fraser left after the first series and was replaced in the role by Donald Churchill. Another newcomer to the cast was Patricia Hayes as a ticket-waving traffic warden.

Produced for ATV, *Spooner's Patch* lasted a commendable three series but couldn't help but feel like a disappointment coming from such esteemed talents as Galton and Speight.

***

Actor Peter Tilbury had always rather fancied having a go at writing, 'although I wasn't desperately committed'.[31] That was until he managed to get Thames Television interested in a potential sitcom about an inept con man. Entitled *Sprout*, it starred John Alderton and a pilot went out in the summer of 1974. It didn't go anywhere, mainly because Peter failed to come up with any subsequent episodes. 'Even so, I was encouraged by the idea that I could do it, even though I couldn't follow up on it.'[32] His next writing project was far more successful, despite the fact it took another five years to reach screens: the creation of James Shelley, a self-confessed layabout and quirky observer of life, which became one of ITV's most popular comedies.

Shelley was based very much on Peter's own experiences:

I was a vague lefty at the time and also out of work a lot and signing on. I really didn't like the signing on part. I just couldn't shake off the business of being supported by people who were working for a living, which is not very lefty. I was very struck by my own confliction about that.[33]

The result was Shelley, a geography graduate who prefers a life on the dole to working a nine-to-five job. He spends much of his time in the pub or the job centre, where he helpfully points out to the staff that, 'It's us hardcore layabouts that are your bread and butter.' He and his girlfriend Frances, played by Belinda Sinclair, live in a tiny north London bedsit, where Shelley's jaded views have little effect on their stern landlady, played by Josephine Tewson.

Another influence on Peter was George Orwell's novel *Keep the Aspidistra Flying*, the central character of which despises the empty commercialism and materialism of middle-class life, takes a stance against it but ultimately doesn't stick to it. 'It was very much in my mind this thing of the woolly liberal who is actually feeling rather unrelaxed about his lifestyle. And it's also true that Shelley can say all those things that I couldn't at the Labour Exchange.'[34]

For Peter, one of the most important things as a writer is to come up with a situation out of which you can get real laughs. 'And Shelley, being a cocky social security scrounger, did seem to work.'[35] The dilemma was, would the public take to this character or be put off by him? 'I suppose it was a challenge I was giving myself,' says Peter, 'could I make him so funny that the public forgave him being this dreadful person?'[36] It also meant they had to find the right actor to play him.

Thanks to Peter's contact at Thames going back to *Sprout*, *Shelley* found a natural home there. 'I may have sent it to the BBC, too, because it did feel like a BBC show. And I wanted to work for the BBC. They were very complimentary about the script but ended up turning it down.'[37] While he was writing it, Peter had in his mind James Bolam, not with the intention of him playing the role, just his speech patterns and the rhythm of his delivery. Peter had been an ardent fan of *Whatever Happened to the Likely Lads?*. 'I thought that was a tremendous show. It was the kind of writing I really liked.'[38]

As it transpired, finding the right actor turned out to be somewhat troublesome, with no suitable candidates. Then one night Peter was watching the BBC serial *Pennies from Heaven* and saw Hywel Bennett playing a rather unpleasant character and something clicked. He suggested him to the producer. 'We had, I think, reached the stage where if we didn't come up with someone it was going to stall.'[39]

Shelley was something of a slow-burner to start with, not helped by the first series being among the many casualties of a technician's strike that blanked out ITV in the late summer of 1979. But audiences soon warmed to his sardonic wit and anti-establishment attitude, and it was a role that Bennett became most identified with. 'I was very worried about him at the beginning,' admits Peter. 'I wasn't confident that he was getting it right. But he was getting it right in spades.'[40] Coming as he did largely from a film background, and making his first sitcom, Bennett was new to the way these things were put together. 'I think he was a little bit shaken on that very first show by the audience being there,' says Peter. 'He used to say that he was playing to the millions through the camera lens. Then I think he found the right balance.'[41]

In series two and three, while Shelley remained his same sardonic self, his partner Frances became pregnant, they got married and she gave birth to a baby girl. It seemed like a good natural end to the story, certainly as far as Peter was concerned. 'Inspiration-wise, I was dried up. Television wants a variation on a theme once a week and that isn't naturally how I am as a writer, so once I'd done something like twenty-one episodes, I knew I wanted to finish with it.'[42]

The public, however, were in no mood to do without *Shelley* and Peter was happy for Thames to make new episodes and for other writers to be brought in. 'It was a surprise to me that they wanted to carry on with it.'[43] Neither did Peter keep a watching brief. 'I thought the last thing they want is me hanging around the fringes. I stayed completely out of it.'[44] There was a rough sort of outline developed with Peter's input to which they kept, including the plot development that Shelley and Frances eventually divorce, which indeed they do. By the sixth and final series in 1984 Frances has plainly had enough and kicks Shelley out of her life unless he can prove he is capable of being a proper husband and father, although we know he's never really going to change.

Thanks to a string of repeats proving popular with audiences, Thames decided to revive the show in 1988. Peter was delighted to see it back but wasn't interested in being involved any more. Again, *Shelley* was a hit and the new series continued into the early '90s. Back from the Middle East, where he's been teaching English, Shelley finds that things have changed in Britain, with Thatcher's yuppie era in full flow. Now approaching middle age, his views on life haven't changed. At one point he lodges with a pensioner whose home is scheduled for demolition. True to his anti-establishment sensibilities, Shelley is only too happy to join the fight against the developers.

Not surprisingly, given the longevity of the show, plenty of guest stars and familiar faces pop up in episodes, including Warren Clarke, Leslie Ash, Fulton Mackay, Max Wall and, in one of his first television appearances Alan Rickman.

One of the longest running of all British sitcoms, Peter puts the success of *Shelley* down to the British public's love for a certain kind of character. Bennett used to say that taxi drivers said to him, 'You do come out with them.' It's the wise cracker, the cheeky chappie, characters that have been stalwarts of British comedy going all the way back to the music halls.

***

People have always been fascinated about what goes on behind the chintz curtains of suburbia and it was Leslie Thomas, the renowned author of *The Virgin Soldiers*, who sated that curiosity with his book *Tropic of Ruislip*. Published in 1974, the story was set in a fictional middle-class housing estate outside of London that was full of frustrated housewives, gossips and unfaithful husbands. Thomas lived on a similar estate in Hertfordshire and said it was all based on true events, if slightly embellished.

The book courted some mild controversy with its take on the British class divide and themes such as wife swapping. In Ruislip inhabitants took particular offence and a public meeting was called in the local library. Thomas recalled attending this meeting and facing an angry crowd. At one point a woman leapt to her feet and shouted: 'This book has blackened Ruislip in the eyes of the world!'[45] A statement that Thomas never quite forgot for the rest of his life.

Thomas had never attempted a sitcom before but that didn't stop ATV asking him to adapt his book to the small screen. With the shortened title of *Tropic*, the series didn't elicit the same kind of protests but was still considered quite saucy for its time. Starring Ronald Pickup and Ronald Lacey, the series was interrupted by the long ITV strike and never managed to make an impression. Only six episodes were made.

September

Had Richard Beckinsale lived there is no question that he would have risen to greater heights of fame as an actor in the 1980s. Sadly this was not to be, and *Bloomers* represents his final television work.

Beckinsale plays Stan, an out of work actor who in a bid to make extra money takes a part-time job in a local florist. It's a job that also gives him a bit of solace away from his complex and neurotic girlfriend Lena (Anna Calder-Marshall) and their messy, cramped flat and domestic life.

Written by playwright James Saunders, the idea came about from his frequent visits to a local garden centre and chats with the man who owned it, a certain John Challis. Back in the late '70s, Challis was a down-on-his-luck actor. Looking for a steady stream of income, he went into business with a friend, opening a small garden centre. Challis often related some of the amusing incidents that happened with his customers and Saunders thought it might make for a good comedy series. Writing a script, probably with Challis in mind for the lead role, Saunders sent it to John Howard Davies at the BBC, where it was viewed as a perfect vehicle for Richard Beckinsale. Challis was not left out completely, getting a small role in one of the episodes. He would, of course, later rise to fame as Boycie in *Only Fools and Horses*.

Five episodes of *Bloomers* had already been recorded when Beckinsale died suddenly from a heart attack in March 1979, just before a planned rehearsal for the sixth and final episode. He was only 31 and had no knowledge of the heart condition that would eventually kill him. *Bloomers* was shelved immediately, though Beckinsale's widow, Judy Loe, gave her approval for the five completed episodes to be broadcast as a tribute.

★★★

Along with the likes of Douglas Adams, David Renwick and John Lloyd, Peter Spence worked for BBC radio, supplying sketches and spending his time writing pilots, 'all supposed to be very ground-breaking and wacky'.[46] To which, of course, the BBC establishment turned their noses up. 'So,' recalls Peter, 'fed up with being turned down John Lloyd and myself thought, let's do something totally traditional that actually obeys all the rules, is wholesome and doesn't try to break ground, is very old fashioned and very BBC.'[47]

Peter already had a gem of an idea that might fit. His main character was lady of the manor Audrey fforbes-Hamilton, who is forced to sell her beloved home when her husband's death leaves her financially strapped. Decamping to a small lodge on the estate, with a butler in tow, she is dismayed when a brash American tycoon takes over the family seat. It was called *To the Manor Born*.

This time the idea was accepted and a radio pilot was made featuring Penelope Keith as Audrey fforbes-Hamilton: 'I wrote it very much with her in mind,' says Peter.[48] In the role of the American, actor and comedian Bernard Braden was cast. Before the pilot was broadcast, Penelope sent it to John Howard Davies, feeling that it might make a good piece of television. At the time the BBC were looking for a vehicle for Penelope to do after the success of *The Good Life*, so Davies listened to the pilot and liked it. The upshot of all this was that Davies hijacked the project from the radio and asked Peter to write it as a television series. This came as a bit of shock. There was an added complication, too, since Peter had just started writing sketches for a proposed new comedy show called *Not the Nine O'Clock News*. 'The BBC took me aside and said, "Look, you're falling behind, we want these *Manor Born* scripts."'[49] So, Peter had to choose, and *Not the Nine O'Clock News* went on without him.

Adapting the show to television, Peter came to the conclusion that the American tycoon idea was a bit obvious. Instead, the estate's new owner would be the nouveau riche Richard DeVere, a wholesale food magnate of Czech descent. The character was a composite of Robert Maxwell, himself Czech born, and Jimmy Goldsmith, who was born in France, both businessmen who morphed into the perfect English gentleman by design. Peter Bowles was expertly cast in the role.

It was obvious to Peter Spence that one had to hint at the possibility that there might be an underlying romance between Audrey and DeVere, but he didn't want it to take centre stage. He knew that if they ever got together as a couple it could spell the end for the series. To this end, pretty much every episode was constructed in the same way:

> The relationship would be going along very nicely until one of them, usually DeVere, did something that seemed unconscionable as far as Audrey was concerned. There'd be arguments, it would resolve, there was a truce, they'd start getting back on together and then suddenly they'd do something else and it all flared up again.[50]

When producer Gareth Gwenlan was looking for a suitable manor house to use, it was Peter who suggested his father-in-law's home in Somerset. Peter had lived on the estate for a while soon after getting married. The experience also proved useful when it came to writing *To the Manor Born*: he had a unique insider's knowledge of the lives of the gentry and the almost feudal way these estates still worked. 'I thought this lifestyle must be out of date by now, but no, it was still going on exactly the same, untouched.'[51] It was, however, beginning to come under threat, as many of these old manor houses were being bought up by entrepreneurs and turned into hotels and health spas. This is something the series touched upon, and what Audrey was all about, upholding tradition and trying desperately not to change.

Peter had written the show with a largely middle-class audience in mind. 'But by the third or fourth episode it had really caught on and we were getting huge figures, which indicated to me that it was being watched by all sorts of minorities and people who it was never really intended to appeal to.'[52] It helped that ITV was in the middle of a protracted strike, so the BBC had the field to itself. But even when ITV returned, audiences stayed loyal to the show and the final episode of series one was watched by an astonishing 23.95 million, the fourth-highest figure for any programme in the UK in the 1970s, and the highest for a non-live event. It was only beaten by coverage of the Apollo 13 splashdown, the FA Cup Final replay between Chelsea and Leeds United and Princess Anne's wedding. It's interesting to note that out of the twenty highest-rated programmes of the 1970s, six of them are sitcoms.

After handing in the scripts Peter didn't have much to do with production after that, save for attending the first cast read through. 'The light entertainment department really was a treadmill back then, a constantly moving production line of shows made under extraordinarily tight schedules and tight budgets.'[53] He found there wasn't much room for levity. Writing something in one of the scripts that was intended as an in-joke, he received a swift rebuke: 'For goodness sake, this is the Light Entertainment department of the BBC, we haven't got time for jokes!'[54]

As the series continued, still attracting huge ratings, Peter was put under pressure to place more emphasis upon the romantic element. But he continued to resist, preferring the antagonism between the two leads as opposed to the romance. 'I could do war very well; I didn't have any difficulty with that. I found peace, particularly lovey-dovey romance, quite hard going. You can't make getting on funny.'[55]

Finally, in the last episode of series three, Audrey and DeVere are married, and she is reinstated as the lady of the manor. The powers that be decided that this neatly concluded the show, although Peter feels that it could have gone on longer. 'Just because you're married it doesn't mean to say the tension's off. It's a different kind of spark.'[56]

Briefly there was going to be a feature film. An official from the Rank organisation announced such a plan at the Cannes Film Festival and Peter was asked to come up with a treatment. In the end nothing more was done.

Then, twenty-five years later in 2007, Peter was asked by the BBC to write a one-off special for Christmas. Worried that it wouldn't work, it was obvious at the first read through that the old fizz was back.

October

Despite running since 1974 and six series, *Happy Ever After*, with Terry Scott and June Whitfield, was still drawing in healthy ratings. However, writers John Chapman and Eric Merriman felt like they were on a treadmill. Chapman was the first to leave, and Merriman had to finish the last few episodes with a new writer, which didn't work out very well. Another writer, John Kane, was brought in but things did not improve. Kane was glad to be working with Scott again after their earlier sitcom *Son of the Bride*, but recalls an almighty bust-up that resulted in Merriman leaving and refusing to allow the BBC to continue with the show or use his and Chapman's characters.

Meanwhile, the BBC were in no mood to lose a hit formula and John Howard Davies instructed Kane to take over the series. *Terry and June* was born. Ostensibly it was the same show as *Happy Ever After*, involving the same lead actors, playing the same characters in a very similar suburban location; all John did was change their surname from Fletcher to Medford and move them to Purley. Dotty Aunt Lucy and her mynah bird, being a Chapman/Merriman creation, was the only casualty, much to the delight of Scott, who hated the creature.

For inspiration, John went back to his childhood. 'At home growing up, family life could be very fraught, so as a child I loved to watch shows about families getting into a mess and then going on happily ever after.' Most of these shows seemed to be American imports of the mid-'50s: *Burns and Allen*, *I Married Joan* and *I Love Lucy*, and then in the early '60s there was the *Dick Van Dyke Show*:

> Despite all the ups and downs you could tune in next week and they would still be getting into scrapes but still loving each other. That's what I wanted to do with *Terry and June* and I think I succeeded because I know a lot of children watched it, possibly children like myself who had a turbulent family life.[57]

As comfortable and as non-threatening as your favourite slippers, *Terry and June* was a fixture of the BBC's early evening schedules for eight years. They remained the archetypal suburban sitcom married couple, their characters having changed not a jot from *Happy Ever After*, with Terry still very much an excitable, delusional, overgrown schoolboy indulging in schemes that threaten to end in disaster, while the vastly more practical June has to quietly and calmly put things right.

John wrote the bulk of the episodes, forty-one in total. 'It was always difficult to come up with ideas,' he says. 'A lot of them were based on things that I had done. For example, I'd ordered a ping pong table and assumed it was going to arrive ready-made but no, you had to assemble it yourself and I found that so difficult and I thought, there's a *Terry and June*.'[58] Another story was based on something that happened to Terry Scott. He'd been to a fun fair with his daughters and won a goldfish. After buying a bowl for it he thought, poor thing, he can't swim around that little bowl, and so he bought a big tank. Now the goldfish looked lonely swimming round this big empty tank, and so he went out and bought some tropical fish. Next Terry thought, that goldfish really lets the rest of those tropical fish down, and so he took the goldfish out and gave it away to one of his daughter's friends. That ended up as a *Terry and June* episode. 'Very often I would go down to W.H. Smith,' says John, 'and I would look at the hobby magazines and think, what would Terry get involved with now?'[59]

John enjoyed working again with Scott:

He was a total professional. He understood the business and understood what he could do and did it very well. And he was an absolute perfectionist. You had to learn your script by the third day if you were doing a sitcom with him. If you couldn't remember the lines you were in big trouble. Terry would have no compunction about saying, 'I can't work with this person, let them go.'[60]

John liked Terry enormously and always valued his friendship and that he remained loyal and supported him, but he does recall one dreadful incident that involved the veteran actress Doris Hare, famous as Mum from *On the Buses*:

She had one scene in this particular episode and she couldn't remember her lines and Terry said, 'She's got to go.' So, she was sacked. And I thought, oh Terry, it's just one scene, what a terrible end to a career, can't you just jolly her along? After all, studio audiences love it when you go wrong and have to go again. But no, he could not stomach it, she had to go. And that was the cruellest thing he ever did.[61]

It was his partnership with June Whitfield, however, that ensured the show's success and longevity. 'It was very popular,' says John. 'They were a much-loved couple. A lot of children loved *Terry and June*, too, because, of course, Terry was a grown-up child and they could associate with that. He had the same passions and the same crazy enthusiasms that kids had.'[62]

Terry and June was also totally out of step with the edgy alternative comedy that had sprouted up in the UK by the early '80s. This new 'alternative' generation of comedians derided the show for its complacent gentility and bourgeois sensibilities. 'It was decried by almost everybody,' recalls John Howard Davies, 'especially the chattering classes. They looked down their nose at it.'[63]

Terry and June themselves were too sensible and long in the business to worry about alternative comedy. They had seen comics and shows come and go and they knew fashions changed. Ironically, Whitfield would later be adopted by one of those very same 'alternative' comedians, Jennifer Saunders, for her '90s hit sitcom *Absolutely Fabulous*.

John knew that they were looked on as old fashioned and scorned in many quarters:

And to my shame, I wasn't ever particularly proud of the show. But that changed somewhat when my mother-in-law told me about a fellow parishioner in Dorking who happened to mention that on the first anniversary of his wife's death that year he had been depressed and had spent the day alone. But in the evening, he told my mother-in-law, he had sat down and watched *Terry and June* and for the first time that day, he had laughed and for that little half hour had forgotten his sadness. That made me feel a lot better about the show.[64]

Unfortunately, the 'spectre' of *Terry and June* didn't help John when he started trying to interest TV companies in other comedy ideas. It just so happened that in 1988 three shows that he had been involved with, *Terry and June*, *Me and My Girl* and *All in Good Faith*, came to an end:

So, I started going round the studios touting my ideas for new series. But my association with *Terry and June* was a huge problem because it represented everything that the companies were no longer interested in. They took my meetings but never took up any of my ideas. It came to a head when one producer that I had worked with on various shows listened respectfully as I pitched my ideas but then said, 'Very nice John, but you see, the age of flock wallpaper shows is over.' And it certainly was for me as I never wrote another comedy show again.[65]

***

Comedies set in hospitals have always worked with audiences, look no further than the Carry On and Doctor film series. *Only When I Laugh* carried on that tradition. Eric Chappell, fresh from his success with *Rising Damp*, came up with the idea after making several hospital visits. 'Also, a confined space is very useful in writing comedy for the interaction of a few characters.'[66]

The series revolved around three patients from very different backgrounds, all congenital hypochondriacs, stuck in a ward together in an NHS hospital. James Bolam, in his first comedy since *Whatever Happened to the Likely Lads?*, plays Roy Figgis, a straight-talking lorry driver, Peter Bowles is the upper-class snob Archie Glover and Christopher Strauli plays the hapless middle-class mummy's boy Norman Binns. When they're not trying to outsmart each other, they are causing grief to the head surgeon Dr Thorpe, played by Richard Wilson in a breakthrough comedy role, and the easily flustered orderly Gupte (Derrick Branche).

For Strauli, this was his first experience of sitcom and it was one of his most nerve wracking. The cast always rehearsed in London during the week before travelling up to Leeds on the train to spend all of Friday in the studio rehearsing and then the recording in the evening. 'We recorded every episode in front of a live audience of 400 people,' Christopher recalls:

> That meant that you would get an immediate reaction just like in the theatre, but you also had to make it look right and work for the 19 million people who would be seeing it in a few days' time. Plus, we only had two hours to record the whole programme and so sometimes with lighting and camera problems, and us forgetting our lines or just messing things up, it sometimes got very close to the wire.[67]

Only When I Laugh was a big hit for Yorkshire Television, thanks to an excellent ensemble cast and sparkling scripts. 'The characters were so well defined and conceived by Eric that you could have put them anywhere and they'd have been entertaining,' says Christopher. 'And it was always genuinely "Family" entertainment with nothing smutty or unpleasant ever.'[68]

By the fourth series Chappell decided he'd pretty much exhausted most possibilities. After all, how long can three patients realistically stay in hospital. 'We went in in the spring with "the daffodils tossing their heads in sprightly dance" and were still there at Christmas!' says Christopher. 'I think we all thought it was best to leave while it was still immensely popular. I think we literally topped the ratings every season for four years – quite an accolade!'[69]

Notes

Chapter One: 1970

1   Ray Galton: Author interview, 2007.
2   Alan Simpson: Author interview, 2007.
3   Galton and Simpson: Author interview, 2007.
4   Ray Galton: Author interview, 2007.
5   Alan Simpson: Author interview, 2007.
6   Ray Galton: Author interview, 2007.
7   Ibid.
8   Alan Simpson: Author interview, 2007.
9   Ray Galton: Author interview, 2007.
10 Alan Simpson: Author interview, 2007.
11 Ibid.
12 Ray Galton: Author interview, 2007.
13 Alan Simpson: Author interview, 2007.
14 Ibid.
15 Ibid.
16 Ray Galton: Author interview, 2007.
17 Alan Simpson: Author interview, 2007.
18 Ibid.
19 Ibid.
20 Ray Galton: Author interview, 2007.
21 Alan Simpson: Author interview, 2007.
22 Ray Galton: Author interview, 2007.
23 Alan Simpson: Author interview, 2007.
24 Ibid.
25 Ray Galton: Author interview, 2007.
26 Alan Simpson: Author interview, 2007.

27 Ibid.

28 Ibid.

29 Ibid.

30 Ibid.

31 Ray Galton: Author interview, 2007.

32 Alan Simpson: Author interview, 2007.

33 Ray Galton: Author interview, 2007.

34 Alan Simpson: Author interview, 2007.

35 *The Guardian*, March 1971.

36 *Reputations*, BBC documentary, 2002.

37 Ibid.

38 Nathan, D., *The Laughtermakers* (Peter Owen Publishers, 1971).

39 Croft, D., *You Have Been Watching* (BBC Books, 2004).

40 David Nobbs: Author interview, 2007.

41 Ibid.

42 Ibid.

43 Ibid.

44 Ibid.

45 Ray Cooney: Author interview, 2007.

46 Powell, V., *From Rags to Gags: The Memoirs of a Comedy Writer* (Apex Publishing Ltd, 2008).

47 Brian Cooke: Author interview, 2007.

48 Ibid.

49 Ibid.

50 Ibid.

51 Ibid.

52 Ibid.

53 Ibid.

54 Ibid.

55 William G. Stewart: Author interview, 2007.

56 Brian Cooke: Author interview, 2007.

57 Ibid.

58 William G. Stewart: Author interview, 2007.

59 Ibid.

60 Brian Cooke: Author interview, 2007.

61 Ibid.

62 Mike Sharland: Author interview, 2020.

63 Ibid.

64 David Kelly: Author interview, 2007.

65 Ibid.

66 David Mallet: Author interview, 2007.

67 Ibid.

68 Mike Sharland: Author interview, 2020.

69 David Mallet: Author interview, 2007.

70 Troy Kennedy Martin: Author interview, 2008.

71 Ibid.

72 Troy Kennedy Martin: Author interview, 2008.

73 Ibid.

74 Ibid.

75 Ibid.

76 Carmichael, I., *Will the Real Ian Carmichael* (Macmillan, 1979) (quotes used by kind permission of the author).

77 Ibid.

78 Ibid.

79 Ibid.

80 David Mallet: Author interview, 2007.

81 Ibid.

82 Perry, J., *A Stupid Boy* (Century, 2002).

83 John Howard Davies: Author interview, 2007.

84 Harold Snoad: Author interview, 2013.

85 Webber, R., *The Complete A–Z of Dad's Army* (Orion Books, 2000).

86 Harold Snoad: Author interview, 2013.

87 Ibid.

88 Ibid.

89 Ibid.

90 Bob Larbey: Author interview, 2008.

91 David Barry: Author interview, 2007.

92 Ibid.

93 Bob Larbey: Author interview, 2008.

94 David Barry: Author interview, 2007.

95 Ibid.

96 Ibid.

97 Bob Larbey: Author interview, 2008.

98 David Barry: Author interview, 2007.

99 Ibid.

100 Ibid.

101 Ibid.

102 Rosenthal, J., *An Autobiography in Six Acts* (Robson Books, 2005).

103 Ibid.

104 Tony Caunter: Author interview, 2007.

105 Ibid.

106 Ibid.

107 Ibid.

108 Ibid.

Chapter Two: 1971

1 Carla Lane: Author interview, 2013.

2 Ibid.

3 Ibid.

4 Ibid.

5 Ibid.

6 Ibid.

7 Nerys Hughes: Author interview, 2020.

8 Ibid.

9 Ibid.

10 Carla Lane: Author interview, 2013.

11 Nerys Hughes: Author interview, 2020.

12 Carla Lane: Author interview, 2013.

13 Ibid.

14 Nerys Hughes: Author interview, 2020.

15 Carla Lane: Author interview, 2013.

16 Nerys Hughes: Author interview, 2020.

17 Carla Lane: Author interview, 2013.

18 Peter Lewis: Author interview, 2013.

19 Ibid.

20 Ibid.

21 Ibid.

22 Ibid.

23 Ibid.

24 Ibid.

25 Ibid.

26 Ibid.

27 William G. Stewart: Author interview, 2007.

28 Ibid.

29 Ibid.

30 Ibid.

31 Ibid.

32 Ibid.

33 Carla Lane: Author interview, 2013.

34 Brian Cooke: Author interview, 2007.

35 William G. Stewart: Author interview, 2007.

36 Ibid.

37 Humphrey Barclay: Author interview, 2013.

38 Ibid.

39 Ibid.

40 Ibid.

41 Ibid.

42 Ibid.

43 Ibid.

44 Ibid.

45 Ibid.

46 Ibid.

47 Ibid.

48 Ibid.

49 Wendy Craig: Author interview, 2008.

50 Ibid.

51 Ibid.

52 Ibid.

53 Ibid.

54 Ibid.

55 Ibid.

56 Ibid.

57 Brian Cooke: Author interview, 2007.

58 Ibid.

59 Ibid.

60 Ibid.

61 Finch, J., *Granada Television: The First Generation* (Manchester University Press, 2003).

62 Richard Briers: Author interview, 2007.

63 Ibid.

64 *Glasgow Evening News*, 9 August 1971.

65 Hunter, I.Q. and Porter, L., *British Comedy Cinema* (Routledge, 2012).

66 David Nobbs: Author interview, 2007.

67 Ibid.

68 Ibid.

69 Con Cluskey: Author interview, 2007.

70 Dec Cluskey: Author interview, 2007.

71 Ibid.

72 Con Cluskey: Author interview, 2007.

73 Dec Cluskey: Author interview, 2007.

74 Dec Cluskey: Author interview, 2007.

75 Ibid.

76 Con Cluskey: Author interview, 2007.

77 David Barry: Author interview, 2007.

78 Ibid.

79 Ibid.

80 Ibid.

81 Ibid.

82 Ibid.

83 Perry, J., *A Stupid Boy* (Century, 2002).

84 Ibid.
85 Jilly Cooper: Author interview, 2021.
86 Ibid.
87 Ibid.
88 Ibid.
89 Ibid.
90 Ibid.
91 Ibid.
92 Ibid.
93 Ibid.
94 Ibid.
95 Ibid.

Chapter Three: 1972

1 William G. Stewart: Author interview, 2007.
2 Ibid.
3 David Kelly: Author interview, 2007.
4 Powell, V., *From Rags to Gags: The Memoirs of a Comedy Writer* (Apex Publishing Ltd, 2008).
5 Ibid.
6 William G. Stewart: Author interview, 2007.
7 *The Guardian*, 21 October 2001.
8 Ibid.
9 William G. Stewart: Author interview, 2007.
10 Brian Cooke: Author interview, 2007.
11 Ibid.
12 Ibid.
13 Ibid.
14 Harold Snoad: Author interview, 2013.
15 Croft, D., *You Have Been Watching* (BBC Books, 2004).
16 *The Age*, 1 January 1973.

17 Richard Stilgoe: Author interview, 2008.
18 Ibid.
19 Ibid.
20 Ibid.
21 Ibid.
22 Eric Sykes: Author interview, 2008.
23 William G. Stewart: Author interview, 2007.
24 Eric Sykes: Author interview, 2008.
25 Ibid.
26 Ibid.
27 Ibid.
28 Ibid.
29 Ibid.
30 Ibid.
31 Ibid.
32 Ibid.
33 Ibid.
34 Ibid.
35 Ibid.
36 Ibid.
37 Ibid.
38 Ibid.
39 BECTU History Project: Johnny Speight interview, 1990.
40 Ibid.
41 William G. Stewart: Author interview, 2007.
42 Ibid.
43 Brian Clemens: Author interview, 2007.
44 Ibid.
45 Ibid.
46 Ibid.
47 Ibid.
48 Ibid.
49 Ibid.

50 Mike Sharland: Author interview, 2020.
51 Ibid.
52 Ibid.

Chapter Four: 1973

1 Dick Clement: Author interview, 2021.
2 Ian La Frenais: Author interview, 2021.
3 Dick Clement: Author interview, 2021.
4 Ibid.
5 Ibid.
6 Ian La Frenais: Author interview, 2021.
7 Dick Clement: Author interview, 2021.
8 Ian La Frenais: Author interview, 2021.
9 Dick Clement: Author interview, 2021.
10 Ibid.
11 Ian La Frenais: Author interview, 2021.
12 Ibid.
13 Ibid.
14 John Howard Davies: Author interview, 2007.
15 David Nobbs: Author interview, 2007.
16 Ibid.
17 Ibid.
18 Brian Cooke: Author interview, 2007.
19 Raymond Allen: Author interview, 2020.
20 Ibid.
21 Ibid.
22 Ibid.
23 Ibid.
24 Ibid.
25 Ibid.
26 Ibid.
27 Ibid.
28 Ibid.
29 Ibid.
30 Ibid.
31 Ibid.
32 Tony Caunter: Author interview, 2007.
33 Ibid.
34 Ibid.
35 Ibid.
36 Trevor Bannister: Author interview, 2007.
37 Ibid.
38 Ibid.
39 Croft, D., *You Have Been Watching* (BBC Books, 2004).
40 Trevor Bannister: Author interview, 2007.
41 Harold Snoad: Author interview, 2013.
42 Ibid.
43 Trevor Bannister: Author interview, 2007.
44 Ibid.
45 Ibid.
46 Ibid.
47 Ibid.
48 Croft, D., *You Have Been Watching* (BBC Books, 2004).
49 Trevor Bannister: Author interview, 2007.
50 Ibid.
51 Ibid.
52 Ibid.
53 Ibid.
54 David Nobbs: Author interview, 2007.

55 John Kane: Author interview, 2021.

56 Ibid.

57 Ibid.

58 Ibid.

59 Ibid.

60 Dacre, R., *Trouble in Store: Norman Wisdom, A Career in Comedy* (T.C. Farries and Co. Ltd, 1991).

61 Bob Larbey: Author interview, 2008.

62 Ibid.

63 Ibid.

64 Melvyn Hayes: Author interview, 2020.

65 David Nobbs: Author interview, 2007.

66 Melvyn Hayes: Author interview, 2020.

67 David Nobbs: Author interview, 2007.

68 Brian Cooke: Author interview, 2007.

69 Ibid.

70 Ibid.

71 Ibid.

72 Ibid.

73 Brian Murphy: Author interview, 2007.

74 Brian Cooke: Author interview, 2007.

75 Brian Murphy: Author interview, 2007.

76 Ibid.

77 Ibid.

78 Brian Cooke: Author interview, 2007.

79 Ibid.

80 Ibid.

81 Ibid.

82 Ibid.

83 Ibid.

84 David Kelly: Author interview, 2007.

85 Ibid.

86 Phillips, L., *Hello* (Orion Books, 2007).

87 Ray Galton: Author interview, 2007.

88 Ibid.

89 Phillips, L., *Hello* (Orion Books, 2007).

90 Alan Simpson: Author interview, 2007.

91 Jeff Rawle: Author interview, 2020.

92 Ibid.

93 Humphrey Barclay: Author interview, 2013.

94 Jeff Rawle: Author interview, 2020.

95 Ibid.

96 Ibid.

97 Ibid.

98 Ibid.

99 Ibid.

100 Roy Clarke: Author interview, 2007.

101 Ibid.

102 Peter Sallis: Author interview, 2007.

103 Ibid.

104 Ibid.

105 Roy Clarke: Author interview, 2007.

106 Ibid.

107 Peter Sallis: Author interview, 2007.

108 Ibid.

109 Roy Clarke: Author interview, 2007.

110 Peter Sallis: Author
     interview, 2007.

Chapter Five: 1974

1   Melvyn Hayes: Author
    interview, 2020.
2   Ibid.
3   Ibid.
4   Ibid.
5   Ibid.
6   Ibid.
7   Ibid.
8   Perry, J., *A Stupid Boy*
    (Century, 2002).
9   Melvyn Hayes: Author
    interview, 2020.
10 Croft, D., *You Have Been
    Watching* (BBC Books, 2004).
11 William G. Stewart: Author
    interview, 2007.
12 Ibid.
13 Ibid.
14 Corbett, R., *High Hopes:
    My Autobiography*
    (Ebury, 2000).
15 David Warwick: Author
    interview, 2020.
16 Ibid.
17 Ibid.
18 Ibid.
19 Ibid.
20 Ibid.
21 Ibid.
22 John Kane: Author
    interview, 2021.
23 Ibid.
24 Ibid.
25 Ibid.
26 Ibid.
27 Ibid.
28 Priscilla Dunn: Author
    interview, 2021.
29 Ibid.
30 Ibid.
31 Wendy Craig: Author interview,
    2008.
32 Ibid.
33 Ibid.
34 Ibid.
35 Ibid.
36 Dick Clement: Author
    interview, 2021.
37 Ian La Frenais: Author
    interview, 2021.
38 Dick Clement: Author
    interview, 2021.
39 Ian La Frenais: Author
    interview, 2021.
40 Dick Clement: Author
    interview, 2021.
41 *The Guardian*, 11 December 2011.
42 Ibid.
43 Ian La Frenais: Author
    interview, 2021.
44 Ibid.
45 Ibid.
46 Ibid.
47 Dick Clement: Author
    interview, 2021.
48 Ibid.
49 Ibid.
50 Ian La Frenais: Author
    interview, 2021.
51 Ibid.
52 Ibid.
53 Dick Clement: Author
    interview, 2021.
54 Patricia Brake: Author
    interview, 2020.
55 Ibid.
56 Ibid.

57 Ian La Frenais: Author interview, 2021.
58 Ibid.
59 Ibid.
60 Ibid.
61 Dick Clement: Author interview, 2021.
62 Ian La Frenais: Author interview, 2021.
63 Ibid.
64 Dick Clement: Author interview, 2021.
65 Ibid.
66 Ian La Frenais: Author interview, 2021.
67 Humphrey Barclay: Author interview, 2013.
68 Ibid.
69 Ibid.
70 Ibid.
71 Ibid.
72 Ibid.
73 Patricia Brake: Author interview, 2020.
74 Ibid.
75 Ibid.
76 Ibid.
77 Humphrey Barclay: Author interview, 2013.
78 Ibid.
79 Ibid.
80 Ibid.
81 Ibid.
82 Ibid.
83 Brian Cooke: Author interview, 2007.

Chapter Six: 1975

1 *The Age*, 4 June 1976.
2 Bob Larbey: Author interview, 2008.
3 Richard Briers: Author interview, 2007.
4 Ibid.
5 Ibid.
6 Ibid.
7 Ibid.
8 John Howard Davies: Author interview, 2007.
9 Richard Briers: Author interview, 2007.
10 Bob Larbey: Author interview, 2008.
11 Richard Briers: Author interview, 2007.
12 Ibid.
13 Ibid.
14 Ibid.
15 Ibid.
16 Ibid.
17 Ibid.
18 Ibid.
19 Bob Larbey: Author interview, 2008.
20 Richard Briers: Author interview, 2007.
21 *Yorkshire Post*, 28 February 2017.
22 Harold Snoad: Author interview, 2013.
23 Eric Chappell: Author interview, 2020.
24 *Evening Times*, 27 August 1975.
25 *The Guardian*, 12 October 2013.
26 John Howard Davies: Author interview, 2007.
27 Humphrey Barclay: Author interview, 2013.
28 John Howard Davies: Author interview, 2007.
29 Ibid.
30 Ibid.
31 Ibid.

32 David Kelly: Author interview, 2007.

33 Ibid.

34 Ibid.

35 Harold Snoad: Author interview, 2013.

36 Ibid.

37 David Kelly: Author interview, 2007.

38 Humphrey Barclay: Author interview, 2013.

39 Ibid.

40 Ibid.

41 Ibid.

42 Ibid.

43 Ibid.

44 Roy Clarke: Author interview, 2007.

45 Ibid.

46 Ibid.

47 John Howard Davies: Author interview, 2007.

48 Ibid.

49 Roy Clarke: Author interview, 2007.

50 Bob Larbey: Author interview, 2008.

51 Tony Selby: Author interview, 2007.

52 Ibid.

53 Ibid.

54 Ibid.

55 Ibid.

56 William G. Stewart: Author interview, 2007.

57 David Roper: Author interview, 2020.

58 Ibid.

59 Diane Keen: Author interview, 2021.

60 Ibid.

61 Ibid.

62 David Roper: Author interview, 2020.

63 Diane Keen: Author interview, 2021.

64 David Roper: Author interview, 2020.

65 Ibid.

Chapter Seven: 1976

1 Liza Goddard: Author interview, 2020.

2 Ibid.

3 Ibid.

4 Ibid.

5 Read, M., *T'rific* (Partridge Press, 1999).

6 Roy Clarke: Author interview, 2007.

7 Ibid.

8 Ibid.

9 Ibid.

10 Ibid.

11 Ibid.

12 John Howard Davies: Author interview, 2007.

13 Harper, S., *British Film Culture in the 1970s* (Edinburgh University Press, 2013).

14 Humphrey Barclay: Author interview, 2013.

15 William G. Stewart: Author interview, 2007.

16 Ibid.

17 Brian Murphy: Author interview, 2007.

18 Ibid.

19 Brian Cooke: Author interview, 2007.

20 Norman Eshley: Author interview, 2007.

21 Brian Murphy: Author interview, 2007.

22 Brian Cooke: Author interview, 2007.

23 Brian Murphy: Author interview, 2007.

24 Ibid.

25 Norman Eshley: Author interview, 2007.

26 Ibid.

27 Brian Cooke: Author interview, 2007.

28 Brian Murphy: Author interview, 2007.

29 Ibid.

30 Ibid.

31 Ibid.

32 Ibid.

33 Norman Eshley: Author interview, 2007.

34 David Nobbs: Author interview, 2007.

35 Ibid.

36 Ibid.

37 Ibid.

38 David Warwick: Author interview, 2020.

39 David Nobbs: Author interview, 2007.

40 Ibid.

41 Ibid.

42 Peter Sallis: Author interview, 2007.

Chapter Eight: 1977

1 Brian Cooke: Author interview, 2007.

2 Ibid.

3 Ibid.

4 David Kelly: Author interview, 2007.

5 Ibid.

6 Ibid.

7 Ibid.

8 Brian Cooke: Author interview, 2007.

9 Ibid.

10 Ibid.

11 Ibid.

12 Ibid.

13 Ibid.

14 Philippa Howell: Author interview, 2020.

15 Ibid.

16 Ibid.

17 Ibid.

18 Ibid.

19 Ibid.

20 Cooke, L., *A Sense of Place: Regional British Television Drama* (Manchester University Press, 2018).

21 Ibid.

22 Harold Snoad: Author interview, 2013.

23 John Kane: Author interview, 2021.

24 Ibid.

25 Powell, V., *From Rags to Gags: The Memoirs of a Comedy Writer* (Apex Publishing Ltd, 2008).

26 Ibid.

27 BECTU History Project: Dennis Main Wilson interview, 1991.

28 Mike Grady: Author interview, 2021.

29 Ibid.

30 Ibid.

31 Ibid.

32   Ibid.

33   Ibid.

34   Lindsay, R., *Letting Go* (Thorogood Publishing, 2012).

35   Mike Grady: Author interview, 2021.

36   Richard Briers: Author interview, 2007.

37   Ibid.

38   Bob Larbey: Author interview, 2008.

39   Richard Briers: Author interview, 2007.

40   Ibid.

41   Bob Larbey: Author interview, 2008.

42   Richard Briers: Author interview, 2007.

43   Ibid.

44   Powell, V., *From Rags to Gags: The Memoirs of a Comedy Writer* (Apex Publishing Ltd, 2008).

45   Humphrey Barclay: Author interview, 2013.

46   Françoise Pascal: Author interview, 2020.

47   Ibid.

48   Ibid.

49   Ibid.

50   Humphrey Barclay: Author interview, 2013.

51   Ibid.

52   Ibid.

53   Françoise Pascal: Author interview, 2020.

54   Humphrey Barclay: Author interview, 2013.

Chapter Nine: 1978

1   Humphrey Barclay: Author interview, 2013.

2   Ibid.

3   Ibid.

4   Ibid.

5   Dick Clement: Author interview, 2021.

6   Ibid.

7   Ian La Frenais: Author interview, 2021.

8   Dick Clement: Author interview, 2021.

9   Patricia Brake: Author interview, 2020.

10   Dick Clement: Author interview, 2021.

11   Humphrey Barclay: Author interview, 2013.

12   Ibid.

13   Ibid.

14   Ibid.

15   David Kelly: Author interview, 2007.

16   Ibid.

17   Ibid.

18   David Roper: Author interview, 2020.

19   Ibid.

20   Ibid.

21   Ibid.

22   Ibid.

23   Daniel Abineri: Author interview, 2020.

24   Ibid.

25   Ibid.

26   Ibid.

27   Ibid.

28   Patricia Brake: Author interview, 2020.

29   Ibid.

30   Ibid.

31   Ibid.

32 Martin Jarvis: Author interview, 2021.

33 Ibid.

34 Ibid.

35 Harold Snoad: Author interview, 2013.

36 Martin Jarvis: Author interview, 2021.

37 Ibid.

38 Diane Keen: Author interview, 2021.

39 Martin Jarvis: Author interview, 2021.

40 Ibid.

41 Susan Jameson: Author interview, 2021.

42 Ibid.

43 Ibid.

44 Ibid.

45 AV Club.com: August 2014.

46 Carla Lane: Author interview, 2013.

47 Wendy Craig: Author interview, 2008.

48 Ibid.

49 Ibid.

50 Carla Lane: Author interview, 2013.

51 Wendy Craig: Author interview, 2008.

52 Carla Lane: Author interview, 2013.

53 Wendy Craig: Author interview, 2008.

54 Ibid.

55 Ibid.

56 Ibid.

57 Carla Lane: Author interview, 2013.

58 Wendy Craig: Author interview, 2008.

59 Carla Lane: Author interview, 2013.

60 Ibid.

61 Wendy Craig: Author interview, 2008.

Chapter Ten: 1979

1   Matthew Kelly: Author interview, 2021.

2   Ibid.

3   Ibid.

4   Ibid.

5   Ibid.

6   Bob Larbey: Author interview, 2008.

7   Ibid.

8   Duggie Brown: Author interview, 2021.

9   Ibid.

10 Ibid.

11 Ibid.

12 Roy Clarke: Author interview, 2007.

13 Ibid.

14 Humphrey Barclay: Author interview, 2013.

15 Ibid.

16 Ibid.

17 Ibid.

18 Ibid.

19 Ibid.

20 Ibid.

21 Robin Hawdon: Author interview, 2020.

22 Ibid.

23 Ibid.

24 Su Pollard: Author interview, 2021.

25 Ibid.

26 Ibid.

27 Ibid.
28 Ibid.
29 Ibid.
30 Ray Galton: Author interview, 2007.
31 Peter Tilbury: Author interview, 2021.
32 Ibid.
33 Ibid.
34 Ibid.
35 Ibid.
36 Ibid.
37 Ibid.
38 Ibid.
39 Ibid.
40 Ibid.
41 Ibid.
42 Ibid.
43 Ibid.
44 Ibid.
45 Thomas, L., *In My Wildest Dreams* (Arlington Books Ltd, 1984).
46 Peter Spence: Author interview, 2020.
47 Ibid.
48 Ibid.
49 Ibid.
50 Ibid.
51 Ibid
52 Ibid.
53 Ibid.
54 Ibid.
55 Ibid.
56 Ibid.
57 John Kane: Author interview, 2021.
58 Ibid.
59 Ibid.
60 Ibid.
61 Ibid.
62 Ibid.
63 John Howard Davies: Author interview, 2007.
64 John Kane: Author interview, 2021.
65 Ibid.
66 Eric Chappell: Author interview, 2020.
67 Christopher Strauli: Author interview, 2020.
68 Ibid.
69 Ibid.

Bibliography

Carmichael, I., *Will the Real Ian Carmichael* (Macmillan, 1979).

Corbett, R., *High Hopes: My Autobiography* (Ebury, 2000).

Croft, D., *You Have Been Watching … The Autobiography of David Croft* (BBC Books, 2004).

Crowther, L., *The Bonus of Laughter* (Hodder & Stoughton, 1994).

David, N., *The Laughtermakers* (Peter Owen Publishers, 1971).

Lindsay, R., *Letting Go* (Thorogood Publishing, 2012).

Lord, G., *Arthur Lowe* (Orion Books, 2002).

Perry, J., *A Stupid Boy* (Century, 2002).

Phillips, L., *Hello* (Orion Books, 2007).

Powell, V., *From Rags to Gags: The Memoirs of a Comedy Writer* (Apex Publishing Ltd, 2008).

Rosenthal, J., *An Autobiography in Six Acts* (Robson Books, 2005).

Webber, R., *The Complete A–Z of Dad's Army* (Orion Books, 2000).

Index

Also by The History Press ...

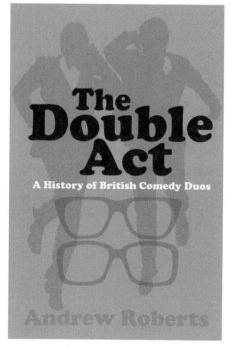

978 0 7509 8432 4

The destination for history
www.thehistorypress.co.uk